SERVICE AND DEPENDENCY IN SHAKESPEARE'S PLAYS

This is an unusual study of the nature of service and other types of dependency and patronage in Shakespeare's drama. By considering the close associations of service with childhood or youth, marriage and friendship, Judith Weil sheds new light on social practice and dramatic action. Approached as dynamic explorations of a familiar custom, the plays are shown to demonstrate a surprising consciousness of obligations and a fascination with how dependants actively change each other. They help us understand why early modern people may have found service both frightening and enabling. Attentive to a range of historical sources and to social and cultural issues, Weil also emphasizes the linguistic ambiguities created by service relationships and their rich potential for interpretation on the stage. The book presents close readings of dramatic sequences in twelve plays, including *Hamlet*, *Macbeth*, *The Taming of the Shrew*, and *King Lear*.

JUDITH WEIL has recently retired from the post of Professor of English at the University of Manitoba. Co-editor, with her husband Herbert Weil, of *The First Part of King Henry IV* (Cambridge, 1997), she has published widely on Shakespeare and Renaissance drama, including essays in *Marlowe, History and Sexuality: New Critical Essays on Christopher Marlowe*, ed. Paul Whitfield White; *The Female Tragic Hero in English Renaissance Drama*, ed. Naomi Conn Liebler; and *Approaches to Teaching English Renaissance Drama*, ed. Karen Bamford and Alexander Leggatt.

SERVICE AND DEPENDENCY IN SHAKESPEARE'S PLAYS

JUDITH WEIL

CAMBRIDGE UNIVERSITY PRESS

CAMBRIDGE UNIVERSITY PRESS

Cambridge, New York, Melbourne, Madrid, Cape Town, Singapore, São Paulo

Cambridge University Press
The Edinburgh Building, Cambridge CB2 2RU, UK

Published in the United States of America by Cambridge University Press, New York

www.cambridge.org
Information on this title: www.cambridge.org/9780521844055

First published 2005

Printed in the United Kingdom at the University Press, Cambridge

A catalogue record for this book is available from the British Library

ISBN-13 978-0-521-84405-5   - hardback
ISBN-10 0-521-84405-3   - hardback

For Herb Weil

Contents

Preface

This book began with a question asked by students in a seminar about Women in the Renaissance. "Why were servants so prominent?" they wondered, reflecting on the anonymous tragedy *Arden of Feversham* and on the poems of Isabella Whitney. They belonged, as does much of the book, to an era of scholarship which encouraged close scrutiny of subordinate actions.

Without the enthusiastic support of students and colleagues at the University of Manitoba, I could never have developed this project: Judith Owens criticized papers and shared research discoveries; John Rempel sent reading lists; George Toles made me take psychological criticism more seriously. For challenging arguments and indispensable information I would also like to thank Adam Muller, Karen Ogden, Arlene Young, Terry Ogden, Jonah Corne, Kathleen Darlington, and Nicola Woolff. Sociologists Charlene Thacker and Raymond Currie introduced me to connections between service and slavery by suggesting studies on Brazil and South Africa.

I am grateful to the Shakespeare Association of America for inviting me to chair a seminar on "Slavery in Renaissance Drama"; strong contributions by seminar members opened up a number of exciting new perspectives. I am also much in debt to Lynne Magnusson and Edward McGee for asking me to present a paper to the Elizabethan Theatre Conference exploring my approach. At a crucial early stage, criticism of the project by Scott Macmillin made it seem more promising than I had thought possible. For happy exchanges of ideas and for their generosity in publishing my essays on related matters I would like to thank Michael Hattaway, Naomi Conn Liebler, and Michael Neill.

Institutional support has been vital as well: a research grant from the Social Sciences and Humanities Research Council of Canada (1991–5) and grants and stipends from the University of Manitoba Research Office, Faculty of Arts, and Department of English. Bye-fellowships at Robinson

College, Cambridge in 1988 and 1995 made it possible for me to work in the University Library. I am also grateful to Michael Best and the Department of English at the University of Victoria for arranging the research privileges of a visiting scholar. At the Cambridge University Press anonymous readers have made extraordinarily thoughtful and incisive suggestions. Sarah Stanton has provided guidance both firm and reassuring.

For permission to reprint a revised version of material in "'Household stuff': Maestrie and Service in *The Taming of the Shrew*," published in *Elizabethan Theatre XIV*, ed. A. L. Magnusson and C. E. McGee, I wish to thank the P. D. Meany Company, Toronto, Ontario.

Permission to reprint a selection from Di Brandt, *Questions i asked my mother* (1987) has been granted by the Turnstone Press Ltd., Winnipeg, Manitoba.

This book has been produced through years of watching and teaching Shakespeare's plays and through dialogue with the fine company of Shakespeareans. I have singled out one of them in my dedication.

CHAPTER I

Introduction: "Slippery people"

Early modern service seems to have been defined through association with various forms of dependency. Loosely congruent types of subordination and support colored and shaped this social practice. My initial concern with service was more dramatic than social; it grew from a sense that here was a way of explaining why Shakespeare's characters are so often more like potencies than identities. I have never understood these characters as essences or even as rhetorical constructs. They excite me as moving intersections of relationships. Through a process delightful to watch but difficult to describe, Shakespeare can suggest that 'character' is something volatile and often shared because dramatic people seem to construct each other. Instead of assuming that service was necessarily archaic and repressive, a common reaction by enlightened thinkers and politicians for two hundred years, I began to see this mobile and adaptive institution as a way of accounting for distinctive features of Shakespeare's craft.

The study that has evolved from these surmises attempts to balance between an engagement with dramatic and with social questions. Because the practice of service may be unfamiliar to many contemporary readers, its customs must be presented in some detail. Whenever possible, I combine social description with dramatic inquiry; I approach Shakespeare's plays as evidence of how he tested and explored cultural attitudes toward service and dependency. These attitudes, reflecting the pervasiveness of early modern service, are highly variable. They correspond to and were probably modified by plays which feature significant conflicts of obligation involving service. Social practice and dramatic form are mutually illuminating.

Such claims may become more persuasive if I begin by setting out several closely connected issues which have emerged through my research and shaped my analysis of it: (1) using definitions of service commensurate with its symbolic and cultural functions; (2) avoiding narrow, utopian prejudices against subordination in general and work in particular;

(3) adopting models of explanation appropriate for the relational, mobile properties of service roles; and (4) using a critical narrative suited to different genres and to the unpredictable agencies of characters who may be active simultaneously or sequentially in several subordinate groups.

Shakespeare's use of terms for service is extraordinarily wide in range. Although a sizeable majority of these terms do refer either to the performance of particular tasks or to functions and agencies generally, service terms can also signify courtly love, sexual intercourse, practical joking, religious ritual, and military conduct, not to mention the formulas of politeness. It may be surprising to notice that a majority of his "servant" references apply to work; only a handful appear in respectful forms of address. The verb "serve" usually means to act as an agent or to work. By far the largest number of "service" references also concern work, followed by politeness behavior and military occupations. Few refer to sexuality.[1]

Shakespeare's linguistic breadth corresponds to the breadth of dependency on service by people at every social level during his life-time. Preliminary definitions need to accommodate this linguistic and social scope. In a massive examination of the feudal society preceding Shakespeare's, Marc Bloch suggests that pervasive needs for service as both aid and protection explain why it was defined in particularly broad terms.[2] Another historian, Edmund S. Morgan, observes that "servant" in the seventeenth century could mean "anyone who worked for another in whatever capacity."[3] Morgan instances people who ran an iron foundry, apprentices, voluntarily indentured servants who sold their own labor, and involuntarily enslaved natives and blacks. Today we satisfy needs for work and service through publically defined institutional and professional agencies, as well as through a private array of labor-hiding practices. But well into the eighteenth century, inclusive, un-rationalized definitions of service would have remained applicable.

For help in mapping so broad a field of action I have turned to historical sociologists as well as to social historians like Bloch and Morgan. When Peter Laslett wrote that finding so many people living in households other than those they were born to "looks to us like something of a sociological discovery" (1972), he had already begun to describe the ethos and conditions of service in chapter 1 of *The World We Have Lost* (1965).[4] Laslett and his followers recovered the significance of service as a life-cycle institution affecting significant numbers of young people and the families they joined. By sending their own adolescent children out to service and employing other people's children, families provided vocational training, shelter, and protection. Laslett added to his revision of *The World We Have Lost* a sharper distinction of the non-permanent master–servant society from the two societies it was "fused" with: husband and wife, parent and child.[5] Other scholars have questioned his statistics or focused on elements of service apparent in different regions, occupations, and economic groups. Nevertheless there appears to be widespread support for his view that the "salience" of servants in households is one of the defining traits of the English family.[6] Where preliminary definitions of service are concerned, this view justifies the expectation that quasi-familial fusions and confusions will create ambiguities and insecurities, both for dependent servants young and old and for masters or mistresses who may have once been servants themselves.

Like Shakespeare's vocabulary, Laslett's discovery shows why definitions of service need to be flexible. He also prepares us to understand why individual servants may not stand out clearly in the records of the past. Kate Mertes remarks in her study of *The English Noble Household 1250–1600* that "Friends, clients, counsellors, retainers, allies, and estate servants can . . . be troublesome to define."[7] Richard C. Barnett points out that the "civil service" organized by William Cecil confused political with domestic status and was "characterized by all the uncertainties of personal relationships."[8] To approach service in Shakespeare's plays, I emphasize "uncertainties" in relationships which develop between public and private, domestic and professional spheres. Encountering servants in Shakespeare's plays can often resemble reading about them in Richard Gough's lively chronicle of *Myddle*; they tend to be both omnipresent and indispensable without arresting much of our attention.[9] Occasionally an individual role will become conspicuous, as with the fall and rise of Autolycus in *The Winter's Tale* or in Gough's wonderfully eccentric tales of village preferment. References to a variety of service occupations and careers occur every few pages in the *History of Myddle*, revealing the versatility of the villagers and the frequent changes in their fortunes.

Laslett has also argued that no servant "was an independent member of society, national or local"; servants of all ages were "'subsumed' . . . into the personalities of their fathers and masters."[10] This argument may be accurate in describing a system the way that masters themselves would have done. But in Shakespeare's plays, as in Gough's Myddle, subsumption can rarely be taken for granted as an instrument of control. Whether subordinate roles are repressive or enabling will often depend on how they interact with one another.

"IN SERVITUDE DOLOR, IN LIBERTATE LABOR"

Gonzalo, the one benign courtier in *The Tempest*, emphatically dispenses with "use of service" (2.1.152) when he tries to imagine a commonwealth without trade or social structure.[11] Suppose, he dreams, that he could institute a utopian "plantation" (144) "Without sweat or endeavor" (161). Suppose that we think for a moment what performances of Shakespeare's plays might be like, were there "use of service none" in their staging. How substantially would these plays be affected were contemporary directors to decide that because early modern service is a lost social discourse, based on practices changed beyond easy recognition, service roles must therefore be adapted or transformed for contemporary audiences? Suddenly, a great many scenes would be set within universities, hospitals, and military camps, indicating not only that a service mentality still thrives in disciplined, hierarchical establishments, but also that it may still be inseparable from urgent human needs for education, care, and security. The persistence of uniforms and quasi-apprenticeships in such institutions suggests that they may continue to resemble the early modern "livery society" so firmly distinguished from our own by Ann Rosalind Jones and Peter Stallybrass.[12] Our professional and familial obligations remain entangled. We are no closer to utopia than was Gonzalo, attempting to distract his king by imposing golden-age equality on an island already dominated by a well-entrenched patriarch, Prospero. Democratic societies still rule and are ruled through 'social services' and 'support staffs' whose responsibilities often motivate public debate. In his novel *The Magus*, John Fowles re-produced Prospero's power for contemporary readers by fusing academy, psychiatric ward, and prison camp.

Much closer than Gonzalo's sense of service to my own is a motto which the traveller Thomas Platter copied down when he visited the palace of Whitehall in 1609. This motto illustrated an emblematic chamber decoration two hounds, one leashed, one coursing a hare and it read, "*In servitude dolor, in libertate labor* [In service pain, in liberty toil]."[13] It implies that although strenuous and unavoidable, voluntary labor should be distinguished from futile, miserable bondage. It uses a gentry sport to question a gentrified association of labor with punishment and pain.[14] I juxtapose Platter's motto with Gonzalo's fantasy, because utopia haunts much more serious discussions of servitude and labor than Gonzalo's.

We find it, for example, in Bruce Robbins' remarkably rich study of service, *The Servant's Hand: English Fiction from Below*. Robbins hopes that his book will continue the literary history, begun by Eric Auerbach in *Mimesis*, of an occulted popular "pressure."[15] Behaving subversively, in ways modelled on the clever slaves of classical tradition, his predominantly comic servants gesture toward an ideal community not yet realized. At the same time, however, they generally function as privileged choral commentators who lack engagement with other characters. Here a utopian approach tends to separate the agency of servants from complex and continuing needs, and to occlude the interpenetration of service with other dependent roles. However inspiring as a prophetic, anticipatory vision of political equality, utopia may not always help us to understand how subordination affects action in specific circumstances.[16]

As a non-utopian principle for approaching service and dependency in Shakespeare, I will be relying on Raymond Williams' notion of the inhabited border. Referring to Hardy's Wessex, Williams writes about "that border country so many of us have been living in: between custom and education, between work and ideas, between love of place and an experience of change."[17] Unlike Gonzalo who plans to be king of his ideal commonwealth, Williams' does not elevate his own position as thinker above the argument he makes. His responsible pastoralism has significant theoretical implications for the following study. First, it obviously questions the use of border metaphor to underwrite an explanatory authority derived from or privileging defense. Williams' border has lost its "fearful symmetry." It functions as a reminder about and warning against the violence of which border-fashioning populations remain capable. But it does not provide a set of authoritative intellectual watch-towers or mine-shafts which might be used to spy upon the center from the margins, or to attack a center so conceived. It implies no necessary allegiance to an avant-garde or to neglected groups. Nor is it an ideological "fault-line," a site for contradictions just waiting to rip apart or explode. Radically ordinary, it suggests that adventure and discovery can be found "where so many of us have been living," that significant agency may occur between and among, as well as above, below, and beyond established social roles or categories.

Second, Williams' "border country" permits dynamic social movement without determining its direction either in or among persons and groups. Optimistic as "love of place" may sound, it scarcely precludes tribalism, snobbery, or nostalgia. Moreover, an explanatory "border" open to a group of movements operating at much the same time produces more understanding than do a series of fixed positions. Apropos of slavery, a recurrent theme in the following chapters, Orlando Patterson argues that the danger of defining "invariant dynamics" in social systems is the neglect of "limiting" or "borderline" cases which "challenge the conceptual stability of the processes one has identified."[18] Although they participate in a social institution so traditional as to be ancient in some respects, many of Shakespeare's characters can also be treated as exciting borderline cases at work in unstable conditions.

RELATIONSHIP AND SERVICE

Williams' inhabited border provides a tentative model for describing complex social transactions. It lends theoretical support to the project of approaching service through fluent relationships as well as through exceptional identities or an invariant master–servant paradigm. It keeps open the possibility that subsumed persons can modify their situations through what Williams' has termed "an active practical consciousness."[19] My approach emphasizes dynamic interactions among dependants: servants, children, wives, and friends. It considers elisions or fusions between and among different types of dependency. Ignorance of fine distinctions in early modern minds may well appear as I examine these fusions. Nevertheless, they can be illustrated through many kinds of non-dramatic evidence: letters, diaries, essays, poems, household records, and conduct books.

My approach has influenced my procedure in several ways. Like M. M. Mahood, I will attend to the actual doings of stage servants, but I will also ask how they function together with other subordinate players.[20] For example, how may the parallel subjections of wife and servants in *The Taming of the Shrew* help us to understand the disturbing conclusion of the play? Why does the fusion between friendship and service in *Antony and Cleopatra* prove to be so deadly? In addition I will look at how children, wives and friends use the languages of service. These characters repeatedly reveal their "practical consciousness" of how they behave by drawing upon service terms and symbols. As the brief reference above to Shakespeare's vocabulary suggests, these terms offer us a stimulating social poetry; shifty metaphors and tropes often shape dramatic passages through the border countries where interdependent agents affect one another.[21]

Still another consequence of my emphasis on social relationships is a de-centered treatment of Shakespeare's plays. "Relationship" itself is an eighteenth-century word. It occurs regularly in sociological and historical discussions of service. For example, generalizing about *The English*

Domestic Servant in History, Dorothy Marshall insists that "the position of servants has always depended more on human relations than on organization or general conditions."[22] "Domestic service is first and foremost a relationship" writes Sarah C. Maza.[23] And so, too, was the service of the friend or ally who followed a great man, described by Mervyn James as "the relationship of responsible dominance and unqualified submission which good lordship implied."[24] Keith Wrightson and David Levine refer to friendship, aid, and "common service in village office" as "densely interlinked" among the inhabitants of Terling.[25] Even more comprehensively, Ronald F. E. Weisman advocates a Renaissance sociology which takes as the unit of analysis "the *social relationship* that links individuals to each other and to groups," and which thinks of meaning as "situational" or defined by placement in an "interaction network."[26]

Relational categories have often come to the fore in scholarship concerned with how dependent people survive through accommodation. The feminist theorists Judith Newton and Deborah Rosenfelt claim that "Women, like men, appear divided from each other, enmeshed not in a simple polarity with males but in a complex and contradictory web of relationships and loyalties."[27] I believe that dramatic actions can be considered de-centered networks in many respects. By potentially exaggerating the inter-relations of characters, I am also trying to compensate for dramatic criticisms based on the roles of one or two characters or on the assumed reliability of a privileged viewpoint. Beset by suspicion of service, conflict with servants, and shame at his own servility, Hamlet is not always a witness we can trust.

Even students of culture and its many discourses may treat these bundles of custom and ideology like efficient central intelligences guiding us through literary works. A static social cosmos replaces dynamic characters. The extreme passivity of some early modern servants and dependents seems to invite such a totalizing procedure. To understand why, let us look for a moment at Walter Darell's defense of the gentle serving man in his "Pretie and Shorte Discourse of the Duetie of a Servingman" (1578), a complaint inspired by the growing practice among the English gentry of hiring personal attendants with non-gentle origins.[28] Having listed "Godlinesse, Clenlinesse, Audacitie, and Diligence" as the "chiefest ornamentes" of his calling, Darell goes on to say that the word "servingman" "hath great relation to his kind," depending on whether he serves God, prince or country. For Darell, "relation" is fully determined by these all-powerful masters. His "Discourse" dwells on the very vulnerability of such dependants as they attempt to maintain "credit": "the least faulte a servingman comitteth is greatly remembered."[29] Darell defines his own identity in terms of his master's needs, hoping through "diligence" to eventually become a master himself.[30]

The masterly perspective addressed (and probably flattered) by Darell is a strong cultural force evident in numerous texts. It readily determines that servants must give up any independent will. Ordered by Antipholus of Ephesus to bring bail money from home, the slave Dromio of Syracuse concludes, "Thither I must, although against my will, / For servants must their masters' minds fulfill" (4.1.112–13). Justifiable resistance to a master's command, while allowed by many givers of advice on obedience, is generally treated as an exception, not as a rule. In a letter counselling his twelve year old daughter, Lavinia, on her behavior at the Court of Savoy, Annibal Guasco warns her to so "subdue her will" that she can guess what her Lady desires her to do.[31] Platter copied down a second emblem at Whitehall, a light burning in a glass of oil, accompanied by the motto, "Je me consume au service d'aultruy."[32] Masters could interpret an agreement to serve as removing the servant's will for most practical purposes. Thomas Fossett (1613) argues that even if treated with "mallice and perversenes," a servant cannot simply leave his (or her) place: "they have not power of their own selves, they covenanted with their maisters, tyed and bound themselves to serve them so long, and in such sort."[33] While service lasts, according to William Gouge (1622), both the persons and actions of the servant belong to the master.[34]

How such views concerning the volition of servants might affect their political status becomes evident in Thomas Whately's conviction (1624) that a servant who desires to marry can not have been "called" to the marriage by God. A man may *only* marry "without wronging any other person, that is, when hee is now become his owne man." "God never crosseth himselfe," Whately proclaims; God doesn't send men into house-keeping before they can afford the expense![35] It is important to remember that precisely because many servants were thought to have given up autonomy, they would be excluded from free citizenship by most seventeenth-century English Levellers and republicans as well as by eighteenth-century French republicans, who also disliked their association with aristocratic privilege.[36] In one of his "Devises," Thomas Howell, the household poet attached to the Pembroke family, develops their motto, "Ung ie Servirey" [to serve one] in celebrating single-minded devotion to one prince and one God. "Who serveth more, he rightly serveth none."[37] Male domestic servants only gained the rights and responsibilities of citizens in the late nineteenth century.[38] In this respect, as in so many others, certain servants could be treated like wives and children, also denied civic responsibility because of their "great relation" to husbands and fathers.

Contemporary readers are no longer likely to accept, much less praise, the docility of servants like Darell. They will feel uneasy with the conclusion reached by Jonas Barish and Marshall Waingrow in their pioneering study of service in *King Lear*. By the end of the play, they believe, the audience functions as "servants of *God*": "we discover the true and whole meaning of service: that by promoting concord between individuals of different rank, it ends by minimizing distinctions of rank."[39] We do? Moses Finley observes that ancient slaves as virtuous and devoted as Seneca and Saint Paul might have wished would have helped to strengthen a malignant system. "Not everyone," he concludes, "will rank the creation of honourable and decent servants as one of the higher moral goals of humanity, or accommodation to enslavement as a moral virtue."[40] If God, according to Whately, "never crosseth himself," what about patriarchs? Why not acknowledge that self-sacrificing servants would have been man-made god-sends and get on with analyzing the destructive contradictions of patriarchy?

In an essay on nineteenth-century domestic service, Leonore Davidoff helpfully suggests that while patriarchy may define an entire society, it may also explain either groups within that society or certain relations in a society which is built upon other norms.[41] As a highly variable part of a network of dependencies, a part which interacts with the functioning of maturation, marriage, and friendship, service reflects and modifies other norms. The early modern churchmen and moralists who rigorously advise selfless obedience do not fairly represent an entire social world.[42] Some prescribers compared the choice of highly valued servants to the choice of friends. While servants were often vulnerable, they were not always passive. They might learn to obey in resourceful, independent ways. As Robert J. Steinfeld has convincingly maintained, early modern people generally distinguished between service and slavery: "One condition was mainly identified in contemporary minds as consensual and limited, the other just as clearly as arbitrary and absolute."[43] *In servitude dolor: in libertate labor.* A totalizing account of contradictions, taking patriarchal service on its own most autocratic, defensive terms, would make it difficult to demonstrate why specific contradictions develop in particular plays, much less acknowledge that tyrannical, saintly and duplicitous motives can ever be qualified or localized.[44] As does a play, the practice of service includes many points of view.

CRISES OF OBLIGATION

Because they function as mediators, servants often participate in crucial dramatic sequences. If we assume that their actions are always secondary, or brief extensions of traditional roles as vices, fools, officials, and companions, we will miss the full significance of their interventions, whether these turn out to be creative or disastrous. The problems which face historians in defining and describing servants suggest that their positions, irrespective of status level, could be volatile. Whether they provided security or received it from their employers, they flourished by imitating behavior through associations where intimacy and loyalty were prized. Adept at crossing the borders of status (or of dramatic plots) they should have been strong candidates for survival. Mertes believes that servants tended to switch loyalties instead of falling with their lords.[45] But Laslett and Gordon Schochet agree that patriarchal power was exerted more strenuously upon servants who were "strangers to the family" than upon kinsmen.[46] A collapse of family fortunes could leave defenseless servants scrambling to find new sources of income and protection. Jean-Louis Flandrin asserts that a servant could have been helpless when caught in a social breakdown: "he would have liked to escape that which would assuredly come crashing down on his superior, but he could do nothing."[47]

To a servant who had literally lost his or her place, my emphasis above on the potentially dynamic interplay of subordinate positions could well seem utopian. Even an aristocratic officer like Cassio in *Othello* may respond to such a loss with intense anguish: "I am desperate of my fortunes if they check me [here]," he exclaims after Othello dismisses him and makes Iago lieutenant (2.3.331–2). Preparing to "shut myself up in some other course, / To fortune's alms" if his suit for reinstatement in Othello's "service" fails (3.4.121–2), Cassio speaks more like an unemployed servingman threatened with poverty and prison than a talented Florentine strategist who will ultimately replace *his* master as the governor of Cyprus. His language evokes the situation of the masterless man, worse off than a beggar according to one I. M. because "farre from his friendes" and ineligible for the license which kept beggars who had established a residence out of jail.[48]

Several plays represent the suffering of servants who have been cast out of their places when households dissolve.[49] In *Timon of Athens*, Timon's servants, "All broken implements of a ruin'd house" (4.2.16), link Timon's fall with beggary, theft, disease, and death, worrying more about their master's fortunes than their own, which they define using the image of a "Leak'd . . . bark" about to sink (19–21). In another of his "Devices," Howell, the Pembroke retainer-poet mentioned above, describes a servant who needs assistance as a "Pynnis smale" at sea in a storm.[50] In *Antony and Cleopatra*, Antony's household servants weep when he tells them,

> Mine honest friends,
> I turn you not away, but like a master
> Married to your good service, stay till death. (4.2.29–31)

Enobarbus actually breaks his heart on the conflict between a "marriage" to his master Antony and an alliance to a new master, Octavius. Comparing his actions to those of a "master-leaver and a fugitive" (4.9.22), Enobarbus dies judging himself as punitively as any patriarchal master might wish.

No one articulates more eloquently than does Enobarbus the warring imperatives experienced by servants when households or regimes collapsed:

> The loyalty well held to fools does make
> Our faith mere folly; yet he that can endure
> To follow with allegiance a fall'n lord
> Does conquer him that did his master conquer,
> And earns a place i' th' story. (3.13.42–6)

This desperately selfless sense of "place," analogous to arguments against vengeance, seems to coincide with that abeyance of individual will which Darell, Fossett, Whately, and a host of other writers all advocate. If masters happen to overlook the merits of humble servants, writes William Basse in *Sword and Buckler: or Servingmans Defence* (1602), "Then we are men of more respect than they."[51] "The servant of a king is a king," according to one especially passive proverb.[52] A terrible crisis drives Enobarbus to accept the possibility of abjection in language resembling that which apologists for ideal order prescribe as normal! No wonder, then, if contemporary scholars who seek to recover the stories of Renaissance subordinates have at times leapt from a dramatic crisis to the cultural discourse it seems to expose, implying as they do so that a disastrous situation is both typical and inevitable, and a dramatic story over before it begins.

Philosophers and historians have been more alert to the fallacy of treating disasters in this fashion. Michael Walzer, for example, has observed that if we say war is hell, we cannot distinguish among wars, showing how they differ in their causes and, perhaps, learning to avoid them.[53] Walzer's strategy is to challenge "a general account of war as a realm of necessity and duress, the purpose of which is to make discourse about particular cases appear to be idle chatter, a mask of noise with which we conceal, even from ourselves, the awful truth."[54] Susan Amussen suggests that more normal social functions must often be inferred from evidence which emphasizes disruption; it may be "virtually impossible to find out how things worked when they went right."[55] There could well be assumptions of warlike emergency and military need behind the long line of sermons and guide books which counsel unswerving devotion; Xenophon's seminal treatise on household order emphasizes parallels between husbandry and warfare.[56] But such prescriptions do not envision complicated conflicts of loyalty, heartbreak and suicide. They do not equip us to find the causes of conflict in particular cases involving servants and dependants. They do not prepare us for Enobarbus and his "place i' th' story."

For Enobarbus, as I will argue in chapter 4, "things" that "worked" include his resemblance to Cleopatra and her women, a household relationship which Roman propaganda will ultimately use as a misogynous weapon against Antony's followers. They include professional status as an officer in a military retinue which is often indistinguishable from a domestic menage.[57] They include his child-like privilege of acutely perceptive speech to Antony himself. They include a friendship between Antony and Enobarbus which Enobarbus nurtures with amazing resilience and wit. If we treat his selfless death as a cultural symptom or necessity, we lose an important part of his dramatic story: a sense of what might have happened had Antony taken this friend and his advice more seriously. To understand the drastically limited choices which characters may make in a dramatic crisis, a modern audience requires a broader vocabulary of obligation than the crisis itself can usually generate. To grasp the significance of service in helping to produce such crises, we need to examine the roles with which service overlapped when it worked.

HISTORIANS OF SERVICE AND LITERARY EVIDENCE

Two themes have run through the preceding consideration of issues: that I frequently depend on the insights of social historians and that I regard plays as composed of actions which are often unpredictable. Before concluding with a few comments on dramatic forms and genres, I will try to clarify my debt to and difference from the historians on whom I rely. These scholars have shown that in Shakespeare's lifetime, contractual obligation was replacing reciprocal personal solidarity, women and yeomen were replacing gentle serving-men, and shorter terms of service were reducing familial intimacy. The numbers of gentle serving-men declined for complex economic and political reasons. These included more opportunities for gentlemen in urban professions and at court and a taste for military adventures abroad, advocated, for example, by the courtier Valentine in the quizzical dialogue, *The English Courtier and the Countrey-gentleman.*[58] At the same time as Laurence Humfrey and others were attacking the vanity of retaining superfluous "cuppeflyes," aristocrats were coming to prefer service by much younger pages and grooms.[59] Then too there was the practical consideration that the sons of farmers often made better country-house employees. More stable throughout the period would have been the traditional contempt of aristocratic followers for manual labor and wages, and the fear at lower levels of becoming wholly dependent on wages as other liberties and customary privileges diminished.[60]

These changes belong to the process through which England slowly became an industrial nation state. They may influence the representation of service in drama but they do not cohere as a narrative pattern. To impose such a pattern upon Shakespeare's plays or to theorize a massive change or crisis in service during his life might well be to ignore how dramatic characters use service to think about or facilitate what they are doing.[61] Too imperative a consciousness of historical movement may credit characters who satirize or rebel against service roles with progressive fore-sight, as if an Iago were riding the wave of the future.[62] As a rule, social historians subscribe to lengthy epochs and slow transitions. I have admired their patience with time and their preoccupation with detail.

Also congenial has been their reluctance to accept myths of "cultural unity" which might enclose many servants in an economic class.[63] This is not to say that servants never behave as a class. But as E. P. Thompson points out, "Class and class-consciousness are always the last, not the first, stage in the real historical process."[64] Dramatically, too, class tends to emerge from conflict or through the loss of place. As an institution which lacks any strict economic or legal definition, service corresponds to what Thompson terms "an indefinite sociological praxis."[65]

Social historians have also shown exemplary discretion in their handling of prescriptions for behavior. Keith Wrightson contends that the early modern ideas of "place" and "degree" employed a "vocabulary of the study," lacking much currency in daily life or "institutional reality."[66] In *English Society 1580–1680* he points out that "Conventional definition of roles and the actual performance of them in everyday life can be quite different things, and as Powell argued long ago about the problem of women's place in society in general, 'we should get a fairer and more fundamental view by examining historical and biographical facts, rather than by studying the writing of moralists, lovers and satirists'."[67] Alice T. Friedman claims that the letters and account books of gentry houses reveal a chaos obscured by prescriptive writing.[68] Paul Griffiths attacks "normative and prescriptive" opinion as "a still-life or model, which assumes a great measure of conformity and passivity."[69]

Historians who have concentrated on areas in which service played a large part, such as households, families, courts, and labor markets, often argue among themselves.[70] They do however seem to have reached an implicit agreement insofar as they make a limited and cautious use of creative literature. And except for some gracious acknowledgments, social historians rarely cite literary studies. One major reason for this professional caution is probably that before Laslett and demographic quantification or the more rigorous investigation of public archives and parish records, some historians used literature naively to support their arguments. By literary evidence, Laslett means all writing not created primarily as a record; his rubric includes sermons, tracts and advice books. Among the many problems he detects in using "high literature" (i.e. Shakespeare and Fielding) are its "mystic authoritativeness" and its "reversibility": one can't tell whether a character or incident is ordinary or extraordinary, representative or fantastic.[71] A second reason for caution and one especially relevant to my study can be detected in scrupulous reluctance by historians to speculate about the personal feelings of people in the past. It would be dishonest, even arrogant, some scholars have suggested, to claim that they could ever accurately describe the subjectivity of subordinated people, especially when such people were often illiterate as well.[72] Even if drama represents probable versions of such subjectivity, an historian may well prefer to cite only those which can be confirmed through other sources as reliably typical.[73]

I think it may be possible to acknowledge these objections without also conceding that plays have little value as historical evidence. Shakespeare certainly does over-turn current rules and regulations insisting that porters be discreet, that stewards be comely and non-puritanical, or that maids be deferential to everyone else. His situations are often extraordinary and fantastic. But I have come to believe that interactions among dependent characters are apt to be more representative than individual trajectories. In a critical reassessment of how Keith Thomas has influenced the study of witchcraft, Jonathan Barry regrets a lack of attention to sources "which might recreate the full social dynamics of a witch episode, for example the plays of the period that incorporate witchcraft cases."[74] Examples of dramatic interaction may give us access to a "full social dynamics" less evident in other sources. Moreover, as Griffiths points out, "it is not a question of devaluing different types of sources, but of exploring the points of contact between them."[75]

SERVICE AND DRAMATIC ACTIONS

The preceding survey refers again and again to dramatic activity; it emphasizes the agency of actors, their relationships as border-dwellers, and their involvement in crises. I have been assuming that plays are actions much like those described by Aristotle in his *Poetics*. Dramas "imitate men doing."[76] "It is by virtue of their characters that agents are of a certain kind, but it is by virtue of their actions that they are happy or the contrary" (13). For Aristotle, plot is the most important element of a play; dramatic action contains an intricate, developing synthesis of characters, ideas, language and events. His basic principle for the crafting of plots, that they should be unified or whole,has been misunderstood as a rigid, dogmatic formalism. On the contrary, his descriptive scheme can theoretically accommodate an infinite variety of plots. The best tragic plots, he believes are those that include both reversal and recognition ("a change from ignorance to knowledge,"20). This concern for surprising sequences which will engage an audience means that Aristotle's remarks on epic probably apply to tragedy as well. Although the tragic dramatist creates possible and likely plots out of familiar stories, he also enjoys the license of choosing "a persuasive impossibility" over an "unpersuasive possibility" (53). Aristotle adds that poets "ought to bring in the unreasonable with regard to what men say and also because at times it is not unreasonable, for what is against likelihood is also likely to arise."

Aristotle's emphasis on constructing unpredictable plots implicitly grants the dramatist a tentative disengagement from society. It gives him or her a space in which to play seriously with customs and cultures, testing them through situations which could indeed occur, given specific combinations of characters and circumstances. I follow this tendency in Aristotle's approach by treating Shakespeare's plays as if they were entertaining, provocative hypotheses, ways of thinking about relationships through actions. Laura Caroline Stevenson begins her examination of Elizabethan popular literature with the argument that such fiction is "exploratory thought in which a problem is disclosed and considered in

time, through the actions of characters."[77] Useful for most plays, this
critical orientation seems to be particularly appropriate for tragedy, the
only dramatic genre Aristotle described at length. The classicist Froma
Zeitlin argues that tragedy "is the epistemological form par excellence.
What it does best, through the resources of the theater, is to chart a path
from ignorance to knowledge, deception to revelation, misunderstanding
to recognition. The characters act out and live through the consequences
of having clung to a partial single view of the world and themselves."[78]
Tragic playwrights can imagine what will happen when characters afflict
each other with attitudes and ideas which have been validated by collective wisdom. They know how to rend the hearts and minds of spectators
who discover that ordinary practices prove especially destructive when
they converge in surprising ways.[79]

A study stressing inter-related, dependent characters might be expected
to concentrate on Shakespeare's histories and comedies, avoiding tragedies where individuals seem to be much more prominent. Why do I begin
with *Hamlet* and end with *Macbeth*? When Gordon Braden distinguishes
Senecan from Euripidean tragedy, he argues that Senecan drama "reaches
its heights not in a vision of ambient, impersonal evil, but in one of furor
concentrated, triumphantly embodied in a single character."[80] Tragedies
by Euripides, on the other hand, present "a diffused communal reality,"
"a network of social nuance and interconnection."[81] *Hamlet* and *Macbeth*
are more Euripidean than Senecan in this regard. Both heros retain a
strong sense of "social nuance and interconnection." Productions make
evident the communal realities from which Hamlet and Macbeth divorce
themselves.

I have also begun with *Hamlet* because Hamlet so often recognizes and
resists servility. Through discussions of *Hamlet, Coriolanus, King John,*
and *Cymbeline,* I show that virtual fusions between youth and service,
apparent in many historical accounts, help to explain why dramatic
characters who are not servants understand their agency in service terms.
The two tragedies of young leaders emphasize fears of being instrumentalized or enslaved. But fusions which prove damaging in one plot or
tangle of circumstances can prove enabling in others. Forms of awareness
promoted by service relations also vary with the specific dependencies
being dramatized. When service intersects with marriage and friendship,
characters acquire different capacities, different strengths and weaknesses.

The first three chapters illustrate some of this variety by including all
of Shakespeare's dramatic genres and genders. They move outward
from service as a component of normal up-bringing and education to

its inter-penetration with marriage and its vital function as a source of security within friendship and alliance. The final chapters concentrate on two tragedies, *King Lear* and *Macbeth*. These plays receive sustained comment because they anatomize social connections so thoroughly. My discussion of *King Lear* draws the major topics stressed earlier into a much more speculative treatment of social poetry and its power. That of *Macbeth* returns to a question raised by *Hamlet*: how are service and dependency linked to the values of freedom?

Feminist critics have identified early modern trafficking in women, while students of material culture have exposed anxieties over status and power. By extending such analyses to include close readings of how different subordinations interact we can more clearly understand how these subordinations influence ethical choice and conduct. We may become less likely to take any labor for granted, more apt to recognize positive parallels between the roles of wives and servants or to admit the complex needs satisfied by service roles. We can also begin to comprehend the negative associations of service with slavery, alienation, parasitism, and demonic possession. An appropriate title for this study as a whole would have been "slippery people." When Antony uses this pejorative phrase to describe his unreliable followers (1.2.185), he adopts a top-down view. But when people are "slippery," autocratic masters may find them much more difficult to control.

CHAPTER 2

Sons, daughters, and servants

Coming of age in Shakespeare's England frequently coincided with a prolonged period of household service or apprenticeship. A comic passage from *The Merchant of Venice* suggests that cultural fusions between the roles of servants and children would have been fertile sources for dramatic conflict and change. In this passage Launcelot Gobbo plays the master to his old, sand-blind father, then persuades his father to play the master by preferring him to Bassanio's service. Old Gobbo does this by helpfully declaring that his son "hath a great infection . . . to serve" (2.2.125–6). Eliding "affection" and "intention" through "infection," he muddles motives which probably came into conflict when parents behaved like masters, either to other people's children or to their own. The following chapter emphasizes two disastrous coming-of-age stories: the tragedies of *Hamlet* and *Coriolanus* are deeply "infected" by relationships between young heros and servants. But even tragedies may represent some dimensions of service as potentially empowering. To show how young people might have survived through resources offered by service, this chapter supplements discussions of *Hamlet* and *Coriolanus* with briefer considerations of *Cymbeline* and *King John*.

A direct plunge into *Hamlet* could immediately stir up Old Gobbo's confusions and many more. To reduce these, I will begin with a survey of social practices linking youth to service. These practices develop with and prepare for the elisions between service, marriage, and friendship to be considered in following chapters. This survey will indicate how customs worked when they were working and provide some sense of the tensions they caused. No substitute for detailed social histories, it has been designed to make unfamiliar material in four specific plays easier to recognize.[1] It also makes the distraction of frequent reference to early modern customs less necessary.

Young people would have mingled regularly with servants, whether or not they became servants themselves.[2] As a vital part of their education, parents placed adolescent children in other households and received young servants into their own. The aristocracy also exchanged children; a prince like Hamlet might be brought up with gentlemen of lesser rank like Rosencrantz and Guildenstern at court or in a great house. A pretentious young land-owner like Osric, termed a "lapwing" by Horatio (5.2.185), might attend kings and queens to school himself in courtship. The establishment of Queen Elizabeth's chief counsellor, William Cecil, described as an "academy" for young noblemen, provides a well-known example.[3] Living together in such a household could mean waiting on tables as well as sharing tutors and sleeping quarters. Such practices often led to a "lifetime of personal attendance, devotion, and intimacy."[4] For a nobleman or prince to see one's school fellows reappear as family follow-ers or court servants would surely have been as common as the death of fathers. There was "nothing servile" about personal attendance as a means of social education, according to Ivy Pinchbeck and Margaret Hewitt.[5]

This social education seems to have had several purposes. Placing children from different ranks together taught them the importance of status and fostered their skill in getting along with one another.[6] Particu-larly after the Reformation, it helped to strengthen religious affiliations. Protestant households catechized servants and children in family groups, enforcing order and possibly nurturing inclinations toward political inde-pendence and sectarianism.[7] Catholics too practised domestic religious instruction. Mervyn James describes one northern Catholic wife, Dorothy Lawson, as building a spiritual household modelled on traditional gentry arrangements.[8]

Many English people may have taken close associations between youth and service for granted.[9] Household ideology taught that the best masters had been servants.[10] Guides to household management regularly pos-itioned advice on the treatment of servants immediately after sections on children. Early modern English vocabularies contained many reminis-cences of the feudal knight or squire as a "childe" of glory and renown. Shakespeare gives a comic servant, Launcelot Gobbo, the name of the greatest Arthurian hero; Falstaff's follower, Ancient Pistol, anachronistic-ally celebrates Henry the Fifth as an "imp of fame" (*Henry V* 4.1.45). In English as in many other languages the terms "child," "boy," and "girl" could mean "servant" or even "slave."[11] Leah Marcus has argued that members of the upper class would have regarded all children as lower class.[12] For Hamlet as for Shakespeare's disguised heroines, knavish speech might summon up remembrance of youthful experience as a page exposed to serving men and lackeys much more threatening than Osric.[13]

We can assume, I think, that relationships between servants and children were often intimate in both physical and personal terms. By the eighteenth century, class barriers and architectural partitions would divide poorer servants from wealthier children more firmly. Mark Girouard has shown how designers of country houses removed servants to wings, attics, and basements.[14] But it would be tendentious to emphasize emerging trends which will rationalize and redefine social roles. Hamlet's one memory of earlier childhood is of having been born "a thousand times" on the back of his father's jester, Yorick (5.1.186). Sir Simonds D'Ewes (1602–50) includes an anecdote in his *Autobiography* about his mother's strong-man cook, John Martin, who at seven was able to carry D'Ewes' grandfather "round about his hall at Coxden."[15] According to Jean-Louis Flandrin, the manuals for confessors from late sixteenth or early seventeenth-century France do not denounce familiarity between children and servants, as do later manuals.[16] The household guide by Gilbert Cousin, translated into English by 1543, apparently has no objection to intimacies like those Hamlet recalls: "Here hung those lips that I have kiss'd I know not how oft" (5.1.188–9).[17] Cousin stresses the loyalty and efficiency of servants rather than their bad manners or the need to disinfect them by keeping them in separate compartments.

Such relationships may have been intimate; they were not always harmonious. Strict household regulations can be taken as evidence that masters struggled to control the unruly behavior of young people living in close quarters. Some servants wished to be treated like family members or at least hoped for more cordial relationships.[18] Mothers, however, often advised that children be kept away from supposedly clever jacks and babbling, promiscuous maids.[19] Grace Mildmay's "Autobiography" describes how she saw her father "with his owne hands . . . scourge a young man naked from the girdle upwards, with fresh rods, for making but a show and countenance of a saucy and irreverent behaviour towards us his children, and put him from his service." Mildmay was urged to beware of servingmen by her cautious governess.[20]

Servants were perceived as potentially damaging to young men as well as to young women. In "Of the Education of Children" Montaigne sees as disadvantages to educating a son at home "the respect the whole household pays the boy, and the consciousness of the power and greatness of his house."[21] Even in late eighteenth-century France, as Sarah C. Maza has demonstrated, philosophes could still object to the "unnatural" mediation of servants between parent and child.[22] Servants often helped to educate children or were held up to these children as models of obedience or skill. In older or traditional noble households, resident retainers might have shared parental authority over their master's children.[23] Claude Desainliens includes in his educational dialogue, *The French School Master*, a speech by a maid, Margerite, scolding a boy, Frances who expects her to wash his hands for him: "Can you not wash in the baason? Shall you have alwayes a servaunt at your tayle?"[24] A disaffected servant could easily revenge him or herself upon a younger child; an inherited household corps might take advantage of an older but unseasoned heir.[25] And of course, servants could also infect households with religious heterodoxy or moral corruption. "What deadly poyson may wicked servants be to our children?" writes Matthew Griffith.[26] Cousin observes in his remarkably benign tract on servants that if they catch the "frenche evil," they "deale the same amonges their masters childern and hole familie."[27]

In considering the associations between youth and service, it is important to notice how points of view have been inflected by status and circumstances. Masters and patriarchs tend to collapse categories, as when William Lambarde describes one danger of war in the low countries: "Now will your sons and servants strive to draw their necks out of the yoke of due obedience."[28] In a particularly conservative dialogue on household order, *A Diamonde Most Precious*, J. Fit John has the speaker, Puer, ask Civis (a master who has been a servant) why he makes no distinction between sons and servants and Civis replies: "Yea all is one, for where there is a child or a sonne named, or a servaunt, all is as one thing."[29] Some servants (often remembered in wills) would have enjoyed adoptive status within households. Oliver Heywood refers to the young woman who served him and his two little boys after his wife died as "my child as well as servant, one of my first and best converts to the faith, and that spiritual relation hath much endeared us."[30] But children sent out to great houses may have wished to distinguish themselves from servants. For example, Robert Plumpton, in a letter written to his mother during the reign of Henry VIII, asks that his parents move a "Lady Gascoin" to request her brother "not to bee only his servant, but of his houshold and attending unto him; for els he wold do as other lords do, knows not half their servants."[31]

For the children of noble households which sheltered court wards or poor relations, or included pages and personal attendants of high birth, discriminating themselves from the servants must often have proved difficult.[32] In a speech addressed to Parliament in 1610, complaining about

Scottish domination of the King's household and bed-chamber, Sir John Holles appears to assume that his audience has experienced such domestic tensions for themselves. "I am not lean because they be fat," he says, "only I wish equality, that they should not seem to be children of the family and we the servants."[33] Then there is the interesting case of Lucy Hutchinson. Brought up in the Tower of London, where her father was Lieutenant, she "despised" playing "among other children;" she used "to exhort my mother's maids much, and to turn their idle discourses to good subjects." But she also became a "confidant" of these maids in their love affairs: "there was none of them but had many lovers, and some particular friends beloved above the rest."[34]

Before turning to young Hamlet and his associates, I would also like to point out that a society so conscious of status probably practised a number of distinctions in the daily treatment of children as opposed to servants, especially those adolescent servants who at lower levels of society preferred to work for shorter terms. Ralph A. Houlbrooke has argued that close emotional relations with servants were exceptional. The rural servants studied by Ann Kussmaul generally failed to renew their year-long agreements and kept their masters as strangers.[35] William Ames' *Conscience with the Power and Cases Thereof* (1630) spells out five major differences between servants and children: (1) Service is contractual, (2) it primarily benefits masters, (3) children do only "ingenuous" work, not all kinds, (4) service is not age-dependent, and (5) "in all things, children are more tenderly and favorably to be used."[36] William Gouge, who believes that children and servants lack agency while "under government," also implies that children, who have other "motives" to love their parents, needn't be made to feel the "trembling feare" recommended for servants in 1 Peter 2:18 and other texts.[37] Yet the examples above suggest that close connections between youth and service could have made specific relationships unpredictable and highly volatile. An early modern audience, familiar with some of these distinctions and connections, might have wondered whether the Ghost who so terrifies Hamlet can possibly love him as a son. Or why Polonius apparently credits his servant Reynaldo with an ingenuity lacking in either his son or his daughter.

Because they so frequently coincided in ordinary life, youth and service interact at some point within most of Shakespeare's plays. I have focused here on characters who are strikingly conscious of service and on two important issues which arise through their behavior: instrumentality and imitation. Although generally ignored by current scholarship, the awareness of using or being used as a human instrument occurs often in representations of service and can convey more anguish than we might expect. Imitation, much discussed as an element of theatricality and disguising, takes on special importance as a form of cultural development propelled by servants who try to imitate their masters. Pertinent to sixteenth and seventeenth as well as to eighteenth-century English society is J. Jean Hecht's sense of the servant as an agent of cultural change, well equipped through many opportunities for imitation: "a whole scheme of life lay open to his inspection."[38] When Rosalind in *As You Like It* or Viola in *Twelfth Night* disguise themselves by imitating servants, they slip easily into schemes of life maintained through networks of reciprocity and mutual support. Hamlet, however, intuits through his encounters with young people and servants a scheme or order which he feels compelled to resist. This resistance helps to explain why he is often acutely sensitive to the dangers of instrumentality and imitation, dangers to which other revengers seem either indifferent or blind. In this enormously complex tragedy, Hamlet's attitude toward service and servants provides one measure of how badly he has been damaged by a deliberate alienation. His resentment of go-betweens and mediators contributes to his most brutal and destructive acts.

SERVICE AND HEROISM IN *HAMLET*

Hamlet's engagement with service takes several forms. The most obvious of these forms is his relation to Polonius, Rosencrantz and Guildenstern, the agents of Claudius whom he treats with increasing contempt. He himself serves as the agent of his father's Ghost, born to cure a country that is "out of joint" (1.5.188) or, in a more significant phrase, used after he kills Polonius, to be a "scourge and minister" (3.4.175). For Hamlet "minister" may well express its Latin meaning of petty servant or slave, the antonym of *magister* or master.[39] The play indicates that like other young masters or leaders, Hamlet feels humiliated by a subordinate position. Orlando in *As You Like It* rebels against his treatment as a "peasant" (1.1.68). Hotspur in *1 Henry IV* consigns those who merely serve royal intentions to the rank of "base second means" (1.3.165). When ordered by Cardinal Pandulph to make peace with King John, Louis, the Dauphin of France protests

> I am too high-born to be propertied,
> To be a secondary at control,
> Or useful servingman and instrument
> To any sovereign state throughout the world. (5.2.79–82)

Other stage revengers who are merely court officials or followers suffer from madness and melancholy but exploit their secondary positions with less discomfort.

To mock his opponents and disguise his rage, Hamlet behaves at moments like a particularly knavish young attendant. In assuming an "antic disposition" to confuse his enemies, he also drops into the liminal ranks of "silken, sly, insinuating jacks" who were generally assigned a low status and treated as lackeys whether they later grew up to be heirs, officers, or servingmen.[40] Licensed to speak as openly as any jester (the Page in *2 Henry IV* is a good example), and able to move through social barriers, the nimble young court servant apparently enjoyed something of the freedom which older youths might seek in cities and universities. This regressive element of Hamlet's conduct provides much of the comedy in the play and must have delighted audiences accustomed to the outrageous pranks of pages and apprentices. From his taunting of Polonius to the performance of "The Mousetrap" to Hamlet's enforced departure for England, his knavish wit intensifies particular encounters. Shamed by his own child-like helplessness and furious with the King, Hamlet often provokes laughter when he takes leave of Claudius with barbed docility:

HAMLET Farewell, dear mother.
KING Thy loving father, Hamlet.
HAMLET My mother: father and mother is man and wife, man and wife is one
flesh – so, my mother. (4.3.49–52)

Hamlet's initial contacts with servants begin to explain his later distrust of service. These contacts are strongly positive. He learns about the Ghost from a group of loyal guardsmen who with Horatio have approached him "[a]s needful in our loves, fitting our duty" (1.1.173). He generously welcomes Horatio, who has introduced himself as "your poor servant ever," by replying "my good friend – I'll change that name with you" (1.2.162–3). Speaking with these companions while they await the Ghost on the battlements, Hamlet uses the phrase "Nature's livery" (1.4.32) to excuse inevitable human failings. His companions try to restrain and protect him when he is summoned by the Ghost; they release him when he threatens to "make a ghost of him that lets me!" (1.4.85); and they are then sworn, in effect, to drop their support of Hamlet and his concerns, through the way that Hamlet (urged on by the Ghost) defines his responsibility: "The time is out of joint – O cursed spite, / That ever I was born to set it right!" (1.5.188–9) This peculiar, sensational swearing ceremony anticipates Hamlet's later disavowals of marriage and friend-ship. Before an audience can grasp his motives, they watch him cut himself off from well-meaning helpers and allies. It is ironic that in this context he calls the Ghost, echoing his command to swear on his sword from beneath the stage, a "boy" and a "truepenny" (1.5.150). Editors have glossed "truepenny" as a term for a "trusty fellow" or reliable servant.

Hamlet's next dramatic encounter is with the King's own truepenny, Polonius. Polonius thinks of himself as a brilliant advisor to Claudius but generally behaves as a more domestic mediator, the sort of over-bearing upper servant or official who could have been perceived as interfering in relations between parents and children. His scheme for having Reynaldo spy on Laertes in Paris may partly inspire his equally home-spun scheme for spying on Hamlet. As if he were following the advice he has given to Reynaldo – "observe his inclination in yourself" (2.1 68) – he accounts for Hamlet's distraught conduct to Ophelia by remembering the "extremity for love" he has suffered "in my youth" (2.2.189–90). He has already anticipated in Laertes "such wanton, wild, and usual slips / As are companions noted and most known / To youth and liberty" (2.1.22–4). And he has apologized to Ophelia for his "jealousy" in forbidding any contact with Hamlet: "it is as proper to our age / To cast beyond ourselves in our opinions, / As it is common for the younger sort / To lack discretion" (2.1.111–14). Hamlet, so violently carried away from any possi-bility of sexual love, fathoms in Polonius a parental obsession with sexual license; he mocks him as a "fishmonger" who has perishable goods on his hands (2.2.174).

While Hamlet is exercising his frustrated wit on this fuss-budget, he is also provoking our attention to changes in his sense of his role. Speaking to Polonius with the deference owed to an inquiring stranger who is "friend" and "sir," Hamlet riddles on the childishness of servility: "for yourself, sir, shall grow old as I am, if like a crab you could go backward" (2.2.202–4). This is again to observe another's inclination in oneself. Hamlet projects upon old Polonius a morbid feeling of infantile helplessness, later repeated when he scoffs to Rosencrantz and Guildenstern, "That great baby you see there is not yet out of his swaddling-clouts" (2.2.382–3). The Ghost has weakened Hamlet in body if not in mind: "hold, hold, my heart, / And you, my sinows, grow not instant old, / But bear me [stiffly] up" (1.5.93–5). He takes leave of his companions on the battlements and later welcomes Rosencrantz and Guildenstern by emphasizing his poverty (1.5.184, 2.2.272). The audience may not see Hamlet as Ophelia describes him to Polonius, with his stockings "down-gyved to his ankle" like chains or shackles (2.1.77). We do see, well before they actually inspire his wrath, that servants remind him of his limited strength and means.

With the entry of Rosencrantz and Guildenstern, Hamlet's feeling of weakness becomes much more intelligible. Quite aside from being bound to plan a secret regicide, Hamlet is constrained, with Rosencrantz and Guildenstern, by membership in a gerontocracy.[41] The first Act of *Hamlet* dramatizes the power of age over youth when Claudius allows Laertes to depart for Paris and keeps Hamlet from returning to Wittenberg, or when the Norwegian king prevents his warlike nephew Fortinbras from attacking Denmark. Polonius confidently supervises his children and servants. In a fit of aged wisdom, Laertes warns Ophelia that Hamlet's will is not his own where marriage is concerned, both because he is heir to the throne ("subject to his birth") and because he is still young and may alter his preference: "as this temple waxes, / The inward service of the mind and soul / Grows wide withal" (1.3.12–14).[42] Fortinbras excepted, these young men will die by the end of the play. Growing up will mean, as Barbara Everett so eloquently writes, "growing dead."[43] When Hamlet discovers that Claudius has summoned Rosencrantz and Guildenstern to court and that their "visitation" is not "free" (2.2.275), he immediately realizes that they have no autonomy. To deflect their offers of service ("I will not sort you with the rest of my servants: for to speak to you like an honest man, I am most dreadfully attended" 2.2.267–9), is to suspect that their circumstances would make them particularly dangerous allies. Hamlet stays well ahead of Rosencrantz and Guildenstern in his growth toward fatal maturity.

I suggested above that young men brought up together might be expected to enjoy lifelong reciprocity or what Hamlet calls "the rights of our fellowship" (2.2.284). Claudius assumes that Rosencrantz and Guildenstern may be able to help find a "remedy" for Hamlet's trans-formation because they have been "of so young days brought up with him, / And sith so neighbored to his youth and havior" (2.2.11–12). It is the very "consonancy of our youth" (2.2.284–5) to which Hamlet appeals when he gets Rosencrantz and Guildenstern to admit, in a moment fraught with great dramatic tension, that they have indeed been "sent for" (2.2.292). This same "consonancy" forces Hamlet to turn away from their service and friendship. Had he been reading the English chronicles, he would have learned that the enemies of Edward II and Richard II attacked them through the beloved friends of their youth. Hamlet does not need to be present when Rosencrantz and Guildenstern, understanding that Claudius can command them, volunteer their services

(2.2.26–32). He knows what any young courtier or prince would know, and can place himself in their position as he explains why they have been summoned: "I will tell you why, so shall my anticipation prevent your discovery, and your secrecy to the King and Queen moult no feather" (2.2.293–5).

In *The Whole Journey*, C. L. Barber and Richard P. Wheeler observe that Shakespeare designed the play to make an audience accept Hamlet's point of view toward people who do not "matter."[44] But Rosencrantz and Guildenstern do matter even if their "consonancy" or harmony with one another deprives them of much individuality. Hamlet has "much talked" of them, says Gertrude: "And sure I am two men there is not living / To whom he more adheres" (2.2.20–1). Hamlet himself appeals to the "obligation of our ever-preserv'd love" (2.2.285–6) and calls them "my good friends" when he leaves them after the player's speech. The tragedy of Hamlet becomes more moving and powerful when Ophelia is either imagined or represented on stage as a woman Hamlet might have married in another life. The fact that Hamlet will later treat Ophelia and his young friends with knavish scorn does not mean that they fully deserve it. They never know what he knows about the great villainy of Claudius. Hamlet cannot afford to have friends who are weak and dependent, any more than he can afford to marry a woman at the mercy of her father, Polonius. Harold Jenkins believes that when Ophelia describes Hamlet's departure from her chamber, with his head turned and his eyes bent upon her, she is in effect describing his agonized farewell to marriage.[45] Why not perform Hamlet's farewell to Rosencrantz and Guildenstern with a touch of ruefulness? As he says "Ay, so God buy to you" and begins his soliloquy with "Now I am alone," he has severed ties between obligation and love, service and friendship, ties which sustain relations in the *Sonnets* and in play after play. His only friend will be Horatio, a Stoic figure who remains steadfast because he depends on no one.[46]

Hamlet avoids being victimized because of his attachments. Instead he destroys the agents of Claudius through a process confused by misunderstandings and accidents. To the extent that other young people and servants deserve pity, the primal tragedy of Cain and Abel, alluded to by Claudius and Hamlet, becomes more inclusive. It certainly becomes much richer than the mighty two-hander perceived by Hamlet as a duel "Between the pass and fell incensed points / Of mighty opposites" (5.2.61–2). Until he kills Claudius, Hamlet changes and grows through interaction with surrogates and substitutes, insiders who obey Claudius and outsiders like the actors and pirates whom Hamlet can employ.

Rosencrantz and Guildenstern may at first remind Hamlet of his own severe limitations. In response to Hamlet's glad question, "Good lads, how do you both?" Rosencrantz replies, "As the indifferent children of the earth" (2.2.225–7). Almost immediately Hamlet asks (in F) why "Fortune" has sent them to "prison" in Denmark (2.2.241). If Rosencrantz and Guildenstern are trying to disclaim self-interest through their obscure wordplay on ambition as a "shadow" peculiar to "shadows" or dependent followers (2.2.262), they are also revealing a weakness Hamlet must overcome and react against. After the success of "The Mousetrap" he treats them as if he were an aristocrat pestered by contemptible syco-phants. His tremendous new authority in chastizing his mother has already appeared in his wrath at Rosencrantz, Guildenstern and Polo-nius when they join in summoning him to Gertrude's chamber. Killing Polonius should have weakened Hamlet irretrievably. Instead it even-tually leads to another liberating reaction against weakness when a "kind of fighting" in his "heart" prompts him to discover that Rosen-crantz and Guildenstern are carrying his death warrant. What rouses him is the feeling that "I lay / Worse than the mutines in the [bilboes]" (5.2.4–6).

A "kind of fighting" well describes the way that Hamlet struggles not only with actual servants but also with his own subordinate role as revenging son. Samuel Johnson maintained that "Hamlet is, through the whole play, rather an instrument than an agent."[47] After the players arrive, he seems to wrestle with his instrumentality, perceiving its contra-dictions. In his great soliloquy beginning "O, what a rogue and peasant slave am I!," Hamlet tries to shock himself into action by accusing himself of servile passivity. He imagines that if he were called "villain," beaten on the pate, plucked by the beard and humiliated in other ways, he would simply "take it" (2.2.572–6). Not to act is to forfeit independence and responsibility: "I / A dull and muddy-mettled rascal, peak / Like John-a-dreams, unpregnant of my cause / And can say nothing" (2.2.566–9). But Hamlet also surmises something that his rash murder of a rash Polonius will bring home to him; a mindless absorption in one's function can be just as instrumental. When he begins to rehearse action within his soliloquy by loudly venting his hatred of the "slave" Claudius, he quickly discovers another sort of servility. Now he blames himself for cursing like a "very drab, / A stallion" (586–7). In the Folio reading, "scullion," Hamlet compares the humblest of servants to a prostitute. Awareness of these contradictions prompts him to develop a plan: using a play to "catch the conscience of the King."

A vital context for this speech and for his meditation, "To be or not to be" is Hamlet's profound admiration for the travelling players who can manage to offer service (2.2.318) while retaining their liberty. He anticipates that "the lady shall say her mind freely" (2.2.324–5) and requests a provocative speech with "Masters, you are all welcome. We'll e'en to't, like [French] falc'ners – fly at any thing we see" (2.2.429–30). A hawk or falcon is a disciplined, princely instrument for active hunting. Better to think of oneself as a hawk ("Come, [bird,] come," 1.5.116) than as a mechanical handsaw or a human tool like Pyrrhus, bludgeoning Priam with the force of "Cyclops' hammers" (2.2.489). The "To be or not to be" speech, which exhilarates audiences with its sweep and breadth, is partly an exercise in free mental flight. After his compassionate survey of universal suffering, Hamlet encounters Ophelia and changes his style. He speaks with the only freedom he can safely use when he turns his knavish sarcasm upon her, treating her as if he were indeed a lecherous servingman like the "saucy" fellow Grace Mildmay describes.[48]

Hamlet is most apt to attack service or speak knavishly when he feels his freedom slipping away. This is why he responds so rudely when Rosencrantz and Guildenstern bring a summons from his mother: "Have you any further trade with us?" (3.2.334). Elated by the success of his dramatic hunting scheme, he cannot tolerate a hurt appeal to former "love" by Rosencrantz or the suggestion that in hiding the cause of his distemper from a friend, "You do surely bar the door upon your own liberty" (3.2.338–9). This complaint, from a secondary cause of his bondage, so angers Hamlet that he accuses his old friends of trying to "play" upon him like a recorder: "You would play upon me, you would seem to know my stops, you would pluck out the heart of my mystery" (3.2.364–6). Observing their inclination in himself and simultaneously criticizing it, he storms, "how unworthy a thing you make of me!" and "Call me what instrument you will" (3.2.363–4, 370–1). He assumes that Rosencrantz and Guildenstern flatter to deceive or, with Polonius, imitate to entrap. ("They fool me to the top of my bent" 3.2.384).[49] Hamlet puns on "mystery" as his secret revenge and as a trade or occupation which must never sink into servitude. A few minutes later, he refuses to kill Claudius at prayer, thereby sending him (Hamlet believes) to heaven. That would be "hire and salary"; Hamlet would be serving Claudius as another of his henchmen!

From the perspective I have been describing, Hamlet's killing of Polonius is more than an accident. It represents a direct attack upon service in the person of the king's chief minister and surrogate. It openly and publically severs Hamlet from the traditional relations of support he has already given up in private. It is a terrible mistake, as Hamlet realizes in the lines cited above: "heaven hath pleas'd it so / To punish me with this, and this with me, / That I must be their scourge and minister" (3.4.173–5). Although an audience, caught up by an intensely exciting sequence, will focus on Hamlet's treatment of Gertrude, it is possible I think that Shakespeare has designed a deadly frame for their interview: old Polonius murdered on the stage and old Hamlet appearing in order to "whet" his sons's "blunted purpose" (as if Hamlet had not just used his knife). Polonius dies of the contradictions Hamlet has tried to overcome, entangled in a thick web or virtual "arras" of relationships, too dependent and too rashly carried away by his office. Old "truepenny," the Ghost, so piteously weak and so obsessed with revenge, may represent this contradiction in a dehumanized and extreme form. After the closet scene, Hamlet seems to become more tolerant of an instrumental, secondary role and its contradictions: action subsumed within the agencies of others on one hand and sudden thrusts of whetted purpose on the other.

Rosencrantz and Guildenstern die from such a thrust when Hamlet re-writes his own death warrant by swiftly exchanging their names for his. He frankly acknowledges the instrumental nature of this act by apologizing for his rashness ("Our indiscretion sometime serves us well" 5.2.8) and for his hand-writing skill ("yemen's service" 5.2.36). Rosencrantz and Guildenstern have never understood why their friendship with Hamlet is incompatible with their services to Claudius. They can make no sense of Hamlet's knavish warning to a "spunge . . . that soaks up the King's countenance, his rewards, his authorities" (4.2.14–16): "When he needs what you have glean'd, it is but squeezing you, and, spunge, you shall be dry again" (19–21). Although we may sentimentalize Rosencrantz and Guildenstern if we regard them, with Tom Stoppard as "bewildered innocents," it is far from certain that they would have become such zealous servants to Claudius without Hamlet's scorn.[50] Nor is it indisputable that they eventually "make love," as Hamlet claims, to the "employment" that will kill them (5.2.57). Rosencrantz is not simply flattering the monarch when he testifies to the vulnerability of followers in a crisis of authority: "The cess of majesty/Dies not alone, but like a gulf doth draw / What's near it with it" (3.3.15–17). John Kerrigan, finding more emphasis on friendship in the Folio text, suggests that this added line on "employment" may show that Hamlet is "less sure of the pair's complicity in F than Q₂" and that he may be shrugging off blame.[51] If early modern audiences were as ignorant about Claudius as Rosencrantz and Guildenstern are, they might have guessed that Claudius sends all three young men off to his tributary monarch in England, not to kill one of them but for their mutual good and Hamlet's cure. In other contexts such a plan would continue their education and accord with the practice of sending young people out to other families for their training, protection, and discipline.

Hamlet's deliberate self-alienation from reciprocal relationships, from service and marriage, compels him to ward off both his young, dependent friends and the woman he loves. The design of Shakespeare's tragedy gives more prominence to the plight of Ophelia than to that of Rosencrantz and Guildenstern; the effects of her madness and suicide make her brother Laertes highly susceptible when Claudius seduces him into killing Hamlet by treachery.[52] Might Shakespeare have noted the irony that in Greek the name "Ophelia" can mean service or support?[53] Seemingly infected by Hamlet's vexed and virulent attitudes toward service and dependency, mad Ophelia sings of the baker's daughter and the Valentine maid as if she herself were a seduced servant girl. Rosencrantz and Guildenstern "go to't" (5.2.56). If the actor playing Horatio pauses before he makes this comment on Hamlet's reported treatment of Rosencrantz and Guildenstern, he could seem to withhold his full assent. His observation could mime, in its curtness, Hamlet's merciless efficiency. Horatio's dramatic timing might prompt an audience to have some second thoughts about this play's tragic fusions of servants and children, Cains and Abels both, all more terribly "soil'd [wi' th'] working" (2.1.40) than Polonius could ever have imagined.

Falstaff and Enobarbus, the dependent friends to be considered in chapter 4, will be fatally vulnerable during a crisis. Otherwise they differ from Rosencrantz and Guildenstern in a number of significant respects: their age, their experience, their deep attachment to those they follow, and their great theatrical appeal. It would have been impertinent for Shakespeare to invoke the fates of Clytus (*Henry V* 4.7.39) or Lichas (*Antony and Cleopatra* 4.12.45), friends slain by Alexander and Hercules, when Hamlet sends Rosencrantz and Guildenstern to their deaths. Hamlet himself may be thirty years old but he is still a young Hercules; he has just reached heroic stature when he dies. Almost single-handedly he has replaced the guards on the battlements of Elsinore and slain Denmark's greatest enemy, its corrupt king. To his enormous credit he has eluded capture by Claudius, his own misery or the constricting, subordinate roles he plays in order to avenge his father. He has used them to understand his opponents and his opportunities. Loyalty to the Ghost, a "thing" that appears by night (1.1.21), could have turned him into a Pyrrhus but he resists such servile mechanization. It will be helpful, therefore to contrast him with another young hero who is far more violent but not so strong. Coriolanus will reduce himself to an instrument when he tries to behave as a dehumanized and vengeful spectre.

PUBLIC SERVICE AND SLAVERY IN CORIOLANUS

Whereas Hamlet struggles with his role as "scourge and minister," Coriolanus seems largely unaware of how accurately Aufidius speaks when he insults his rival: "Wert thou the Hector / That was the whip of your bragg'd progeny / Thou shouldst not scape me here" (1.8.11–13). Hector scourged the Greek enemies of the Trojans; Coriolanus will punish his own people as well (which they intimate at 2.3.91–3), turning into a machine for death. This exaggerated instrumentality is already implicit in the terms of the challenge which Coriolanus hurls at Aufidius early in the play: "Let the first budger die the other's slave, / And the gods doom him after!" (1.8.5–6). When such references to slavery occur in English Renaissance literature they have generally been understood as little more than crude insults. According to Moses Finley, the references to slavery in classical plays are virtually worthless as evidence about the actual social attitudes.[54] This is emphatically not the case where *Coriolanus* is concerned. Such references not only show how characters understand subjection; they also indicate that Shakespeare, developing minimal suggestions in his probable sources, Plutarch's *Lives* and Livy's *History of Rome*, knew that slavery could change people into things. In dramatizing the Rome of Coriolanus, he seems to have drawn upon a general English aversion to serfdom as well as upon a more aristocratic contempt for low status and physical work.[55] Resemblances between early modern and ancient Roman attitudes toward service would have been more accessible to audiences then than now, for as Jean-Louis Flandrin writes: "All that appears unfamiliar to us, in the status of the domestic servant, was already characteristic of that of the slave."[56]

Comparisons of Hamlet and Coriolanus have been rare; when they are approached as individuals their differences are likely to stand out.[57] Coriolanus may echo Hamlet when he objects to his mother's advice on how to behave in appealing for popular support: "Would you have me / False to my nature? Rather say, I play / The man I am" (3.2.14–16). Hamlet opposed his mother's argument for limited, conventional types of mourning with: "I know not 'seems'" (1.2.76); "they are actions that a man might play" (1.2.84). But while both know that imitation can deceive, Hamlet also knows that circumstances and character prevent most people from performing their natures. Unless one happens to be an Horatio, so constant and so oddly autonomous, seeming will rarely coincide with being. Hamlet's ethical sophistication is only one of many qualities which distinguish him from Coriolanus. Their social roles, rather than their personal traits, justify considering them together. Both young men are cast as the scourges of their societies. Both are compared to Hercules, that most servant-like and over-worked hero. Fratricidal conflict in Denmark summons up memories of Cain and Abel; in Rome it may evoke the primal myth of Roman origins, the murder of Remus by Romulus. Both young men are tested or "put on," proved to be capable of self-sacrifice, and killed.

Given these similarities in the roles they play, it is fair to suggest that the social worlds of young Hamlet and Coriolanus can be used for cross-reference and mutual illumination. Hamlet, as we have seen, feels imprisoned in a large Danish ménage. As revenger and exile, he distances himself from this establishment but he still seems susceptible to as well as suspicious of servants and young people. A Jacobean audience might have noticed that because Coriolanus has been given a military education (he was sent by his mother to "a cruel war" while "he was but tender-bodied" 1.3.13, 5–6), he has been spared the domestic entanglements of a normal young English aristocrat. Had he tumbled with Yorick or been "of so young days brought up" with Rosencrantz and Guildenstern, he could never have earned his oaken garlands.

The military education of Coriolanus helps to explain his scornful view of underlings. By achieving a precocious early heroism, he has missed an immersion in contexts where children, servants, and other dependents interacted. He would not have experienced the prolonged youth typical of early modern England. There are several reasons for thinking that this hypothesis about his education might be more useful than psychological approaches in explaining for his attitudes and actions. Psychological interpretations don't account for his reluctance to be a political leader or to accept reward. They miss the significance of his encounters with slaves and slavery. They tend to blame his mother for causing his downfall when it is Aufidius who can ultimately destroy him by calling him a "boy."

Plutarch traces the disposition of Coriolanus to his military upbringing. He writes that "lack of education" made Coriolanus, who was gifted with "natural wit and great heart," "choleric and impatient," "churlish, uncivil, and altogether unfit for any man's conversation."[58] He implies that if Coriolanus had sought to become learned rather than valiant, he would not have succeeded as a warrior. Learning, Plutarch believes, "teacheth men that be rude and rough of nature, by compass and rule of reason to be civil and courteous and to like better the mean state than the higher." But "in those days, valiantness was honoured in Rome above all other virtues" (297). To a degree, the faults of the warrior are those of his world. Shakespeare revises this anti-heroic perspective by indicating that Coriolanus is rude to almost everyone beneath the "higher" ranks and that he represents Roman "valiantness" or *virtus* in an exaggerated form. In Plutarch's "Life of Coriolanus" it is the people who fear to become "bondmen, notwithstanding all the wounds and cuts they showed" from battles, and who rebel when the Senate allows them to become "slaves and bondmen to their creditors" (301). Shakespeare transforms this Roman resistance to bondage by giving his scarred hero phobic responses to servitude. Shakespeare could have read later in the "Life" that at this period of their history, the Romans "did use their bondmen very gently, because they themselves did labour with their own hands and lived with them and among them; and therefore they did use them the more gently and familiarly" (340). Deprived of a social education which would make him familiar with ordinary dependants, Shakespeare's young warrior treats them with aversion.

Perhaps because he was accustomed to the subordinate status of most young people, the dramatist can develop a contradiction which the ancient biographer does not seem to identify. Having, as his general Cominius says, performed as a warrior while still in his "pupil age" (2.2.98), Coriolanus seems content to follow Cominius and boasts repeatedly of his "services" to Rome. His education has created the radical dependency of someone who scorns dependants on those who can use his talents as a fighter. He defines himself as a "sword" wielded by Rome (1.6.76); when his mother wants him to lead, not follow, by standing for consul, he protests, "I had rather be their servant in my way / Than sway with them in theirs" (2.1.203–4). Psychological interpretations of Coriolanus have been preoccupied with his dependency on a mother who has deprived him of nurture and threatened him with castration. In psychoanalytic readings, Coriolanus denies any physical weakness because he is horrified by his bond to his mother. He hungers, writes Stanley Cavell, "to lack nothing, to be complete, like a sword."[59] But this does not explain why so self-contained an individual prefers not to rule others, a preference which will dispose him to serve Aufidius as an instrument of vengeance when he is driven from Rome by the "voice of slaves" (4.5.77), that is, the Roman people who are ungrateful for his "painful service" (4.5.68) to his country. "Make my misery serve thy turn," he urges Aufidius:

> So use it
> That my revengeful services may prove
> As benefits to thee; for I will fight
> Against my cank'red country with the spleen
> Of all the under fiends. (4.5.88–92)

Central to this tragedy is the unanswered question of how to reward a public servant who refuses to be thanked but who, by saving the state, has created an overwhelming sense of obligation. Plutarch provides two different explanations for this hero's view of rewards. First, Coriolanus and other Romans have been so "bred" that they value "not to receive reward for service done, but rather take it for a remembrance and encouragement, to make them do better in time to come." Second, Coriolanus is distinct from other Romans because "the only thing that made him to love honour was the joy he saw his mother did take of him" (299–300). Shakespeare's play emphasizes the first explanation when Cominius praises Coriolanus by saying that he "rewards / His deeds with doing them" (2.2.127–8). It gives the second to a hostile citizen: "he did it to please his mother, and to be partly proud" (1.1.38–9). Such allegations will be echoed by the enemies of Coriolanus, the tribunes and Aufidius. His mother obviously rejoices in his victories, but imagines heroism and reward in mundane *georgic* terms. She describes her son as a worker employed by others when she visualizes him on the battlefield:

> His bloody brow
> With his mail'd hand then wiping, forth he goes,
> Like to a harvest-man [that's] task'd to mow
> Or all or lose his hire. (1.3.34–7)

Coriolanus, however, suspects that demonstrating his wounds to the people will suggest that he received them "for the hire / Of their breath only!" (2.2.149–50). Not his mother, then, but the youthful military initiation, rehearsed at length by Cominius (2.2.87–98) probably causes him to confuse honorable rewards with shameful wages. When he refuses to accept gifts and praise after his victory at Corioli, Cominius replies,

> If 'gainst yourself you be incens'd, we'll put you
> (Like one that means his proper harm) in manacles,
> Then reason safely with you. (1.9.56–8)

His antipathy to reward is indeed a kind of madness. In this Roman society, some of the people who worked without reward might well have been manacled. They would have been slaves.

No play creates a more disturbing connection between nobility and servility than does this one. Even in a world riven by social prejudice, Coriolanus stands out for the virulence of his aristocratic disdain. Could Shakespeare have been recalling *The Rape of Lucrece* when Comenius, in his oration to the Senate, speaks of young Martius driving against the enemy with his "Amazonian [chin]," saving a Roman life, and striking Tarquin himself on the knee (2.2.91–5)? "In that day's feats," he continues,

> When he might act the woman in the scene,
> He prov'd best man i' th' field, and for his meed
> Was brow-bound with the oak. (2.2.95–8)

Tarquin overcomes Lucrece by threatening to bind her raped corpse to that of a dead slave. In consequence she suffers from a sense of morbid abjection analogous to what Orlando Patterson, in his brilliant book on slavery, calls "social death." By thoroughly conquering his own tender-bodied and much-violated weakness (he received seven wounds, according to his mother 2.1.150), Coriolanus has acquired a *virtus* tainted with servility. His devotion to state service as a living weapon means that he both resists and reveals an affinity with the human things who would have been the living victims of his conquests.

This social pathology emerges when Romans try to reward him for his victory over the Volscians. He has entered and then emerged from the gates of Corioles, a Volscian city, eager to rally the Romans and looking, says Cominius, like "a thing of blood" (2.2.109; cf. "flea'd" 1.6.22). As the Romans show gratitude, first by giving him the surname Coriolanus and then by asking him to stand for consul, his isolation, scorn and instrumentality grow stronger. It is as if his new stature places hero and Romans in false positions. Their first failure occurs when Coriolanus wants to rescue from slavery a Volscian who had been his "poor host" (1.9, 87). The fact that he can't save this man (as he does in Plutarch's "Life") because he literally forgets his name suggests to some readers that he disdains social inferiority or that he is somehow rejecting a father-figure.[60] In Plutarch, this generosity to an "old friend," along with his "abstinence" from rewards, persuades Roman soldiers of his "virtue" (312–13). I would surmise that his forgetfulness, which he blames on his wrath at Aufidius, occludes his defensiveness toward slaves and their helplessness. That he sees the obligations of hospitality as contaminating emerges later when he resolves to be calm with the people "as an hostler, that [for th'] poorest piece / Will bear the knave by'th' volume" (3.3.32–3). Coriolanus has been challenging Aufidius with "Let the first budger die the other's slave" (1.8.5) moments, it would seem, after the host who "us'd me kindly" cries out to him for help and is led away as a prisoner (1.9.83–5). It takes no Hegelian theory of the master-slave dialectic to sense through this juxtaposition how slavery damages the reciprocal relations maintained by the customs of service, hospitality, and friendship. Heroic warriors become more inflexible while a generous care-giver is enchained.

Asking Coriolanus to stand for consul precipitates a sequence of mutual failures: conflict between Coriolanus and the people (burdened, it is clear, by their feeling of debt); the banishment of Coriolanus; his alliance with Aufidius and near-destruction of Rome. This sequence splendidly illustrates Naomi Conn Liebler's understanding of the interactive process through which tragedies are generated. "*Hamartia*," she writes, "is misrecognition not only by the protagonist, which could still be interpretable as a 'flaw' or an 'error', but also *by the community* of the identity and social function of the protagonist."[61] When Coriolanus confronts the plebians, they expose in one another the effects of promising development, personal and political, stunted on both sides by fears of extreme vulnerability and coercion. The play indicates that Coriolanus and the people are beginners, sharing a botched initiation into civic adulthood. The Tribunes, confident about their own mastery of political skill, regard Coriolanus and the people as naive, manipulable; in a caricature of husbandry (Menenius calls them "herdsmen of the beastly plebeians" 2.1.95) they speak of the people as sheep and of Coriolanus as a sheep-dog (2.1.257); later, they openly condescend to the people for their "childish friendliness" in yielding their "voices" to Coriolanus (2.3.175–6). "Have I had children's voices?" Coriolanus asks (3.1.30) after the people are persuaded to retract their approval. The candidate for consul who must stand in the market place wearing the symbolic "gown of humility" (2.3.40) or "woolvish [toge]" (115) feels thoroughly dishonored by having to "crave the hire which first we do deserve" (2.3.114) from those he later terms, citing his mother, "woolen vassalls, things created / To buy and sell with groats" (3.2.9–10). Beneath these evocations of seventeenth century hiring fairs and feudal bondage, we may find, I think, that Coriolanus sees himself, decked out in sheep's clothing, as a thing for sale in a slave market.[62]

In this crisis over service and reward (Coriolanus has been a "petty servant" to the Tribune Brutus 2.3.178, a diseased but curable limb or "gangren'd" "foot" to Menenius 3.1.294–5, 304–5), we are never far from the horrors of abjection, focused though these may be through a *pharma-kon* or living bearer of social sickness. The execution of Coriolanus by Romans would be, Menenius states, "A brand to th' end a' th' world" (3.1.302). Coriolanus reveals how deeply he has been touched in his ordeal by the brand or stigma of slavery when he expresses an encyclopedic sense of shame:

> Away, my disposition, and possess me
> Some harlot's spirit! My throat of war be turn'd,
> Which quier'd with my drum, into a pipe
> Small as an eunuch, or the virgin voice
> That babies lull asleep! The smiles of knaves
> Tent in my cheeks, and schoolboys' tears take up
> The glasses of my sight! A beggar's tongue
> Make motion through my lips, and my arm'd knees,
> Who bow'd but in my stirrup, bend like his
> That hath receiv'd an alms! (3.2.111–20)[63]

This speech prepares us for his swift reduction to instrumentality once he and Romans have banished each other. His references to harlots and pipes recall Hamlet's shame at being manipulated; "tent" and "take up" convey his feeling of being occupied and owned. Appropriately, he enters the service of Aufidius by passage through a company of knavish figures, the household corps of the Volscian leader. They scorn him and he taunts them. His conduct, according to Ruth Nevo, is "a repudiation of all that is menial, slavish, and dependent by one who senses that his own inde-pendence is founded upon quicksand."[64] When Coriolanus goes looking for a "world elsewhere," he finds a congenial home with a brutal, servile tribe whose leader has already vowed to "Wash my fierce hand in's heart" (1.10.27). The insults which he had earlier heaped upon the Roman people, calling them "quarter'd slaves" or "fragments" who "change a mind" about their leaders, seem inclined to cannibalism, and sit by the fire gossiping about political factions (1.1 182–99, 222), would more fairly describe the Volscian servingmen. They quickly change their tune after his welcome by Aufidius and the Volscian lords, discrediting Aufidius and beginning to idolize Coriolanus, who will "sowl the porter of Rome gates by th' ears" and "mow all down before him" (4.5.200–9). In war, says the Third Servingman, men really "need one another" (231–2).[65]

Exiled from his city, Coriolanus welcomes the role which Hamlet plays in a more reluctant, unconventional manner. He turns into a spirit of retribution, more like the Ghost than like Hamlet himself in resembling "a thing / Made by some other deity than Nature" (4.6.90–1). Aufidius, who actually regards this monster as the "foot / Of our design" (4.7.7–8), exploits his services as a deadly weapon against Rome. Coriolanus never becomes aware of how he has enslaved himself to Aufidius, but his language, I believe, does, during his reply to the supplication by Menenius:

> Wife, mother, child, I know not. My affairs
> Are servanted to others. Though I owe
> My revenge properly, my remission lies
> In Volscian breasts. (5.2.82–5)

Glossed in recent editions as referring to the possibilities of pardon or of release from obligation, "remission" can also mean liberation or deliverance from captivity.[66]

The fact that an inhuman, thing-like quality has long been an element of this hero's *virtus* makes the climax of *Coriolanus* particularly surprising and painful. Before she begs her son to spare Rome, Volumnia points to his own small son who may in future "show like all yourself." Coriolanus responds with a prayer whose terms express the most admirable characteristics of this self:

> The god of soldiers,
> With the consent of supreme Jove, inform
> Thy thoughts with nobleness, that thou mayst prove
> To shame unvulnerable, and stick i' th' wars
> Like a great sea-mark, standing every flaw,
> And saving those that eye thee! (5.3.70–5)

Then Volumnia, who earlier objectified her son as an instrument of slaughter ("Death, that dark spirit, in's nervy arm doth lie" 2.1.160), recalls him to his humanity. By persuading him to honor his responsibilities to his family, thereby saving Rome, she undoes the military education which culminates when he recreates himself by exploding from the gates of Corioli as an isolated "thing of blood" (2.2.109).

This remission from slavery to Aufidius is brief. A nascent sense of fellowship and reciprocity cannot arm Coriolanus against insults by treacherous, servile Volscians. Aufidius justifies assassinating his "joint-servant" (5.6.31) by maintaining that he, not Coriolanus, has been made a degraded "follower" (38). Asserting that "[h]e wag'd me with his countenance as if / I had been mercenary" (5.6.39–49), Aufidius and Shakespeare evoke for seventeenth-century audiences the fate of soldiers neither protected nor rewarded by mighty leaders.[67] But Coriolanus rarely leads in this play as he has done in Plutarch's "Life." It is his masterful enslaver Aufidius who speaks when he openly accuses Coriolanus of enslaving Volscians: "At a few drops of women's rheum, which are / As cheap as lies, he sold the blood and labor / Of our great action" (5.6.45–7).

Because Coriolanus has just parted from his "nurse"/mother and "boy"/son, an audience may well wonder why the accusations of Aufidius can so swiftly infuriate him:

> at his nurse's tears
> He whin'd and roar'd away your victory
> That pages blush'd at him, and men of heart
> Look'd wond'ring each at others. (5.6.96–9)

Indicating that he, too, dissociates military service from personal dependency, Aufidius can demolish his rival by invoking the familiar roles and ordinary relations of young people in early modern England. Because both men scorn these normal rites of passage, "boy of tears" (5.6.100) can provoke Coriolanus into shouting, "Cut me to pieces." He boasts of killing Volscians in Corioles, Aufidius and his conspirators slaughter him and he reverts at last to his role as a "thing of blood." "Boy" literally means "slave" to Coriolanus. "'Boy'! O slave!" he rages. "Boy" to Shakespeare's audience might have meant a low menial servant, an actor, or a catamite, but it could also refer to a page or personal attendant.[68]

It might be objected that I have over-emphasized the power of slavery to infect dependent relationships in *Coriolanus*. Had he wished to stress its deadly force, Shakespeare could have made its presence much more explicit. He could have introduced loyal, humane slaves (like the duteous vassal in *The Rape of Lucrece* or Eros in *Antony and Cleopatra*) in order to undermine patrician attitudes. He could have developed the threat of captivity with which Coriolanus curses Rome (3.3.127–33) by following Livy rather than Plutarch and making the women who intercede expect "untimely death or long enslavement."[69] I have tried to show that the servility latent in a promising young man becomes malign through specific circumstances and dramatic conflicts. Like psychological arguments which explain his contradictions in oedipal and pre-oedipal terms, my interpretation does include a largely unconscious hero, but with these key differences. I would emphasize that whereas his behavior to women is generally dutiful and chivalrous, his behavior to plebeians and servants is vitriolically defensive. Moreover, it reveals attitudes which are widely shared by other Romans and Volscians. Without diminishing the claims of those who find so much terror of women in Shakespeare's tragedies,

I would urge that the terrors of extreme subjection are also important in this particular play because Coriolanus has been isolated from more ordinary dependencies and constantly exposed to threats of conquest and enslavement. To believe that his mother destroys him by persuading him to make peace is a mistake. Aufidius destroys him by treating him as a tool and then throwing him away.

The English word "hero" descends from a Greek word meaning a "guard" or "protector," like the great sea-mark imagined by Coriolanus in advising his son (5.3.74). The Latin word *servare*, meaning "to guard," is cognate with this Greek term. Our words "serve" and "servant," on the other hand, descend from the Latin word for "slave" which is *servus*.[70] In Roman language, then, as in the mind of Coriolanus, we find a barrier between the guardian and the lowly worker, between the protector and those who most need protection. The tragedies of *Hamlet* and *Coriolanus* question such barriers but represent service as a dangerous border country for young leaders. In two of his English plays, *King John* and *Cymbeline*, Shakespeare shows that young characters can survive by partially reconciling *servare* and *servus*. But the death of Prince Arthur is another tragedy. *King John* confirms and clarifies Hamlet's intuition that in a crisis of authority or conflict of loyalties, vulnerable children and servants may weaken one another.

SURVIVAL THROUGH SERVICE IN *CYMBELINE* AND *KING JOHN*

Because of his scorn for nurses and pages, whom he lumps with harlots, schoolboys, and beggars as examples of "inherent baseness" (3.2.123), Coriolanus refuses to practice the arts of imitation: impersonation as well as adaptation and adjustment. Studies of courtship like Frank Whigham's *Ambition and Privelege* which chart the twists and turns of machiavellian verbal art can make us forget that courtiers were ever young or that imitation of one's superiors in all walks of life was then, as now, a vital part of education. To his credit, the Page that Prince Hal assigns to Falstaff in *2 Henry IV* disturbs this process by making Falstaff and his crew look ridiculous; he condemns his masters when, presumably, he reappears as their "Boy" attendant in *Henry V*. That pages were normally expected to emulate their masters is suggested through Hotspur's complaint in *1 Henry IV*; when the "lords and barons of the realm" noted Northumberland's support for Bolingbroke, he recalls, they "Gave him their heirs as pages, followed him / Even at the heels in golden multitudes" (4.3.66, 72–3). As we have seen, Hamlet falls back on skills which

Coriolanus has never learned and can speak more freely by playing the knave himself. When he becomes a follower of Queen Elinor in *King John*, the Bastard satirizes, but also resolves to use "compliment" and "observation" (I.I.201, 208):

> . . . not alone in habit and device,
> Exterior form, outward accoutrement,
> But from the inward motion to deliver
> Sweet, sweet, sweet poison for the age's tooth,
> Which, though I will not practice to deceive,
> Yet, to avoid deceit, I mean to learn;
> For it shall strew the footsteps of my rising. (I.I.210–16)

That service was a form of social imitation, a customary practice which could teach wary young attendants to avoid deceit (and deceivers) is regularly assumed by those who advise servants and children. Servants at all levels are incessantly urged to avoid mere "eye-service," or a deceptive appearance of duty. Such counsel for upper servants attending in noble households or at court appears at times in personal letters. For example, Roger Manners, advising his thirteen year old niece, Bridget, recently appointed as a maid of honor, tells her to be "dyligent, secret and faythfull" and to "be no medeler in the cause of others."[71] In another such letter to a twelve year old daughter sent to the Court of Savoy (mentioned above p. 8), Annibal Guasco urges her to love her lady's favorite if she wants to be loved herself, to imitate the older servants, and to study others in order to accommodate herself, while avoiding calumny or gossip.[72] He supplements his own advice by giving her the conduct books of Baldesar Castiglione, Giovanni Della Casa, and M. Steeven Guazzo, where verbal negotiations often keep practitioners out of trouble. That young attendants did not always slip easily through the mazes of court intrigue is suggested by Francis Osborne when he advises his son not to bring to court or public places "boys not wise or strong enough to decline or revenge affronts, whose complaints do not seldom engage their masters, as I knew one of quality killed in the defence of his page."[73] Richard Brathwaite, objecting to a current preference for fewer attendants who are also younger and less well-bred ("pages and groomes"), insists that they be "well countenanced" (i.e., supervised).[74]

Cymbeline, one of the most idealistic plays in its representation of service, treats the survival of a young page countenanced by a good master more realistically. Because it appears to reduce her power and say little about her gender, Imogen's disguise has interested critics far less than have the more subversive roles of characters like Portia or Rosalind. The fact that her disguise also involves areas of experience relatively alien to current audiences or readers accounts for its neglect. We do not expect to be rescued by servants or to use service as a means of saving our lives. *Cymbeline* dramatizes a world where servants protect masters from themselves, children from their parents, and a wife, Imogen, from her husband Posthumus. These crucial interventions make it fitting that Britain ultimately returns to a dependent position as a Roman tributary. It is obviously germane to the topic of this chapter to consider, if briefly, how a princess who has married a poor and worthy orphan, bred by Cymbeline to serve in his own bed-chamber, preserves herself through imitating such a figure (her former "playfellow" 1.1.145) and being virtually adopted by her master, the Roman general, Lucius. Here, if anywhere, we may see how the fusions of youth and service might have worked when they were working, and why.

To "lose so bad employment" (3.4.110) as it would have been to obey Posthumus and kill his supposedly adulterous wife, Pisanio helps her escape from court, then instructs her on how to behave as a page:

> You must forget to be a woman; change
> Command into obedience; fear and niceness
> (The handmaids of all women, or more truly
> Woman it pretty self) into a waggish courage,
> Ready in gibes, quick-answer'd, saucy, and
> As quarrellous as the weasel. (3.4.154–9)

Dressed in her disguise, she is, "with what imitation you can borrow / From youth of such a season" (3.4.171–2), to present herself to Lucius, "desire his service," and "tell him / Wherein you're happy" (173–4). In the event, Pisanio's scheme turns out better than he could hope. Lucius discovers Imogen prostrated upon the corpse (of Cloten in the clothes of Posthumus) which she takes to be her husband's, and she is remarkably quick at translating her grief into terms suitable for a devoted page:

> Alas,
> There is no more such masters. I may wander
> From east to occident, cry out for service,
> Try many, all good; serve truly; never
> Find such another master. (4.2.370–4)

In consequence of her devotion, Lucius vows to "rather father thee than master thee" (4.2.395). When he is sentenced to death, he begs Cymbeline to spare the life of his page, "so kind, so duteous, diligent, / So tender over his occasions, true, / So feat, so nurse-like" (5.5.86–8), and it is as Cymbeline's page that Imogen can expose Iachimo and recover Posthumus, who strikes her as if she were a "weasel" for interrupting his grief. Eventually she saves Lucius too: "My good master / I will yet do you service" (5.5.403–4). Had Cymbeline always treated his young dependent, Posthumus, with the kindliness which Lucius uses toward Imogen or Belarius toward the princes he has kidnapped and fostered, there could have been no play.

Imogen has little in common with the wives whose relations with servants will be the subject of chapter 3. Instead, she escapes wifeliness and becomes an adolescent boy, replaying in some sense her husband's pre-history and encountering her blood brothers, striplings like herself who immediately love her as if she were their brother. There is not much opportunity for gender conflict lurking in this particular cross-dressed role, which instead brings out the talents and skills ("wherein you're happy") of the one who plays it. A coming-of-age through service, which in *Hamlet* threatens heroism, now tests and toughens the social fabric. Wales functions as the "world elsewhere" which Coriolanus could never have found, as a refuge for a youthful victim of sophisticated deceit. What would Coriolanus have thought of Belarius, a warrior whose only "treason" lies in educating royal boys and marrying the "nurse" who has stolen them for him? Service, Belarius tells them, "is not service, so being done / But being so allowed" (3.3.16–17). He means, I think, that only those helped by it are in a position to judge it as something other than a routine duty or obligatory performance. *Cymbeline* may have the plot of a fairy-tale ("infantile," George Bernard Shaw called it), but the play is serious where responsibilities to young servants and children are concerned.

Like Imogen, the Bastard in *King John* has recently figured in post-modern readings which emphasize the construction of national subjects.[75] But the play also shows, as Graham Holderness has argued for the second tetralogy, how thoroughly Shakespeare understood feudal customs and mentalities.[76] I would emphasize that the play is very much a work of the 1590's in revealing how treacherous for young people service within their own families and households might become. In the face of much advice to the contrary, people often drew upon their own relatives and children for service and attendance.[77] It is difficult to judge where kinship ends and service begins when reading the letter which Christopher Hatton sent along with his cousin and servant Peter Dutton, to Peter's father, John. Hatton urges him to receive and encourage a promising future courtier whom he vows to befriend later ("After he hath been with you a while, and discharged some part of his duty by presence towards you").[78] When even biological parentage can be made to sound like an adoptive arrangement, the Bastard's experience may be distinctive only because he prefers himself so aggressively in becoming the follower of his grandmother, Queen Elinor, and of King John.

Having chosen a vaguer service placing over a legitimate kinship role, the Bastard enjoys the kind of protection which licences a degree of free speech.[79] He is sheltered by his retainer's position when he brashly advises the Kings of France and England to attack Angiers (2.1.373–96). He provokes Hubert, sheltered by the walls of Angiers, into arguing (so disastrously for Arthur's cause) that John's niece Blanche should marry the Dauphin (2.1.423–55). Like Hubert, who soon becomes another of John's servants, the Bastard seems to be closely associated with the term "hand." Regarded by Emrys Jones as elements of Senecan style, the many "hands" referred to in *King John* also invoke the agency of retainers in a world of manual work, warfare, and communication.[80] To expound *The Housholders Philosophie*, Torquato Tasso idealizes the good servant as a "hand" that responds immediately to the master's "mind" (obeying him "at a winck of the eye, or bent of the brow"), and he praises this animate, ensouled "instrument of instruments" as a "lively and several instrument of action."[81] The Bastard boasts of his role when he threatens the invading French by referring to

> That hand which had the strength, even at your door
> To cudgel you and make you take the hatch,
> To dive like buckets in concealed wells,
> To crouch in litter of your stable planks,
> To lie like pawns lock'd up in chests, and trunks,
> To hug with swine, to seek sweet safety out
> In vaults and prisons, and to thrill and shake . . . (5.2.137–43)

Just such terror may drive Prince Arthur to seek his own "sweet safety" by disguising himself as a ship-boy and jumping to his death from the walls of his prison. In responding to the "heinous spectacle" of Arthur's body, seen by John's rebellious barons as clear evidence of murder, the Bastard says, "It is a damned and a bloody work, / The graceless action of a heavy hand – / If that it be the work of any hand" (4.3.57–9). After echoing the Bastard's last line in a tone of outraged disbelief, Salisbury promptly links "Hubert's hand" with John's mind ("The practice and the purpose of the King") and vows to "set a glory to this hand," namely his own, "By giving it the worship of revenge" (4.3.60–72). An audience will probably hesitate between the Bastard's doubt and Salisbury's conviction. We have seen John try to use Hubert as a mind-reading instrument who will intuit his murderous desires and kill Prince Arthur, placed in his care. But we have also seen Arthur persuade Hubert to change his mind.

Arthur's puzzling death draws to our attention the unpredictable, even spectral process by which mind becomes action in *King John*. In contrast to the often dismembered hands of other histories and tragedies, the "hands" so repeatedly mentioned in *King John* remain attached to bodies and minds. They are prominent in assurances of alliance or support or as symbols of personal strength; they join when characters attempt definitive actions by making marriage or peace. But with the Bastard's doubt, "If that it be the work of any hand," the play questions that direct link of hand to mind which the barons and John himself seem to take for granted. In this de-centered and indeterminate play, containing a series of beginnings which perform less than they promise, the obscure connection between Arthur's death and the behavior of John's "hands" provides a fascinating example of how dependents interact. The characters directly involved are too frightened, furious, or confused to understand how this process works. Hubert and the Bastard are "amazed" and lost at Arthur's death (4.3.140) and at the ensuing chaos of John's sickness, the French invasion, civil war, and impending defeat, which they later report to one another in Act 5, scene 6. The utter blackness of this brief scene hints that these "hands" have been in and will remain in the dark about their obligations during such a crisis. John's imminent death merely accentuates the oddly masterless empowerment of his agents.

How then does Arthur's death activate the opposing "hands" of the barons? In order to answer this question, we need to consider briefly a function of service relations which will be stressed in chapter 4. Arthur is the most tragic among those few young characters who in Shakespeare's plays seek protection through service. Notably they do so when kinship either vanishes or becomes an active threat. Viola believes that she has lost her brother in a shipwreck when she imitates him and serves Orsino. Edgar escapes violence at his father's hands by impersonating a crazed serving-man. Imogen, as we have seen, disguises herself as a page when her husband tries to have her killed. It would be specious to argue that these dramatic responses to emergency must typify common behavioral patterns. The only group of people who appear to have regularly sought cover through service were Jesuit spies.[82] What could have made Arthur's death more disturbing four hundred years ago would be a wide range of experiences through which service and security converged in people's lives.

Early modern children were often nursed, transported, disciplined, and rescued by servants or attendants. Associations of servants with food, warmth, and shelter would have been inevitable. A host of preachers and elders identified ideal service with selfless kindness. The very dependence upon the will of another which might disqualify a servant from adult political responsibilities might also re-qualify him as a trusted source of help. Tasso writes that servants, being reasonable like children, need reason more than children do "to rescue many times and asist their Maisters in the Perill of some civill broyle or other troubles, that may oftentimes betide them."[83] While such moralism is unreliable in documenting social practice, a few stories and anecdotes do support what might otherwise appear to be a nostalgic fantasy or, in the tradition of Roman comedy, a dramatic cliché.[84] Moreover, contemporaries often suggest that being protected is one of the benefits enjoyed by servants.[85]

It seems that Hubert's reference to Arthur's "innocent prate" (4.1.25) has often shaped interpretations of Arthur's response when threatened with blinding. But Arthur knows what he is doing here; he does not deserve to be treated as a weak, unpromising prince whose death is meaningless and pathetic. His conduct shows evidence of the "crafty love" or "cunning" which he himself acknowledges (4.1.53–4).He has emphasized that he and his uncle, King John, fear each other, even before he reads John's instructions to Hubert. What is crafty is not his affection for Hubert but his reminder, in these circumstances, of how he served him. Because of his repeated attentions to Hubert and Hubert's headache, "you at your sick service had a prince" (4.1.52). Can Arthur be ignorant of the fact that Hubert, assigned to act as his "keeper" (3.3.64) is himself dependent on John? Again, before seeing the "warrant" for his torture, he has exclaimed "I warrant I love you more than you do me" (4.1.31), whereupon Hubert hands him John's order. A. R. Braunmuller notes that he "unconsciously echoes another use of *warrant* at the beginning of the scene (4.1.6).[86] I would replace unconscious dramatic irony with Arthur's "crafty love." His wariness, prescience (so strong in Shakespeare's young victims) and intimacy with Hubert enable Arthur to grasp and exploit a complex interplay of loyalties and roles.[87]

Having just lost his royal protector, the French King who initially supported his claim (and the "powerless hand" of a child-claimant), Arthur seems to be seeking another one. Like the Bastard he is a son in need of a master. Hence the bitter irony of his argument that the very instruments of torture are more humane than Hubert is: the heated iron has cooled and "like a dog that is compell'd to fight" may "Snatch at his master that doth tarre him on. / All things that you should use to do me wrong / Deny their office" (4.1.115–18). For L. A. Beurline, "the childish illogicality of his argument and its wishful thinking are what make it reach Hubert," who perceives its "psychological truth" with his "newly activated conscience."[88] But in social terms there is nothing illogical in figuring Hubert's own dependent agency through the tools he would employ. Like Tasso's cited above, the discourses of service often emphasize the instrumental hands and feet of a pre-industrial economy. By placing himself within this discourse of office and use, Arthur can get that other servant, the iron, on his side and use it to remind Hubert, as master, of his responsibilities, thereby taking "possession" of Hubert's "bosom:" "O, spare mine eyes, / Though to no use but still to look on you!" (4.1.101–2). This less-than-innocent prating eloquently forges the interdependency of a servant and child who sense that in a crisis their roles as instruments of mediation make them acutely vulnerable to dismemberment.

Then, instead of sleeping "doubtless and secure" as Hubert tells him to do (4.1.129), Arthur escapes again. He assumes a more literal servant role, dresses himself as a ship-boy, jumps, and dies. No sense that Arthur is in effect already dead, killed by the miasmal insecurities of feudal politics, should mute our pain and disappointment at this event. Given his resourcefulness (a child may know his house, castle, or prison well enough to turn up a disguise), Arthur has surely deserved his chance on the high seas, along with other youthful survivors. There he might have found the protective master he was seeking when he asked, "Is it my fault that I was Geffrey's son? No, indeed is't not; and I would to heaven / I were your son, so you would love me, Hubert" (4.1.22–4). Imogen is much luckier.

Nor should we underestimate the response of the barons to what they see as Arthur's murder. The crisis which his death brings about deepens so quickly because it reflects a profound violation of a working practice, a set of customary links between the subjection of children and servants. Reverence toward a parent as opposed to awe or "trembling" towards a master, the two kinds of fear so carefully distinguished by William Gouge and others, are confounded in rampant terror when Arthur can find no security in a service role. He also exemplifies the mood of the English people reported by the Bastard ("Not knowing what they fear, but full of fear" 4.2.146) and again by Hubert (4.2.191–2). In their explosion of rage, the barons, described as red-eyed (4.2.163), seem to turn up the heat which cooled on Hubert's iron. Scenting pollution in Arthur's death (4.3.112), they respond by attacking their master like Arthur's righteously disobedient dog. "Now," the Bastard can predict, "for the bare-pick'd bone of majesty / Doth dogged war bristle his angry crest / And snarleth in the gentle eyes of peace" (4.3.148–50). When the death of Arthur releases the agencies of many hands, a medieval power struggle plunges into tragic anarchy. As in *King Lear* or *Hamlet*, the quasi-familial loyalties of followers fan the flames of family violence. But these hands also work to restore the lion's heart, said to have been ripped out in "fury" by King Richard's "hand" (1.1.265–7). By the end of the play, the frightening image of a young prince, Arthur, kneeling to his murderous servant, Hubert, has been recast in the tableau of a young prince, Henry, surrounded by his kneeling supporters, the Bastard and the barons.

CHAPTER 3

Wives and servants

Because service has so often coincided with coming of age in western societies, our languages contain terms which refer simultaneously to young people and to servants. This is not the case with the English word "wife" nor with the concept. Although at law an early modern wife might have been regarded as having few more rights than a servant, advice manuals often object to husbands who treat their wives like servants.[1] Robert Cleaver emphatically criticizes husbands "that through evill and rough handling, and in threatning of their wives, have and use them not as wives, but as their servants."[2] William Gouge protests that "Such as will not give a blow to a servant, care not what load they lay upon their wives."[3] Wives are often allotted greater responsibilities and control over property; both wives and servants can admonish, Thomas Gataker decides, but the wife "may much more."[4]

Recent scholarship on households and families has stressed the degree to which patriarchal supervision must have been eased as wives tacitly negotiated strict rules on obedience.[5] Without such *de facto* adaptation, it would be difficult to explain why wives apparently had considerable freedom to work, do business, run estates, go to market, or meet with their friends. One of the chief responsibilities of the wife would have been the management and training of servants. Because wives spent much of their time in the company of servants, their roles must often have overlapped and interacted. But when plays seem to indicate that the wife's role has been wholly fused with that of a servant, we may suspect that social order has been strained in important ways.

By a virtual fusion of wife and servant roles, I refer to dramatic plots in which a wife acts *as* a servant or a servant (male or female) takes the place of a wife. Such plots could have functioned as cautionary tales for patriarchal masters, often reluctant to have wives supervise male servants.[6] This might well have been the case when plots presented aristocratic women who marry stewards or wives who plan to murder husbands with the help of their servant-lovers.[7] Fusions between the roles of wives and servants could also have confirmed the views of those prescribers who believed that both groups shared the burden of Eve's sin or that Christ himself was born to serve.[8]

Unpleasant as such dramatic warnings might have been to an over-burdened patriarch or anxious moralist, he need not be granted the only valid perspective upon them. Shakespeare's audience would have contained many wives, servants, and former servants who had become wives. Moreover, these dramatic fusions of wife and servant roles have a significance which may not be visible from an authoritarian perspective. Wives who serve produce surprising, unpredictable disruptions which can be liberating as well as disastrous. In almost every case where these occur, the play is asking what happens when the potentially creative agencies of wives and servants converge. Shakespeare did not monopolize this question, which is also vital in such works as Thomas Dekker's *Patient Grissil* (considered below), or Ben Jonson's *Epicoene.*[9] But he did pursue it at length through different genres and social contexts.

The four plays emphasized in this chapter, *The Taming of the Shrew*, *All's Well That Ends Well*, *Othello*, and *The Winter's Tale*, all present male figures of authority who are absurdly, even fatally fallible. But a critique of their power cannot fully explain the behavior of their wives and servants. Plays about rulers who maintain an absolute domination over households and kinfolk do of course dramatize the interactions of wives and servants in moving and persuasive detail. What distinguishes the four plays above from works like Jonson's *Sejanus* or Webster's *The White Devil* is that they represent dynamic, temporary fusions between wife and servant roles. Such fusions transform characters and directly influence events. These four plays do correspond at many points to current discourses about wives and servants, but by eliding their roles in more than incidental ways, they also unsettle preconceptions about subordinate roles.

As with his treatment of friendship (chapter 4), Shakespeare uses service to sound the depths of affection and loyalty within unbalanced pairs, between people who would seem to have been unlikely candidates for either marriage or friendship. Valuable as psychological studies may be in conjecturing prior causes for emotional bonds, they do not show how specific differences in status can both intensify such bonds and make them particularly susceptible to corruption. When service is added to the vocabularies of gender and identity which have been applied to the marriages in these plays, their unconventional, even embarrassing nature may become more apparent.

HYPERBOLIC MASTERY IN SHREW PLAYS

As Petruchio violently carries off his new wife, Katherina, he proclaims that she is "my goods, my chattels, she is my house, / My household stuff, my field, my barn, / My horse, my ox, my ass, my any thing" (3.2.230–2). Through repeated references to shrew-taming and a final celebration of Katherina's submission, the play invites readers and spectators to find what may look like unchecked patriarchal force. Many of Shakespeare's comedies feature strong heroines, capable as Peter Erickson and others have shown, of teaching male characters or disturbing male audiences.[10] Modern spectators can view such functions as reassuring, even revolutionary. But *The Taming of the Shrew* alters this comic scenario by presenting a heroine who is disciplined by a masterful male. Even when the play is considered to be, in Anthony Fletcher's words, "the most profound statement about early modern courtship that we have," contemporary readers are apt to regard this "statement" as harshly alien, confined to a world we should all rejoice to have lost.[11]

Historical readings like Fletcher's do not go far enough. By limiting their focus to the issues of gender control, they reflect current preoccupations with sexual politics and its injustices. I will argue that the play resists such a reading because it couples the lots of women and servants, opening up questions about whether power corrupts love and whether the loving, grateful professions of subordinates can ever be trusted. If we come at the play through its literary contexts, through works which either anticipate *The Shrew* or show its direct influence, we may be better prepared to recognize its full significance as a cultural icon.

In 1590, *Book Three* of Edmund Spenser's *Faerie Queene* strongly reasserted the argument, derived from Chaucer's "The Franklin's Tale" (764–6), that love may not be "compeld by maisterie."[12] Spenser examined "maestrie" through a wide range of possessive and lustful lovers of both sexes; his Britomart escapes compulsion by active pursuit of her own prophetic destiny as Artegall's mate and the mother of kings. Concurrently, the anonymous author of *Arden of Faversham* (1592) reworked "The Franklin's Tale" in a tragedy of passionate love and murder. Early in this tragedy, the advice of Arden's friend (aptly named "Franklin") not to interfere with his wife's affections ironically releases her lust and allows her to plot her husband's death (1.44–53).[13] Shakespeare, too, turned idealistic assertions about love into dilemmas raised by the use of force in *Richard III*, *The Rape of Lucrece*, and *Venus and Adonis*. Then in a play which might well be treated as a companion piece to *The Taming of the*

Shrew, he submitted another "faerie queene," Titania, to violent and humiliating coercion at the hands of her lord, Oberon. My point in locating the *Shrew* within a literary series less familiar than its acknowledged sources is to suggest that it treats love and "maestrie" with comparable hyperbolic, myth-making verve. "Was ever woman in this humor won?" Richard asks when he wins Anne's love by inflaming her resentment in *Richard III* (1.2.228). The successes of Oberon and Petruchio could well prompt a similar response.

Like the *Shrew*, *Arden of Faversham* and *A Midsummer Night's Dream* emphasize a politics of domesticity in which servants play very active, if often thankless parts. The plight of Susan Mosby, suddenly ordered to mop up and tidy over buckets of blood in the wake of Arden's murder (14.255), epitomizes reliance in these plays upon a kind of household corps. Although Alice Arden is the step-daughter of the Kentish magnate, Sir Edward North ("All Kent knows your parentage and what you are," says her conspirator, Greene, 1.491), she seems to prefer the company of servants. She passionately loves a steward, employs his sister as her waiting woman, and engineers Arden's murder through a group of disaffected servants and masterless men.[14] The quarrel between Oberon and Titania concerns both her authority over and loyalty to her independent ménage. Reluctant to turn her changeling boy over to Oberon, she nurses the memory of his dead mother, her attendant, and is finally tricked into obedience by the Puck, a figure who specializes in disrupting households and driving poor females mad. It is notable that the two plays most directly inspired by the *Shrew*, Dekker, Chettle and Haughton's *Patient Grissil* and John Fletcher's *The Woman's Prize or The Tamer Tamed* (1611) also make the roles of servants especially prominent. They exploit the reputation of Shakespeare's taming tale but use it to expose the kinds of sycophancy and misogyny to which servants and subordinates are susceptible. They remind us that while the battles of Katherina and Petruchio may distract our attention from a large supporting cast, this supporting cast works to define these notorious lovers and their actions.

The first servants we encounter in *The Taming of the Shrew* capably and quickly transform the identity of a drunken tinker. Some difficulty seems to be anticipated by the very length and care of the Lord's instructions to his page, Bartholomew. In great detail, he sends orders to his young servant, "as he will win my love," to

> bear himself with honorable action,
> Such as he hath observ'd in noble ladies
> Unto their lords, by them accomplished. (Ind. 1.110–12)

The Lord's confidence that "the boy will well usurp the grace, / Voice, gait, and action of a gentlewoman" (131–2) is premised on social factors which are almost as important as Bartholomew's gender ambiguity. For this page should probably be regarded as a young aristocrat in training to become a master himself. The Lord takes it for granted that his page has practiced the skills of imitation, stressed in the last chapter, and can therefore impersonate a gentlewoman on short notice. Clearly, the cast of servingmen who support his imitation have also, like the wise fool Feste in *Twelfth Night*, learned to "observe their mood on whom he jests, / The quality of persons, and the time" (3.1.62–3). They are able to persuade Sly (uncertain whether to name his wife, in village terms, as "Al'ce madam, or Joan madam" Ind. 2.110) that his village companions have never even existed, because the servingmen have noted the villagers and can tick off the exact names of all the locals Sly must forget (Ind. 2.89–95). Shakespeare is much more careful to specify this social conditioning than is the anonymous writer or writers who concocted *The Taming of A Shrew*. There, the Lord simply borrows a "Boy" from the visiting troupe of actors for the part of Sly's wife (i.72).[15]

Shakespeare's servingmen and page anticipate the fact that, within the play proper, a convergence of wife and servant roles will become a means of transformation:

3 SERV. O, this it is that makes your lady mourn!
2 SERV. O, this it is that makes your servants droop! (Ind. 2.26–7)

Contrariwise, the ingenious substitutions in Lucentio's scheme to win Bianca reinforce the social order.[16] As Lucentio's "trusty servant, well approv'd in all" (1.1.7), who has grown up with his master, Tranio is ready to take his place. "Would I were so too!" quips the Page, Biondello (1.1.238), who is Tranio's "fellow" in ambition. Such fellows can jump up and down on the ranks of hierarchy without shaking the ladder itself, an activity which promotes energetic and violent competition. This violence is suggested by the gratuitous lie that justifies Lucentio's disguise: "I kill'd a man, and fear I was descried" (1.1.232). His new-comedy intrigue against the patriarchy he hopes to join presupposes the rigid, even fortified domesticity of Padua, symbolized by the family house. Tranio becomes "serviceable" (214) as a gentleman who keeps "house and port and servants, as I should" (1.1.203), while Lucentio pretends to be another kind of servant, a school master, so he can get at Bianca, locked away from her suitors.[17] These schemes, along with the creation of a surrogate father who keeps his real father from entering his own son's house, derive from Gascoigne's *Supposes*, but in the earlier play their aggressiveness is tempered by the mutual loyalties and strong affections of servants, sons, and fathers.

Shakespeare re-locates homosocial civility where competitive patriarchs and conventional spectators might least expect to find it: in Petruchio's "taming school" or country house. This house is staffed (stuffed), as Ann Thompson notes in her edition, by "a total of thirteen servants, far more than are ever likely to have appeared on stage."[18] Such an all-male organization reflects the traditional large English household (or Italian *famiglia*) in which even the most capable wives could feel isolated or distrusted.[19] John Hoskyns was probably not untypical both in delegating management to his wife while he was away ("I troble you with to much husbandry") and in worrying about her susceptibility to flattering servants.[20] Henry Percy advised his son to manage household affairs through reliable officers. He believed that rule by women in great houses would produce "factions" because servants would always rather please a passionate woman than a rational man: "womens humors are stepps nerer there reaches then wyse mens can be."[21] Conflict between wives and servants would have been as common as collusion, and was probably exacerbated by the growing prominence of women (and yeomen) in positions of authority, as gentlemen found employment in the professional sphere, rather than as domestic officers.[22]

According to a number of accounts, associations with a husband's servants could have been difficult for wives. Anne Clifford often battled with her husband's favorite agent Matthew Caldicott, who on Easter 1617 was "continuing still to do me all the ill offices he could with my Lord."[23] Joan Thynne resented being treated like a servant by her husband's family, while her daughter-in-law, Maria, presumably defending one "Digory" from "uncivil" words by other servants, ironically apologized to her husband, "thou doth many times call me a fool for yielding to the enticing of fair words."[24] In her lively account of the Willoughby household, Alice T. Friedman describes a sustained marital conflict ("ongoing melodrama") to do with the wife's property, a conflict exacerbated by ambitious, competitive servants.[25]

The earlier courting scene between Katherina and Petruchio prepares audiences for a "taming school" where Katherina will be treated like a servant or worse. Petruchio's initial attempt to change Kate into "household stuff" makes him sound ominously possessive. She responds to the mercantile calculation latent in his flattery ("Kate of Kate-Hall," "my super-dainty Kate," whose "mildness" is "praised in every town") by reducing him to a "moveable" or "join'd-stool" (2.1.197–8). He wants, she thinks, what the writer of a household *Breviate* may have wanted when he referred to the attendance of gentlewomen "in the greate chamber for the better furnishinge the same."[26] She rejects him with "Go, fool, and whom thou keep'st command" (257) because she hears the threat of her own servility in "O, let me see thee walk. Thou dost not halt" (2.1.256). Petruchio seems to be shopping for a wife in a spirit more appropriate for buying a horse or hiring a laborer.

The taming process begins when Petruchio turns himself into a "jolly surly groom" (3.2.213) and carries his new bride away. From a story told by John Manningham, we might infer how a real Katherina would have felt after a humiliating and miserable journey. His "cosen," riding on a horse behind her husband, slipped off. Because the husband failed to notice she was gone, she was forced to walk so far that she considered seeking "a service in some unknowne place."[27] Grumio tells Curtis, a member of the large staff Petruchio keeps in his country house, the "tale" of how Katherina " . . . was bemoil'd, how he left her with the horse upon her, how he beat me because her horse stumbled, how she waded through the dirt, to pluck him off me; how he swore, how she pray'd, that never pray'd before; how I cried, how the horses ran away, how her bridle was burst; how I lost my crupper – with many things of worthy memory . . ." (4.1.75–82).

Petruchio's surprising country-house (as productions often suggest) is a genuine world apart, a setting for change which is not simply ridiculous or superficial. Although the servingmen have supposedly made "all things neat" (114) and are themselves "spruce companions" (113), instructed by Grumio to welcome master and mistress in their "new fustian, [their] white stockings, and every officer his wedding garment" (47–9), Grumio has to apologize: "There were none fine but Adam, Rafe, and Gregory; / The rest were ragged, old, and beggarly, / Yet, as they are, here are they come to meet you" (4.1.136–8). Petruchio draws into his scheme a group distinguished from the servants who follow the Lord of the Induction or Lucentio by their good will and inefficiency. They are quick to understand that Petruchio kills his new wife "in her own humor" (4.1.180), and through their participation they can help audiences understand why her "humor" needs such killing. For this antidotal cure to succeed, Katherina must see herself in the way Petruchio treats third-party servants. Her change begins when, as Grumio reports, she "waded through the dirt to pluck him off me" (4.1.78). Her first line in this new company is her defense of the servant struck by Petruchio: "Patience, I pray you, 'twas a fault unwilling" (4.1.156). Her second is a defense of the meat the servants have prepared for the new couple to eat (168–9). Equally significant is the way that Grumio collaborates with Petruchio in getting Katherina, "who never knew how to entreat, / Nor never needed that I should entreat" (4.3.7–8) first to ask for food, and then to thank those who serve her: "The poorest service is repaid with thanks, / And so shall mine before you touch the meat" (4.3.45–6).[28]

Petruchio's taming school reverses the conventional wisdom that wives should instruct servants in their duties. It alters the implications of a pattern in the comedies of Plautus. Erich Segal observes that the slaves of Plautus love to hear "the sound of *orare*" coming from their masters.[29] The slaves enjoy a brief, sensational reversal of rigid roles. By learning to entreat and pray, Kate ("that never pray'd before") becomes capable of reciprocity. Through her subordination to servants, she discovers how dependent she is on those who help and care for her. It is unfortunate that spectators and critics often discover a submission to power they have been led to anticipate instead of witnessing the genesis of ethical insight. As if he took a different view of servingmen, the author of *A Shrew* developed the common theme of resentment between servant and mistress. He motivated the scene in which the master's attendant starves the wife by turning Grumio into Sander. This foolish glutton has been warned that a new mistress may reduce his rations (viii.24–5) and he seems eager to prolong her fast (ix.22–3, 34–5). *A Shrew* concludes, predictably, with a didactic sermon by Kate on the necessary obedience of all fallen women.[30]

In Shakespeare's version of the tale, Kate's experience in the "taming school" charges her final performance with imaginative hyperbole. If she had been tamed into thinking of herself as a chattel ("my goods, my chattels . . . my any thing" 3.2.230–2), would she compare herself to a fountain?

> A woman mov'd is like a fountain troubled,
> Muddy, ill-seeming, thick, bereft of beauty,
> And while it is so, none so dry or thirsty
> Will deign to sip, or touch one drop of it. (5.2.142–5)

Fountains tend to suggest free and generous action of a more heroic nature: Othello will apply the metaphor to his initial love of Desdemona; Achilles will contrast it to his own troubled and dysfunctional mind. If she had been fooled into thinking herself grateful for domination, would she be able to describe the role of her "keeper" (146) as "painful labor, both by sea and land" (149)? Kate creates myths of reciprocity here (for the shared labors of the taming school have been far more humble); she cajoles Petruchio by treating him like the Herculean figure Gremio said would be needed to tame her (1.2.255). Dilating upon female softness, she speaks like a pygmy ("our lances are but straws") rather than like an amazon. Hercules, as we have seen in chapter 2, is in many respects a glorified servant.[31]

The Taming of the Shrew leaves us with a sharp choice between two kinds of marriage which have been defined, to a large degree, by the kinds of service which bring them about. One, appropriate for maze-like Padua and the captivities, literal and emotional (1.1.219) of its lovers, recalls the rigid archaic family along with the slavery from which serfs and servants developed. The other illustrates what Bruce Robbins calls "the positive unreality of utopianism."[32] Kate's assimilation to the household, a process which may have been historically regressive in 1594, can work as a progressive resource by challenging marriages based on competitive marketing or, like Lucentio's, on theft.[33]

Petruchio predicts that Hortensio and Lucentio are in for a lifetime of sexual warfare: "Come Kate, we'll to bed. / We three are married, but you two are sped" (5.2.184–5). "We three," meaning the three former bachelors, can also be understood as part of a riddle: "Kate and I and a third party are married; you two men (who think you have merely lost your wagers) have really lost yourselves." This mysterious third party could be a figure for Petruchio's household, or more specifically, for his "ancient, trusty, pleasant" servant Grumio. Grumio ushers Petruchio into Padua when he refuses to obey his master's command: "knock me here soundly" (1.2.8). Petruchio beats him, in effect, for scruples which initiate a recurrent theme in Shakespeare's plays, that of a servant who will try to keep a master from injuring his own better self. At this point, the servant refuses to put the master in his own place (that of one who gets beaten) and prevents a confusion of roles. But later it is Grumio who introduces us to the taming disciplines of the household with his carnivalesque account of hierarchy confounded in mire, riders under their horses, and a new wife protecting a servant from his master by force. Grumio also fetches Katherina for Petruchio so that she can then bring into the room the other wives who will be reprimanded by her speech.

The possibility that Kate may be changing into a female Grumio, rather than a Petruchio or a brilliant and erotic boy actor, is unlikely to console modern audiences or students.[34] From a distance of four hundred years, it may be more interesting to believe that the wife or servant who ministered to or even created the more positive inclinations of a master was merely perpetuating hierarchy and subjection. Yet, by joining the ordinary homosocial world of the "spruce companions," secure in their positions and loyalties, Kate escapes the perpetual farce and domestic rivalry of conventional marriage. Group membership promotes greater freedom to please oneself by pleasing others, a kind of in-house theater based on responsiveness to the needs of a small audience.[35] However, Kate does not thereby escape all questions about her sincerity and her future happiness. The most serious question concerns the extent to which her love has been produced by her submission: Do the constraints so evident in the claim that women are "bound to serve, love, and obey" (5.2.164) warp the effects of desire? It will be taken up by plays which respond directly to *The Shrew* and given some disturbing answers by *All's Well That Ends Well*.

SERVANT-WIVES AND INCIPIENT MONSTERS

According to John Fletcher's continuation of the *Shrew* story, *The Woman's Prize or the Tamer Tam'd*, Petruchio's second wife, Maria, revenges Kate by humiliating Petruchio. Fletcher imagines that the marriage of Kate and Petruchio has become a living hell when both her shrewishness and his violence escalate. In order to purge Petruchio of raging resentment and misogyny, Maria drives him beyond childish helplessness to the desperate ploy of pretending himself dead, whereupon she offers him obedience: "From this houre make me what you please: I have tam'd ye, / And now am vowd your servant" (5.4.45–6).[36] Ostensibly, the lesson taught by this play, says its Epilogue, is that the "Sexes," being equal, are bound to "love mutually." But as in all the successors to *The Shrew*, happy endings appear less convincing than unresolved problems. Fletcher's Petruchio has spouted vitriolic loathing for women, supported by his servants and friends. Because neither wife nor servants share directly in his taming experience, the play offers miraculous rebirth for the husband but no household community for the wife. Fletcher's wife may or may not be aware that Petruchio's death is a pretense. She weeps, she claims, because he is better off dead, his life having been "poore unmanly wretched foolish" (5.4.20). This is a bitter-sweet variation on the tragi-comic practice of creating affection through self-sacrifice or death. Petruchio's second marriage bears as much thinking about as his first.

Patient Grissil and *All's Well That Ends Well* focus upon the responses of women humiliated by their husbands. Both plays probe the strength of affection in wives conscious of their social inferiority. With rampant inquisitorial passion, Marquess Gwalter tries the patience of his wife Grissil for many years. He outrages modern sensibilities, but he also violates early modern advice against turning wives into servants. Grissil herself complies readily with this violation. She refers to her new bridal costume as the "liverie" of a "humble servant" (2.2.69–70) and passes her first test by tying the shoes of Furio, a gentleman attendant.[37] In a confusing of mistress / servant positions much harsher than Petruchio's, the Marquess pretends to be enraged with both Furio and Grissil who are, he claims, alike (104); when he threatens to kill Furio, Grissil begs for his life (2.2.110 ff.). She then waits upon two courtiers, Mario and Lepido, who have despised her from the outset for her low birth. "It is the overthrow of many families," writes William Gouge, "that servants are trusted, and not wives."[38] In *Patient Grissil*, the Marquess delegates Furio to chase his wife's father and brother from court (3.1.23–5) and (after Grissil and her two infants have also been dismissed to poverty) to take away her children. Gwalter announces and Grissil believes that they die (4.3.262, 5.2.194). Grissil's trials come to an end when she obliges Gwalter by handing over to him a new and beautiful bride whom he reveals to be her long lost daughter.

As an exercise in wife control, Gwalter's behavior would seem sadistic and cynical: Grissil never indicates that she needs any testing, Gwalter's sister and cousin object strenuously, and Gwalter concedes that he has wronged Grissil all along. But wife-control is not, I would argue, wholly the point here.[39] Gwalter's treatment of Grissil is part of his strategy for testing the loyalty of his courtiers and of his agent, Furio. Like Grissil, the two courtiers, Mario and Lepido, have been raised from poverty through Gwalter's power (3.1.129–32) and should, as he points out, "simpathize" with Grissil's "passions" (133–4). Recognizing their malice when they constantly harp on Grissil's base origins, Gwalter, in effect, acts out its consequences. By granting the envy of these flatterers the power to torment Grissil for (presumably) most of her married life, the playwrights emphasize, I think, its form and pressure. When Gwalter takes Grissil back, he also rewards Furio and rejects Mario and Lepido: "Arise flatterers get you gone, / Your soules are made of blacke confusion" (5.2.209–10). This may sound like yet another tale about patriarchs who achieve civility at the expense of women. But Dekker and company complicate their story of courtiers put out of flattering humours by representing persuasively the precarious status of servants and by articulating Grissil's position through Furio's.

Like *The Merry Wives of Windsor*, *Sir Thomas More*, and the two parts
of *Henry IV*, *Patient Grissil* engages us with the plight of servants and
followers threatened with unemployment or outright rejection. Rice, the
ever-hungry "longcoat" or page to Sir Owen in the Welsh sub-plot, quips
"house keeping you know is out of fashion: unlesse I ride post, I kisse the
post" (2.1.31–2). When Babulo, Grissil's servant, is driven with her family
from court, he cashiers *his* own servant with "I must give over houskeep-
ing" (3.1.109–10). In the next scene, Julia, Gwalter's sister, who has told
her suitors "followe me and love not, and ile teach you how to find
libertie" (2.1.299–300), discharges her "servant" Emulo for bragging.
Hence, when Gwalter finally packs off his own court-followers, we have
a climactic action fully as important as his reconciliation with Grissil, and
inseparable from it. Fear of "kissing the post" (or of "dining with Duke
Humphrey" or being given "John Drum's entertainment"), that is, of
being cast from the favor and protection of a service role, explains the
aristocratic snobbery of courtiers who were once poor themselves. The
play suggests that when subordinates of either sex are constantly required
to please and appease, the line between loyalty and sycophancy becomes
difficult to draw.

In one particularly complex sequence, Gwalter reveals by his comments
to Furio that he recognizes Mario and Lepido to be flattering parasites.
Nevertheless he orders Furio to keep Grissil from touching her babies;
Furio fails this test and hands one over to her, saying in an aside, "I would
I were rid of my miserie, for I shall drowne my heart, with my teares that
fall inward" (4.1.139–40). Gwalter pretends for the parasites' benefit to
berate his servant; he then requests their willing assistance in banishing
and disrobing his wife. They will be the next to lose their livery. After
Gwalter sends Furio to take Grissil's babes away from her, he resolves to
test both servant and wife: If Furio is "unblemisht," "I have found two
wonders that are sildome rife, / A trusty servant, and a patient wife"
(4.1.238–40). Putting on the disguise of a basket-maker, he pretends to
intervene on Grissil's behalf. Grissil, however, sides with "my deare Lords
servant" (4.2.177), whereupon Gwalter concludes that servant and wife
have both proved true (4.2.208–9).

The good servant Furio plays a more active part than Grissil herself as
he juggles together a range of roles. He has to please and identify with
both Master and Mistress, simultaneously becoming a nursemaid and
carrying out Gwalter's patriarchal rigor. His very name symbolizes just
how much he is up against. Furies are tragic beings, mythical embodi-
ments of raging women who have suffered the contradictions of injustice.

(Gwalter's cousin Owen calls his shrewish wife a "very furie," 3.2.232.) Recalling harpies, "Furio" may sound monstrous, as well as sexually ambiguous or effeminate. Grissil's angry family assume that his name matches his cruelty (3.1.52–4); "Princes," says Grissil's brother the scholar, are at least compassionate towards those they must punish (3.1.58–9). More emphatically than Grumio in *The Taming of the Shrew*, Furio becomes a figure for a marriage defined through service relationships, a marriage all but sacrificed to the forces of social fear and hatred. Furio's inward falling tears parallel Grissil's grief that "burnes inward" (4.2.204). Trusting Furio with her babes because he "lookes gently," she nevertheless says, "God can tell, / My heart saies my tongue lyes, farewell farewell" (4.2.179–81).

Patient Grissil serves here as a prologue to *All's Well That Ends Well* for several reasons. Both plays are distorted when read too narrowly through the sexual desires and actions of romantic leads. Both show how deeply the identities of wives could be shaped by a personal history of subordination. Grissil is inseparable from her pitcher, empty at the time she met and married her lord, hung as a monument in the palace, and her only bit of "houshold stuffe" when Babulo finds her cast out and crying in a grove like a "begger woman" (4.2.27; cf. 1.2.170, 3.1.84). Grissil gives her family cold comfort through an analogy between her pitcher ("My Pitcher is unhurt, see it is fill'd / With christall water of the crisped spring" 4.2.79–80) and "this cup full of teares" (85), sent them by Gwalter; she talks about herself. Her language recalls Katherina's fountain, but in terms of a sturdy icon for service.[40] Helena employs another such item of household stuff to express her endless love for Bertram, poured out into a "captious and intenible sieve" (1.3.202).[41] Both of these female vessels have bodies and brains moulded by service. Helena may have been a doctor's daughter and an attendant to a countess. But before she can be accepted as a wife, she must play and outgrow many features of a servant, including the menace of servility.

We have seen how Hamlet and Coriolanus feel instrumentalized when they submit their agencies to the designs of superior powers. Grissil and Helena bring out the extent to which, in a culture relying on service, all dependent positions are potentially fraught with sensations of monstrosity and self-alienation, with a kind of "Furio" effect. Helena's social progress is crossed with and contaminated by the career of Parolles, degraded from her husband's gentleman-companion and a "noble captain" (2.1.46) to a contemptible, de-humanized lackey. Both characters will speak of themselves as "things." The extreme contrast between Grissil and the courtiers illustrates, I think, what household advisors were trying to formulate in arguing that a wife's "fear" of her husband should never be "slavish" (Carter) or "trembling" (Gouge).[42] Wifely fear, wrote Gataker, is "not a servile or slavish dread, but a liberall, free and ingenuous feare" comparable to the love of God.[43] Grissil becomes a faithful female Job, awed more by her husband's responsibility than by his power. She is resiliently secure in a poverty which frightens the courtiers more than their master does. But with *All's Well*, we can begin to understand why "servile or slavish dread" could have been suffered by masters as well as by wives and servants. This play and *Othello* uncover a daily ugliness in dependent relationships which can make a wallow in the mud of *The Shrew* appear positively refreshing.

Lest this sound like an apology for masters, who were ever vigilant to condemn the sins of their servants, I must emphasize that a fusion of service with either marriage or friendship could magnify the power of the subject. As Guido Ruggiero has maintained, "the acceptance of subservience seems to have been perceived as virtually forcing the support of the superior power. This was because power was to a great extent determined by relationships; in other words, it was less something imposed from above than a reciprocal set of generally accepted relationships whose web tied all who fell within its bounds to certain obligations, even lords and the Lord."[44] More pragmatically, William Fleetwood could point out that masters "cannot do all things necessary themselves, therefore they trust others to do what is wanting."[45] As we have seen in chapter 2, these trusted "others" often practised a highly observant and flexible form of imitation. "Good and faithfull servants, liking and affecting of their Maisters, understand them at a becke, and obey them at a winke of the eye, or bent of the browe, not as a water-spaniell, but as the hand is sturred to obey the minde." Here Robert Cleaver seems to imitate Torquato Tasso, who had also argued that a servant is a "Reasonable Creature, by participation, even as the Moone and the Starres receive light by participation with the Sunne."[46] Kate's willingness in *The Taming of the Shrew* to agree that the sun is the moon if Petruchio says so may signal her grasp of subservience as power.[47]

While the dual subordinations of Helena and Parolles have been recognized by many critics, few have appreciated their social roles as potential sources of strength. Sheldon Zitner lays the groundwork for such an approach by terming the play "an anagram of New Comedy construction," where "the clever servant figure turns out, in the case of Parolles, to be a fool" and "in the case of Helena to be a victorious protagonist."[48] For the most part, Helena's cleverness has been regarded as suspiciously manipulative, although Paula Neuss notices that Bertram's farewell to his mother, "The best wishes that can / Be forged in your thoughts be servants to you" (1.1.74–5), may offer Helena "the idea of giving body to good wishes."[49] That is, instead of "wishing well" (1.1.181) to the body of absent Bertram, she resolves to follow his body with her own, serving her desires (184) rather than remaining shut within them by "baser stars" (183).[50] Brian Parker shrewdly observes that verbal sparring with Parolles, whose language is military and sexual, makes Helena more aggressive.[51] Luckily her status as "gentlewoman" to the Countess does not insulate her from encounters with crude "companions" like Parolles, and she can begin to rehearse a strategy for losing her virginity "to her own liking" (150–1). She receives another kind of support from the Steward who has overheard her confessing her love for Bertram, and carried his tale to the Countess "sithence in the loss that may happen, it concerns you something to know it" (1.3.119–21). The Countess will send her to Paris with "leave and love, / Means and attendants" (1.3.251–2). Just as she has reassured the Countess that Bertram is her master and "dear lord" with "I / His servant live, and will his vassal die" (1.3.158–9), she will ask the King of France to let her choose "such a one thy vassal" who is suited to her "low and humble name" (2.1.199, 197). In terms of her social skills, she is no "weak" or "debile minister" as Lafeu and Parolles will call her after she cures the King (2.3.33–4). Her resourcefulness derives from her ability to flourish within and gain power through a web of domestic obligations.[52]

The servant who quickly becomes the agent of her own wishes, as if they had somehow been created by Bertram's parting instructions (he emphasized Helena's subordination by ordering her to "make much" of his mother) anticipates the wife who carries out Bertram's orders on how to conceive his child. Parker is right, I think, in implying that her servility continues to offend Bertram, both when she betroths herself by giving "[m]e and my service" and later when she speaks of herself as "your most obedient servant," apologizing for her "homely stars" (2.3.103, 2.5.72,75).[53] Neither Helena nor Bertram pays much attention to the King's opinions about inherent nobility or his elevation of Helena's rank. If Helena were not a servant in her own mind and in Bertram's, the test which he sets her could indeed be regarded as an exclusively personal and sexual business. Abandoned by her new husband, Boccacio's Giletta goes back to Rossiglione and sets the country to rights. Helena, however, has only used authority through her father's learning and the king's power. Wife and servant roles remain fused as Helena carries out Bertram's conditions. She shows his letter to the Countess with "here's my passport" (3.2.56), that is, a license to wander as a vagabond or cashiered servant, what Parolles will temporarily become.[54] She refuses to stay at home "although / The air of paradise did fan the house / And angels offic'd all" (3.2.124–6). This delightful image, as G. K. Hunter explains, probably means that "angels acted as domestic servants."[55] The Steward who reported her passion brings her sonnet of farewell to the Countess. In Florence, Helena forms an instant friendship with Diana the "maid" and her mother the inn-keeper, who vows, "You never had a servant to whose trust / Your business was more welcome" (4.4.15–16).

Part of the joke on Bertram must be that, given Helena's background, she will try hard to obey an order. Indeed, a disposition to carry out instructions exactly makes Malvolio an invaluable servant, worth "half of my dowry" to Olivia in *Twelfth Night* (3.4.63). Of course, it also makes him a predictable gull. Only when Helena proves her ability to marshal a wagon-load of ring-bearing women back to Rossillion does she become more of a mistress and a wife than a servant. Skill in orchestrating a large domestic corps distinguishes Olivia and enables the merry wives of Windsor to triumph over Falstaff.

While Helena is using the skills of a servant to establish herself as a wife, Parolles is refusing to be identified by the courtier, Lafeu, as Bertram's servant (2.3.188 ff.) This confrontation with Lafeu immediately precedes and seems to shape his influential flattery of Bertram when he attacks marriage and celebrates the "wars":

> He wears his honor in a box unseen,
> That hugs his kicky-wicky here at home,
> Spending his manly marrow in her arms,
> Which should sustain the bound and high curvet
> Of Mars's fiery steed. (2.3.279–83)

Parolles is quite as absurd in his denials to Lafeu as he is in his clothes; the roles of friend and servant often overlapped and Helena has been a servant-companion to the Countess. Here the potential strength and value of the role Parolles repudiates is born out by Lafeu's desire to warn Bertram against him and by the determination of the French Lords to test him. "It were fit you knew him" the First Lord counsels Bertram, "lest reposing too far in his virtue, which he hath not, he might at some great and trusty business in a main danger fail you" (3.6.13–16). In suggesting that "servant is too broad a character to be usefully defining" where Parolles is con-cerned, David Ellis may underestimate the versatility of good servants and the menace of bad ones. He does imply, however, that Bertram has seen his relation to Parolles in terms of personal service. Otherwise, why, as Ellis points out, would Bertram be much more disturbed by Parolles' violation of trust as a messenger to Diana than by his cowardice?[56] Like Marquess Gwalter, Shakespeare brings together the trials of wife and servant, accomplishing in one Florentine night what in *Patient Grissil* had taken a generation. Helena's reliability gets her a ring and a baby, while Parolles is exposed, confirming Lafeu's insight, as a "light nut" without a "kernel" (2.5.43); he resolves to find "place and means" to live as a kept fool, thereby remaining "the thing I am" (4.3.338–9, 333).

But what if Helena echoes Parolles when her first words to the King, after her return, announce that she is but the "shadow of a wife," the "name, and not the thing" (5.3.307–8)? To become "the thing" in her sense, she must be acknowledged as the physical body in Diana's bed, a body that has played dead and undergone the degradation of being treated as an expensive sexual object. In the process of testing Helena and Parolles, Shakespeare suggests disturbing similarities between the two characters, similarities which may help to explain why the agencies of subservient characters might at times generate near-phobia. When they act out the implications of Bertram's attitude, his confidence in Parolles and aversion to Helena, Parolles and Helena reveal the perversity of their master's views in ways which go far to explain such views.

It would be a misunderstanding of this triangle to think that it is premised on normal misogyny, a patriarchal code which determined that femininity be repressed in order to strengthen male bonds. Such a theory can often have great usefulness; it may help us to understand complex relationships in certain conflicts involving women and male servants or companions. But as a theory, it relies too exclusively on male gender psychology. When Bertram at first rejects Helena, he is not behaving *only* as a snob and misogynist influenced by a companion:

> I know her well;
> She had her breeding at my father's charge –
> A poor physician's daughter my wife! Disdain
> Rather corrupt me ever. (2.3.113–16)

What does he mean by "breeding at my father's charge"? Two things: One, that like Hamlet with Rosencrantz and Guildenstern or Imogen with Posthumus, he may have grown up with Helena.[57] Already resenting his own subjugation as a royal ward, he is ill prepared to watch this domestic hanger-on succeed at his expense. Second, that as a creature bred by his father, Helena is an alien being incapable of honor and unthinkable as a sex partner in marriage.

This second meaning is no doubt intensified by the context of an enforced marriage; the aversion it articulates ("my hate to her" 2.3.287) has been explained psychoanalytically as a fear of incest by Richard P. Wheeler.[58] Marriages regularly trigger acute attacks of familial anxiety in Shakespeare's plays. A special case resembling Helena's is that of Posthumus in *Cymbeline*. Although he has been carefully bred (for service in the bedchamber, 1.1.42) and educated by Cymbeline, the King calls him "Thou basest thing" and a "poison to my blood" (1.1.125, 128) after he marries the King's daughter. Cymbeline, too, is saying that Posthumus is unfit for a marriage, and his reasons, like Bertram's, derive from something other than conventional snobbery or gender prejudice. Sodometrical phobias which confound fears of treachery, sexuality, and social ambition, have been thought to express terror of a feminized body.[59] But perhaps we can also explain how Bertram and Cymbeline react here by positing a different sort of body, like the one figured in Helena's desire to put a "body" into "wishing well" (1.1.181).

Repeatedly the discourse of service imagines the body of the servant as participating in that of the master. This is what the common image of a hand directly linked to the master's brain ideally signifies. I. M. also compares the need for service to Adam's need for Eve, created from his rib. Though not "so serviceable as Eve to Adam," the servants of gentlemen are "yet so needeful" as to be made of their own "metal" or "dough".[60] (All youth are also "unbak'd and doughy," says Lafeu, excusing Bertram's susceptibility to Parolles, 4.5.3.) To be forcibly reminded that such a convenient presence or human instrument has a body and intentions of its own seems to provoke Bertram and Cymbeline into an attitude for which we have no one name. "Misanthropy," if that is the word for an intense disgust at a dependent part of oneself suddenly recognized as having independent power and strength. "Perversity," if the creatures bred by fathers, a process that either by-passes or appropriates maternal nurture, can be thought of as monstrous implements or animals. "He's a cat to me," says Bertram (4.3.238) when Parolles reveals that instead of functioning as a reliable go-between, he has mocked Bertram to Diana and wooed her for himself.[61] An agent who carries out orders in self-serving ways does not simply extend the material substance or power of a master, as prosthetic substitutes and instruments might do. Instead, he or she shares directly in and transforms the master's will.

All's Well That Ends Well does not concentrate exclusively on such disturbing alienations of agency. The play represents service in many different contexts: courtly, feudal, military, domestic, amatory, commercial. It features particularly generous relationships involving servants: the Countess treats Helena as her own child, Lafeu buoys up the morale of his master, the King, Lafeu and the Countess give Parolles and Lavatch lifetime protection. Helena shares a strong consciousness of dependent status with many other figures above and below her in rank. Lafeu's ability to perceive the servant in Parolles, who so strenuously contradicts him, indicates that such a consciousness runs deep, touching attitudes unfamiliar to modern audiences. I have drawn attention to the ugliness in the interactions of Helena, Bertram and Parolles in order to suggest that what is at work here is a strange parody of creative and/or sexual behaviour. It derives primarily from Bertram's de-humanizing view of Helena and misplaced trust in Parolles, but takes its specific course through Helena's servile ability to redirect Bertram's will. By bearing tales about Bertram's lascivious designs on Diana, Parolles accepts his own servile status and supports Helena's schemes. The play suggests that wives and servants can indeed take back and alter the male appropriation of conceit and conception which occurs in tragedy after tragedy throughout the period. When she wins the King's trust, he promises to do for her what she is already doing to and for Bertram: "Thy will by my performance shall be serv'd" (2.1.202).

Whether performances so deeply compromised and accommodating can change Bertram or only publicize him remains doubtful. On a more comic note, Helena the servant has actively and impatiently died into Helena the capable wife and mistress, Juno-like (as her sonnet at 3.4.12–13 may hint) in her ability to control the "labors" of others in more than one sense. And it is all to the good that the ending sweeps away not one but two false motives for attachment between Helena and Bertram: her idolatry, and his sentimental nostalgia ("she whom . . . myself, / Since I have lost, have lov'd" 5.3.53–4). As David Kastan has observed, this play refuses to end.[62] But perhaps it does make new beginnings possible.

GUARDIAN WIVES AND SERVANTS

Othello owes much of its dramatic power to the great speed with which its new beginnings change into horrific endings. Tormented by the loss of happiness promised through his recent marriage, Othello laments,

> I had rather be a toad
> And live upon the vapor of a dungeon
> Than keep a corner in the thing I love
> For others' uses. (3.3.270–3)

He uses a similar language of loathing to Desdemona herself when he distinguishes the afflictions he could probably endure (capture, poverty, disease, and humiliation) from her intolerable whoredom:

> But there, where I have garner'd up my heart,
> Where either I must live or bear no life;
> The fountain from the which my current runs
> Or else dries up: to be discarded thence!
> Or keep it as a cestern for foul toads
> To knot and gender in! (4.2.57–62)

Such language must have seemed alien to an audience already familiar with many features of this tragedy: passionate love, rebellious daughters, travellers' tales, household factions, or fiendish Italians. Othello's speeches turn his marriage into an vile entrapment worse than literal captivity.

In provoking Othello's jealous rage, Iago sends the imagination of this famous adventurer to an obnoxious place. Iago's wife, Emilia, brings Othello back. By becoming a self-sacrificing, loyal servant, she reminds Othello of his public responsibility as protector of the state. In *The Winter's Tale*, Paulina replaces the king's counsellor and keeps the queen alive for sixteen years. Through the exceptional strength and courage with which they serve, these wives achieve the stature of heroic guardians. In dramatic terms, Emilia's sudden bravery is almost as startling as Othello's sudden hatred.

For all of their banality, it is worth examining how Iago uses the customs of service to wreck a marriage. Unless we recognize that Emilia reverses Iago's behavior, changing her own and Othello's, we are apt to find the play's conclusion sensational and nihilistic. Through Emilia we can perceive distinctions between service and slavery which Iago has tried to efface. Both Iago and Othello seem to have been damaged by practices related to slavery. Scholars who have begun to consider the pertinence of slavery to *Othello* have brought out a significant and neglected dimension of the play.[63] Evidence for its damaging effects emerges through metaphors like the dungeons and cisterns above. Freedom, often an implicit value in tragedy, becomes an important motive in *Othello* and (I will argue in chapter 6) *Macbeth*. Both plays will be approached in light of an idea affirmed by Nicole Loraux near the end of her inspiring book: "But there is this special feature of tragedy, that because it notably exalts the role of liberty, the effect of constraint in it – however subtle it may be, however covertly present in this or that signifier – is all the more powerful because it shows up in words rather than in institutions."[64]

We might begin, then, with the institution of service, understood by Iago as thoroughly repressive. Until Michael Neill insisted that military and domestic "offices" belonged to the "same system," it was customary to take Iago on his own terms as a professional soldier.[65] Consequently, the menace of his early attack upon service has not been widely perceived. Re-examined as preparation for the events and images he will produce, this attack begins to expose a nightmare version of normal social dependencies.

"I follow him to serve my turn upon him," Iago explains (1.1.42). His punning cliché mutes his violence in perverting any code of service, old or new, by acting only for his own interest ("turn") in ways that will injure his master. He seeks revenge because Othello has chosen Cassio over Iago as his lieutenant and appointed Iago to the lower rank of ensign or "ancient." Warning a son that "all most all trecheries have bene wrought by servants," Sir William Wentworth advises him to select "Onelie some auncyentt honest servants of our fathers whose welth and creditt depend most upon your hous."[66] When he caricatures the "duteous and knee-crooking knave" cashiered in old age despite "obsequious bondage" (1.1.45–6) and praises those who thrive by "throwing but shows of service on their lords" (1.1.52), Othello's new ancient overturns countless prescriptions for masters and servants. It is the constant emphasis in this discourse upon the servant's abeyance of personal will which may best explain Iago's famously cryptic line, "Were I the Moor, I would not be Iago" (1.1.57).[67] He believes that service wholly destroys identity (i.e., "I would become the Moor"), and that he can only be himself through a pretense of service, a form of behavior widely excoriated in the household guides as "eye-service." His mockery of sincere devotion converts the heart to a badge of carrion worn on a servant's livery:

> For when my outward action doth demonstrate
> The native act and figure of my heart
> In complement extern, 'tis not long after
> But I will wear my heart upon my sleeve
> For daws to peck at: I am not what I am. (1.1.61–5)

Both from his disgust with the "curse of service" evident in Othello's hiring procedures ("Preferment goes by letter and affection / And not by old gradation" (1.1.35–7) and from his later contempt for "huswifery," it seems clear that Iago finds the muddle of personal and professional roles which typified many service roles insufferable. By making Iago his ancient, Othello gives him an office which does in fact require him, whatever its military function as flag-bearer, to fetch women and baggage, carry letters, and act as an intimate personal attendant. Roderigo tries to confirm his sense of aversion and dishonor by chiming in with "I rather would have been his hangman" (1.1.34), that most polluting of social offices. Iago is already violating a more intimate trust and breaking a ground-rule for servants of all sorts when he speaks so harshly of Othello behind his back.[68]

Because his professional honesty has been established, Iago can gain Othello's personal and private trust by pretending to be selflessly loyal. Iago's victims behave as if they were conspiring to support his deception. Othello has had little contact with household enemies or with that easy fusion of military and domestic establishments which appears to be a way of life for Antony when he lives with Cleopatra. As governor of Cyprus, he is quick to associate Cassio's drunken conduct on the "court of guard" with political insurrection or to punish Desdemona, a supposed whore, for threatening the morale of his soldiers.[69] Desdemona seems to have managed her father's household in Venice but has not yet learned what Emilia can surmise: that to "get some office," a "cogging, cozening slave" has slandered the general's wife (4.2.132–3). Emilia may have been appointed Desdemona's attendant on leaving Venice, but her first loyalty is to another master, her husband, for whom she filches Desdemona's handkerchief. In their unaccustomed roles of suppliant and mediator, Cassio and Desdemona are persistent; seasoned subordinates might have been more cautious. All of these characters behave as Iago expects them to, thereby confirming his contempt for marriage and his view of service as a foolish and "obsequious bondage." He has designed a situation in which customary practices work well enough to be deadly.

Because his schemes succeed, Iago believes that he fully controls his master. Othello changes with his verbal "poison" or "medicine," falls at his feet in a fit, and strangles Desdemona according to his suggestion. At the end of the play, Othello picks up Iago's favorite metaphor for domination when he asks Cassio, "Will you, I pray, demand that demi-devil / Why he hath thus ensnar'd my soul and body?" (5.2.301–2) It may seem that by bringing a "monstrous birth to the world's light" (1.3.404), Iago has in effect fathered Othello's jealousy. When he wholly commits himself to "wrong'd Othello's service" (3.3.467) it is possible to feel that the servant has become both master and husband. Could any corruption of service be more demonic than this one?

Yes, I will claim when examining how Shakespeare treats possession in *King Lear*. An advantage of considering related dependencies together is that it allows for a sharper discrimination among types of agency. Characters speak of possession, as we shall see, when one person seems to wholly co-opt the will of another or even drain it away. What Iago does to Othello could be thought of as a more temporary and partial enslavement. He poisons Othello's view of marriage, already assimilated to his public service, with servitude, causing Othello to regard Desdemona as a treacherous subordinate. This fantasy represents a full-blown version of the phobia glimpsed in Bertram's attitude toward Helena and Parolles, subsumed creatures who run away with his intentions. Iago helps generate Othello's monstrous conception of Desdemona. Yet the subsequent dramatic life of this fantasy owes more to the Moor's passions than to Iago's power. From his speeches in the present, it is possible to infer that Othello's passions have been molded by enslavement in the past. His orientation is that of a slave who escapes to freedom. Iago, with no actual recollections of captivity, has a different orientation: that of the slave master who captures and binds. This crucial difference helps to explain why Othello's response so exceeds Iago's provocation.

In his fine edition of *Othello*, E. A. J. Honigmann notes in Iago's speeches a number of tags from the clever slaves of classical comedy. But Iago often sounds more like an en-slaver than a slave. To describe Othello's elopement as boarding a "land carract" (1.2.50), he invokes both piracy and capture ("lawful prize" 51). To "ensnare" Cassio, he resolves to "gyve" him in his own "courtship" (2.1.168, 170). Othello, he imagines, is so "enfetter'd" to his love of Desdemona that she can "play the god / With his weak function" (2.3.345, 347–8). Her goodness will "make the net / That shall enmesh them all" (2.3.361–2). Iago both thickens his disguise as a scrupulous servant and arouses Othello's curiosity about his private thoughts by insisting, "I am not bound to that all slaves are free [to]" (3.3.135); given his view of true service as self-destructive, he is probably equivocating on "free" meaning entitled by membership and stigmatizing slaves as mentally bound (like all servants!) by their very status. Later, when Othello falls in a trance at his feet, Iago scorns him as a fool who is "caught" (4.1.45).

These references imply that for Iago slavery entails abjection and dishonor. Brabantio, Desdemona's father, would have agreed; he vents his profound shame at Desdemona's elopement with "if such actions may have passage free, / Bond-slaves and pagans shall our statesmen be" (1.2.98–9). When Iago warns Othello that Brabantio will find "cable" in the law where with to oppress him, an audience might surmise that Iago and Brabantio are thinking of the Venetian galleys manned by slaves. The Moor and his bride travel by galley in Cinthio's tale. Characters who picture vessels arriving in Cyprus through metonymic sails and masts ("tall ship") occlude the slaves and criminals working the oars.[70] It is also possible that Shakespeare associates Iago with the trade in black slaves developing in the Atlantic world. According to Samuel Purchas (1613), blacks were trying to help their parents by selling them in the Portuguese city of "Jago," the slave-trafficking port of Santiago on the Cape Verde islands off the west coast of Africa.[71] However he comes by his penchant for domination, Iago enjoys himself enormously. When Othello proposes to poison Desdemona, Iago eagerly suggests as an alternative strangling her in her "contaminated" bed (4.1.207–8). Othello's hands would then become a fatal collar around her neck, analogous to the collars and shackles used to bind slaves.[72]

As the play begins, slavery seems to be something Othello has survived and escaped. It represents at least one and perhaps several episodes in the "[battles], sieges, [fortunes]" he describes to Desdemona and the Senate (1.3.130). In his accounts of his "[travel's] history," the experiences of "being taken by the insolent foe / And sold to slavery," then redeemed (1.3.137–8), figure in a survey of "disastrous chances" (134) as just so many facts about his life in Africa and the Near-East before his Venetian career. This positive attitude would resonate with English determination to buy captives out of Mediterranean slavery.[73] It would seem to be consistent with the view, widely held, that physically subjected persons might remain spiritually free.[74] An audience would have no reason to suspect that Othello has been damaged by an enslavement so overshadowed in his seductive tale by Anthropophagi and other exotic wonders.

Othello does not allude again to capture and confinement until Iago has ensnared him. Then he tells Desdemona that he could better have endured a hopeless captivity than keeping his marriage as "a cestern for foul toads / To knot and gender in!" (4.2.61–2) The terrible speeches cited at the beginning of this section suggest that Othello may well have been hurt by confinement in dungeons and cisterns.[75] Tragedy, writes Bernard Williams, "is formed around ideas it does not expound."[76] This one is premised on a man's passionate love for a woman who pities him because of the sufferings he has escaped. The fountain of his life, the renewable resource of Desdemona's faith in his being, depends vitally on his experience of being set free. Love as a form of release and relief gives him an exhilarating but precarious happiness. When Othello celebrates the absolute "content" of his soul after he and Desdemona survive the storm at sea, he admits, "If it were now to die, / 'Twere now to be most happy" (2.1.189–90) This disturbs Desdemona ("The heavens forbid"), as well it should: Shakespeare's sonnets and a number of his plays question loves that are nurtured through anticipations of loss or enhanced by death, real or otherwise. If Othello can't imagine an escape which makes him loveable, he can't imagine mutual love.[77]

Iago the enslaver does not know that Othello's peculiar, powerful love will make him react so furiously. Neither he nor the audience could be prepared for the rage with which Othello begins to hate Desdemona when he begins to see his marriage as bondage rather than as redemption. Aside from her capacity to serve his turn by defending Cassio, Desdemona is nearly incidental to Iago's schemes. Indeed, Iago is a misogynist only if we are willing to grant, with F. L. Lucas, that "the true misogyny is indifference."[78] Wives are trivial functionaries; the best woman in the world is "a wight (if ever such [wight] were)—To suckle fools, and chronicle small beer" (2.1.158, 160). He doesn't realize when he uses his "jealousy" or zeal of honest service to make Othello jealous just how vulnerable Othello will be. Othello's jealousy will include not only sexual anxiety and possessiveness but also his anger at insubordination: "my fair warrior" has slept with "mine officer" despite her being one of "these delicate creatures" (3.3.269) he believed he could own. The responsible public servant will feel confounded with "toads" while Desdemona copulates with his army. This monstrous vision could well be called a "jealousy of service." Iago likes to rattle chain metaphors when he plans to trap Othello, but a handkerchief will ultimately do the trick.

Cassio and Desdemona feel cast out of the social order in much more ordinary ways. Believing that he is "desperate of my fortunes" if he loses the Moor's support, (2.3.331), Cassio hopes "I may again / Exist, and be a member of his love / Whom I, with all the office of my heart, / Entirely honor" (3.4.111–14). Otherwise, he anticipates a kind of beggary, "shut . . . up in some other course / To fortune's alms" (3.4.121–2). The worst fate Desdemona can foresee is that Othello might shake her off to "beggarly divorcement" (4.2.157–8), as if she were another Grissil. Sympathetic to victims and inclined to blame herself, she remembers the song of her mother's forsaken maid, Barbary. As she sings it, she seems to feel that it "expressed her fortune" as it had Barbary's, attacked by her lover for loving him in return. Desdemona adds words fully approving her own lover, Othello, before singing the final ironic lines. These may express her own muted protest, for the "mad" male lover is trying to justify his promiscuity: "If I court moe women, you'll couch with moe men" (4.3.57).

In this intimate moment, Emilia hears what Desdemona is reluctant to think (that Othello desires other women), and responds by giving her a bed-time dose of misanthropy, an angry lecture on sexual double-standards. Emilia's satire identifies her as older and far more conventional than Desdemona. Who could have expected her to sing the willow song and die for her mistress one scene later? Emilia has never been particularly stupid or timid. She has practiced as wife and maid a milder version of Iago's rule: eye-service coupled with self-preservation. She has heard Desdemona "so bewhor'd" by Othello that "true hearts cannot bear it" (4.2.115, 117) but she is still quick to follow her husband in calling Bianca a strumpet (5.1.121). She may love Iago, she may be afraid of him, and she may believe that all husbands are much the same. In any case, she seems better equipped to recognize corruption than to fight it.

Yet by exposing Iago's plot, she makes it possible for Othello to escape his domination. Moreover, her heroic actions anticipate Othello's return to his former role as public guardian. Through Emilia an audience inclined to accept many conditions approximating slavery could discover why service and slavery should never be identified. Iago connives at trapping Othello by urging him to "hold" Desdemona "free" (3.3.255); if Desdemona then confirms her supposed guilt by defending Cassio, Othello will in effect be shackled. Emilia begins to undo Othello's chains when she speaks "as liberal as the north" (5.2.220). In defying Iago and defending Desdemona, she chooses one form of subordination over another, exercising her own freedom of will. In acting for herself as well as for her mistress, she gives the lie to the alternatives initially posed by Iago: service as self-destructive abjection or as self-advancement. No writer of household advice books ever advocated so courageous a rebellion against a spouse (Iago) or imagined that absolute loyalty to a mistress could revive the heroism of a master. Such resistance as servants are allowed on questions of conscience is generally treated as passive in style. Emilia's is active and prolonged.

That Emilia can move through and beyond her rage at a filthy, foolish Moor who has treated his wife as a prostitute, and become a champion of love and truth is also extraordinary. To react through rage and horror is one thing; to produce an accurate account of events, ignoring threats against her life by Othello and Iago, is another. Through Emilia's courageous response, Othello can see the power of Desdemona's loyalty to himself. He can recognize the capacities for which Desdemona loved him, now clarified in their rare and ideal form. Staging such a recognition would enhance the pity and terror of all three deaths.[79] When Othello murders Desdemona, he carries out the ultimate logic of enslavement, which, as Jean Bodin said, is an "unmitigated catastrophe," a cruel and detestable form of behavior analogous to human sacrifice.[80] But when he imagines punishing a "malignant" enemy of Desdemona's Venice, he escapes from slavery by emulating Emilia's courage:

> And say besides, that in Aleppo once,
> Where a malignant and a turban'd Turk
> Beat a Venetian and traduc'd the state,
> I took by th' throat the circumcised dog,
> And smote him – thus. (5.2.352–6)

From the outset, Camillo and Paulina, the good servants of *The Winter's Tale*, oppose the jealousy of King Leontes. In protecting his marriage and disobeying his orders, they recreate a web of relationships around Leontes, saving him from himself. They fulfill a development which Richard Strier sees as beginning with Emilia: that of the loyal virtuous servant who resists a rebellion within the very character of the master.[81] Emilia's sudden heroism gives an audience little time to ponder the implications of her disobedience. That of Camillo and Paulina stretches throughout sixteen years, five acts and two countries.

For all their constancy and courage, these courtiers can do nothing to check the mad jealousy of their ruler. They become implicated in the mystery of what makes Leontes jealous through no fault of their own. Similarities with *Othello*, including servants closely linked to marital obligations and suspicion both of a friend and of a wife acting as a mediator, make it probable that a jealousy of service helps to motivate Leontes. After Camillo disobeys Leontes and escapes with Polixenes instead of poisoning his cup, Leontes discovers monstrosity in the supposed collusion of wife and servant:

> There may be in the cup
> A spider steep'd, and one may drink; depart,
> And yet partake no venom, (for his knowledge
> Is not infected), but if one present
> Th'abhorr'd ingredient to his eye, make known
> How he hath drunk, he cracks his gorge, his sides
> With violent hefts. I have drunk, and seen the spider. (2.1.39–45)

There are strong parallels between the crudeness with which he denigrates Hermione and the disdain with which he treats Camillo when Camillo firmly denies the truth of his suspicions. "I hate thee, / Pronounce thee a gross lout, a mindless slave" (1.2.300–1), Leontes bursts out, quickly reminding Camillo how he has been "bench'd and rear'd to worship" from "meaner form" (1.2.313–14). Here again a master's inclination to suspect and confuse his dependants has turned into a virulent phobia.

Because there is no obvious cause for the King's jealousy of Polixenes and no explanation from other characters, we have assumed that he suffers from generic misogyny or personal neurosis. It seems to me that the spider he visualizes may suggest that reciprocal bonds among dependants have been and remain particularly strong within this play. These webs of connection which Leontes can't destroy may in some sense cause as well as cure his jealousy. To understand why Hermione makes Leontes jealous in the first place, we need to consider what the play subsequently represents: marked similarities between the labors of Camillo and Paulina and a powerful conjunction between the agencies of Hermione and Antigonus.

Camillo immediately rejects the King's jealousy of his wife, Hermione, and his old friend, Polixenes as a "diseas'd opinion" (1.2.297). He slips out of his promise to poison Polixenes through equivocation ("I . . . will fetch off Bohemia" 1.2.334), like wives resourceful enough to avoid open protest.[82] Because he has "keys of all the posterns" (1.2.464), he can "whisper" Polixenes and his "followers" out of the city. Polixenes accepts him as a "pilot" (448), respects him as a "father" (461), and after sixteen years treats him as an indispensable servant and friend (4.2. 13–20; cf. 4.4.493). Yet Camillo still speaks of Leontes as "my master" (4.2.7) and engineers the escape of Florizel to Sicily, in part to "serve my turn" in that he will thereby "[p]urchase the sight again of dear Sicilia / And that unhappy King, my master, whom / I so much thirst to see" (4.4.509–13). This thirst, which he terms "a woman's longing" (667), is another of his wifely traits.

Camillo's role as what Florizel terms the "preserver" and "medicine of our house" (586–7) is matched by that of Paulina, an "honorable minister" for Hermione who brings Leontes his new-born baby and insists that her own words are "medicinal" and "honest" (2.3.37–8).[83] She professes that she is "your loyal servant, your physician, / Your most obedient counsellor" (2.3.54–5). Although her angry protests fail to move Leontes, she too becomes a guardian figure. She replaces Camillo as a trusted "confessor" (cf. 1.2.235–8), and enforces the oracle ("the King shall live without an heir, if that which is lost be not found" 3.2.134–6) by dissuading Leontes from re-marriage. Moreover, she maintains Hermione for sixteen years in a "remov'd house" (5.2.107) and keeps the King in a repentant frame of mind. Leontes fully acknowledges how justified Camillo and Paulina have been in their actions and speech (3.2.156–72, 232–4, 5.1.51–2). Camillo virtually stages the final reunion in Sicily; Paulina stages Hermione's return to her family.[84]

The agencies of Hermione and Antigonus converge when Antigonus, the husband of Paulina, arrives on the seacoast of Bohemia. Before he obeys Leontes and abandons the supposed bastard of Polixenes, he reports a terrible dream vision. Hermione has appeared as a "vessell of sorrow," weeping in "fury," commanding him to abandon her child in Bohemia, and virtually predicting his death (3.3.19–36). At this turning point in the play, we hear of a figure almost as frightening as the ancient Greek Furies, one capable of redirecting the will of Antigonus who soon loses his life by obeying her. Like the servant Furio in *Patient Grissil*, he suffers inwardly ("Weep I cannot, / But my heart bleeds" (3.3.51–2); unlike Furio, he serves the wife in carrying out the husband's "ungentle business" (3.3.34).

If servants can repeatedly stand in for a wife, a wife must be able in some circumstances to act as a servant. When Perdita entertains her guests in Act 4, the Old Shepherd urges her to welcome them as the "mistress o' th' feast" by recalling his own dead wife:

> This day she was both pantler, butler, cook;
> Both dame and servant; welcom'd all, serv'd all;
> Would sing her song and dance her turn; now here
> At upper end o'th' table, now i'th' middle;
> On his shoulder, and his; her face o'fire
> With labor, and the thing she took to quench it
> She would to each one sip. (4.4.56–62)

The daughter's situation illuminates her mother's. In his jealousy of service, Leontes may have repudiated his wife because she has played "dame and servant" so effectively, because he could mistake her hospitable "entertainment" of Polixenes for pliant ingratiation. The idea that Leontes could become jealous of Hermione because she serves as a mediator and persuades Polixenes to extend his visit may be less persuasive than the idea that he becomes jealous through sexual rivalry and competition. Both explanations were available to Shakespeare's culture, and the second is now widely accepted. The first becomes more plausible when the potent affiliations of wives with servants are considered. Like Helena, Hermione ingeniously carries out a masterful desire. In *The*

Winter's Tale, wives and servants mediate the physical and emotional distances separating royal males: the two old friends Leontes and Polixenes, and the father and son, Polixenes and Florizel. Isolated by his rank and dependent on the agencies of others to embody his intentions, Leontes could be quick to spy an alien will in his queen and his counsellor. He might infer from the surprising eloquence of his pregnant helper ("Tongue-tied, our queen? Speak you") that her body is being used by an independent force.

After the oracle is proclaimed and his son Mamillius dies, Leontes recognizes Camillo's honor in refusing to poison the cup of "my kingly guest" (3.2.166). But it is too late to prevent his most inhospitable act, the exposing of Perdita. Then, as if to re-define hospitality from the ground up, the Clown reports on a "land service," the dinner furnished by Antigonus to the bear. After the sheep-shearing feast in Bohemia, it is appropriate both that Paulina acts as hostess to the reunited characters and that her supper party provides the occasion for Hermione's return to life. The "affliction" of seeing Hermione's statue "has a taste as sweet / As any cordial comfort" to Leontes (5.3.76–7); her recovery is "an art / Lawful as eating" (5.3.110–11).

CHAPTER 4

Friends and servants

"Blessed are they that have been my friends." Falstaff's hopes take the form of a beatitude when he learns from Pistol that Prince Hal will soon be crowned King Henry V (5.3.137–8). That any great man's rise buoyed up his followers would be axiomatic in early modern England. Access to power through subordination, so provocative when accomplished by Helena in *All's Well That Ends Well,* was a more predictable type of advancement for male servants who planned to become masters, or for followers who expected to lead.[1] What concerns me in this chapter is not so much the operation of patronage, a subject of much recent study, as it is the fusion of service with friendship roles.[2] How can Henry V break the heart of Falstaff by treating him like a servant who is to be dismissed with a pension or "competence of life" (5.5.66)? How can Antony break the heart of Enobarbus by behaving to him as a good lord and sending after this "master-leaver" his worldly goods? Answers to these questions which are based too narrowly on individual psychology miss, I believe, the significance of customary social dependencies in creating relationships of trust. By looking more carefully at how service intersects with friendship both ideologically and in more local, pragmatic terms, we may understand why characters like Enobarbus and Falstaff become particularly vulnerable to the great pains of lost service through the blessings they have experienced.

My argument below begins with *2 Henry IV,* a history play which includes a probing examination of ambitious retainers and their hopes. Most of the characters in this play, female as well as male, share with Falstaff a desire to be protected and supported or, as they often say, "countenanced." Shakespeare also anatomizes virtual mergers between friendship and service in the tragedy, *Antony and Cleopatra*; minor characters play a major role in the tragic destruction of Antony and Cleopatra themselves. These two plays comment upon one another, and both may be clarified through incessant attempts by Shakespeare's contemporaries to define and differentiate service and friendship. It is possible to identify sweeping historical trends in these discourses, as emergent autonomy challenges residual feudalism, or to offer systemic explanations for such comprehensive mixtures of personal with professional, ideal with instrumental motives.[3] But while such approaches are ambitious, they often distort one vital process occurring in tragic or tragicomic plays: a sustained testing of social codes and customary practices. Instead of merely reassuring us that specific kinds of relationship are unjust or fraught with contradictions, tragedies are apt to suggest that the most satisfying, even productive relationships may be the most treacherous. I suspect that this is why, as Mario DiGangi points out, "Renaissance playwrights more frequently represent the spectacle of court favoritism in a tragic mode."[4]

This chapter will attempt to show why normal fusions of service with friendship might have had deadly consequences. Although mediators and go-betweens often become victims in more tragic plays, few of them seem conscious of imminent risk. Falstaff and Enobarbus would probably be sceptical if forewarned of their ultimate responses to the behavior of King Henry or of Antony. These responses surprise us, as Emilia surprises us with her commitment to Desdemona. It would be fatuous to use such conduct as if it might illustrate the devotion recommended for ideal servants and friends alike, given the fact that these men are improbable candidates for heart-break. Indeed, Shakespeare develops Falstaff and Enobarbus as self-protective figures, especially adept at maneuvering in ambiguous social territory on the margins of family life beyond the more natural bonds of childhood or the civil bonds of marriage. Their very flexibility is anti-heroic, an agile adjustment to shifting circumstances until it suddenly and fatally snaps. Enobarbus gives the lie to commonplace wisdom on how supple undergrowth is able to weather political storms in which rigid colossal oaks crash down. Throughout *Henry V*, when they are deprived of Falstaff's protection as "Fortune's steward" (2 *Henry IV* 5.3.130–1), his "friends" follow their leader into disease and death.

"THE SMILE OF SAFETY": COUNTENANCING IN 2 *HENRY IV*

Just how deeply the practice of service permeates 2 *Henry IV* may be suggested by the case of Bardolph. First mentioned in *Part 2* when the Page answers Falstaff's "Where's Bardolph?" with "He's gone [into] Smithfield to buy your worship a horse" (1.2.48–51), Bardolph is immediately identified as Falstaff's personal servant. "I bought him in Paul's"

(52), that is, in the nave of the London cathedral where masterless men gathered to seek employers. Throughout *Part 2*, Bardolph runs errands, tends to horses and accompanies Falstaff, no doubt reminding some spectators that these two old men share a long past together. In *Part 1*, Falstaff ends a speech on Bardolph's red nose by claiming, "I have maintain'd that salamander of yours with fire any time this two and thirty years" (3.3.46–8). The red nose, Giorgio Melchiori has surmised, was probably suggested by "Rossill," the name given to the companion of Sir John Oldcastle in the original performances of *Part 1* and then altered when "Oldcastle" became "Falstaff."[5] But "Rossill" or "Russell," Melchiori also indicates, would have implied good family and a knighthood. He points out that the main followers of the Prince in *The Famous Victories of Henry the Fifth* (a dramatic analogue) are all knights.[6] Bardolph, however, seems to be a much more humble attendant like another prototype in the play's best known analogues. Alluding to a notorious incident in the legend of King Henry's wild youth, when he was said to have quarrelled with the judge who arrested one of his followers, the Page warns Falstaff, "here comes the nobleman that committed the Prince for striking him about Bardolph" (1.2.55–6). John Stow cites Sir Thomas Elyot who in describing this incident refers to the offending follower as "one of his seruants, whom he fauored."[7] And in *The Famous Victories of Henry the Fifth*, the Prince comes to the rescue of "my man," one Cutbert Cutter, and sets him free by boxing the ears of the Judge.[8]

The representation of Bardolph as a more humble man servant has two important functions in *Part 2*. First, it magnifies the scope of his expectations when he learns that Prince Hal is now King. Anticipating Bardolph's preferment, Justice Shallow has already instructed his own servants to use Falstaff, a potential "friend i' th' court," and his men well (5.1.30–3). They begin to address Bardolph as "Master," toasting him as if he were a gallant London gentleman (5.3.58–9), and when Bardolph promises to "stick by" Davy, Shallow exclaims "Why, there spoke a king" (5.3.68–9). Bardolph heralds his own happiness and luck even before Falstaff does: "O joyful day! I would not take a [knighthood] for my fortune" (5.3.126–7). From humble manservant to royal favorite or favorite's friend: this escalation would have seemed unlikely, yet not impossible, to an audience familiar with current debates about yeomen hired by noble employers in preference to gentlemen, or arguments over the vocational usefulness of service as a profession. A decline in the sizes of retinues had already occurred, reducing the numbers of gentle servingmen. But fundamental changes in attitudes toward such service were still to come.[9]

The second function of Bardolph's service role is more interesting, but also more difficult to understand. His introduction as a servant once protected by the Prince comes immediately after a scene in which Northumberland, fired with desperate rage by the news of Hotspur's death, must be reminded of his responsibilities toward followers who need his protection:

> Sweet Earl, divorce not wisdom from your honor,
> The lives of all your loving complices
> [Lean] on [your] health, the which, if you give o'er
> To stormy passion, must perforce decay. (1.1.162–5)

Such paternalism, a legacy of feudal obligations, survived in the honor codes of "good lordship" studied by Mervyn James and flourished in the military profession.[10] Near the end of *Part 2* we find it motivating a sordid, yet common, transaction: Davy's success at persuading his reluctant master Shallow to "countenance" the knavish William Visor. "I grant your worship that he is a knave, sir; but yet God forbid, sir, but a knave should have some countenance at his friend's request . . . I have serv'd your worship truly, sir, this eight years; . . . The knave is mine honest friend, sir, therefore I beseech you let him be countenanc'd" (5.1.43–51). Davy's speech resonates with the fellowship initiated between Davy and Bardolph as well as with Falstaff's confidence that the Prince will in effect "stick by" him after the coronation. "Friend" as used so emphatically by Davy and Falstaff means more than simply ally or supporter. Friends protect and support one another both in spite of and because of differences in status or rank.

So practiced, friendship converges with service. In a nostalgic lament (contemporary with *Part 2*) for the days when large companies of serving men derived more exclusively from the gentry, I. M. celebrates this fusion, writing that servants are tied by masters in an "undessolvable bonde of assured friendshyp."[11] I. M. obviously idealizes this bond, characterized by "no servile, but as it were a filial feare" (C2v). He evokes a state of bliss when he describes the condition of the gentle servingman as "swimming in the calme" or "being (as it were) even the meane or midwarde of all degrees and callinges" (C3v). He also conjures up a remarkable picture of the "comfort of companions" when he describes them virtually attacking a "Beefe" chine to the "tune" of "It is merrie in Haul when Bear[d]es wagges al" (C1v). I. M.'s elegiac memory is just as unreliable as the nostalgia of characters in *Part 2* or in *Antony and Cleopatra*, but it may also be of value in indicating what many men and women must have sought for: security with honor. "They do not go together," Cleopatra will reply when Antony, dying, advises her, "Of Caesar seek your honor, with your safety" (4.15.46–7). Security in a time of civil warfare, English or Roman, goes, it seems, with a large measure of "accommodation," a slippery synonym, as it happens for being countenanced.[12]

Bardolph may know what he is talking about when he answers Shallow's polite inquiry concerning Falstaff's "lady" by saying "a soldier is better [accommodated] than with a wife" (3.2.66–7). Bardolph defines his word by staunchly repeating it; this provides matter for laughs at his expense but also evidence that a meaning so familiar and obvious needs no more explanation. His own life has been so fully "accommodated" or countenanced. How, without imagination or a dictionary, should he be expected to find many synonyms for a term which so effectively captures the anxious pleasures of status in the "midwarde," fitted comfortably into a social place which one can never take wholly for granted? To convince Claudio that no life is worth living, the Duke in *Measure for Measure* argues, "Thou art not noble, / For all th' accommodations that thou bear'st / Are nurs'd by baseness" (3.1.13–15). Not to be "nurs'd," on the other hand, is to become the spectre recognized by King Lear in the outcast bedlam beggar: "Thou art the thing itself: unaccommodated man is no more but such a poor, bare, fork'd animal as thou art" (3.4.106–8).

"Assured friendship," we might think, sounds like a perpetuation of childhood dependencies. But as I attempted to demonstrate in chapter 2, the youthful characters who seek refuge in service roles may also seek relative strength through positions where they can observe and care for others. Anecdotes of servants as potent helpers and saviors seem more pertinent to their situations than a sense that they need to be "nursed" because of insufficiency or immaturity. "Assured friendship," like the feudal system it derives from, entails reciprocity within "unequal obligations."[13] Falstaff, remembered by Shallow as a page for Sir Thomas Mowbray, now employs a page who enjoys the spectacle of Falstaff's corruption while tending Falstaff and his urine samples. As numerous metaphors of fluidity in *Part 2* or in *Antony and Cleopatra* hint, the bonds of such friendship were anything but "undessolvable" (I. M.'s view) and required artful, vigilant maintenance by all parties.[14] Directors often treat Silence as grotesquely drunken and senile in the penultimate scene of *Part 2*, but like Bardolph, he knows what he is saying, or in this case, singing: a version of I. M.'s beef-eating carol (Shallow apologizes for a shortage of meat) with its homosocial refrain, "'Tis merry in hall when beards wags all" (5.3.34). Silence throws his ancient person and voice into the serious business of courting Falstaff's friendship and securing a powerful ally.

Silence, then, sings a love-song of sorts. Where *Part 2* is concerned, the love in question appears to be inconsistently comprehensive, filling all the purposes carefully distinguished by the theorists of friendship, and analogous to the attachments of marriage or family. Aristotle, Cicero, and Montaigne, among others, tried to exclude familial and instrumental relations from true friendship.[15] Montaigne's friend, Étienne de La Boétie, the apparent inspiration of Montaigne's great essay on this theme, maintained in his own extraordinary treatise, *Discours de La Servitude Volontaire*, that "What makes one friend sure of another is the knowledge of his integrity." It is the inability of the tyrant to love that "impoverishes his own spirit and destroys his own empire;" he is "beyond the pale of friendship."[16]

Like Hamlet, wearing his friend Horatio in "my true heart's core," Montaigne and La Boétie idealistically reject the more inclusive ambiguities to be found in that border-land where service and friendship overlap. But as David Konstan points out, "sundry conceptions of friendship coexist" at any one time.[17] The English aristocrats who advise their sons are inspired by domestic diplomacy rather than by the ideal freedom of kindred spirits. "And be not willingly attended or served by kinsmen, friends, or men entreated to stay," writes Burghley.[18] Similarly, Raleigh warns his son that "those that will serve thee without thy hire will cost thee treble as much as they that know their fare."[19] Raleigh distrusts both friends and servants; friends superior in status are more reliable but are also disposed to forget or resent the services one has done for them.[20] "Friend" in these contexts can mean a more independent supporter or a more dependent follower, and it shifts in political or emotional valence with context and occasion.[21] William Wentworth, for example, wants his son to hire servants born of "good and honest friends." With a sense of such friendship approximating Falstaff's blessedness, this calculating country gentleman recommends choosing as "frendes" three to five knights or esquires "faithfull to your father" who will be "youre strengthe and comfortt under God."[22] In her adaptation of the one hundred and thirtieth Psalm (*De profundis*), Mary Sidney, Countess of Pembroke achieves an unpolitical, ceremonial, and reassuring effect by referring to God as a "frend" on whom to "attend."[23]

Somewhat lower on the social scale, we can find dependants like Thomas Howell, poet/servant of the Herbert family, who wants a new generation and their "friends" to work hard at serving a protective lord ("a wyght that so his servaunt stayes").[24] But we can also find figures who are ill-equipped for a selfless relationship. With bitter realism, the Italians M. Steeven Guazzo, in his *The Civile Conversation* and Giovanni Della Casa (an Archbishop), in *The Arts of Grandeur and Submission,* both assert that for servants who normally resented subjection, "friendship" could rarely be disinterested. In contrast to the courtier, Guazzo and his interlocutor agree, the gentleman has a common servant who hates both his master and service *per se.*[25]

Indeed, for Guazzo's interlocutor, Annibal, the vexations of any servant seem sufficient to preclude mutual emotional attachments: "And in truth that constraynt to eate, to speake, and to goe, by the mouth, by the tongue, and by the feete of others, that estate never to have rest eyther of bodye or mynde, to loose ones selfe in the service of hys Mayster, to bee short, those incommodityes, vexations, troubles, and annoyes, rehearsed in a Letter of yours, wherof you have indured in your own person a greate parte, fill up the Cuppe with so bitter a potion, that the smell of it, yea, the very rememberaunce of it, offendeth nature."[26] Della Casa is more dispassionate. He insists that in a "Friendship" or "Amity" founded entirely upon "Riches, Dignity, and Power" (as opposed to "Learning, Age, Nobility, or intrinsique worth and vertue"), it would be an "intollerable oversight" to exact the attitudes of "vertuous friendship" and "folly" to believe in any disinterested service. He concludes by urging great men to remember that they are served, not by slaves, "but Friends of a lesser degree" who have been subjected through fortune and choice, not nature.[27]

How many English people, on or off-stage, would have been so judicious in sorting out their affiliations? Asserting (with little originality) that the life of a "serving-creature" is "like the life of a water-spaniel," the musician Thomas Whythorne tries to distinguish himself from his fellow-servants by emphasizing his professional competence as well as by courting a succession of mistresses.[28] At one point he manages to "covenant" that "I would be used as a friend, and not a servant," meaning that he would be permitted to eat with the family in the absence of special guests.[29] It is apparent from the *The Autobiography* that "lopsided" friendship "oils the wheels of hierarchical societies" and can make inferiority more acceptable.[30] Eventually Whythorne decides that "I should not keep company with my greaters." One of his poems, "Of fruitless friends or foes," included near the end of his *Autobiography*, reveals his muddled values when it resolves: "As ill I count the helpless friend, / As foe, who harms to me none seeks."[31]

Good cousin Silence would probably agree. The love this old man offers to Falstaff, another old man whom he scarcely knows, may suggest that the love among Prince Hal and his companions or between Shallow and his steward, Davy, is not wholly individualized or personal. Shakespeare represents the customary bonds among these characters as both intimate and strained. The Prince, beginning to withdraw from what he and his father consider "vile company" (2.2.49) and to feel shamed by his knowledge about Poins' supply of stockings or shirts, addresses Poins as one "it pleases me, for fault of a better, to call my friend" (2.2.41–2). He takes offense at a letter in which Falstaff warns him, "Be not too familiar with Poins, for he misuses thy favors so much that he swears thou art to marry his sister Nell" (2.2.127–9). That the wary Poins could have expressed such absurd hopes seems unlikely; he ironically identifies himself as the Prince's "shadow," i.e. follower and servant, toward the end of this uncomfortable scene (2.2.159). Davy, however, so obviously shares domestic authority with Shallow that Falstaff can mock their relationship as a marriage: "It is a wonderful thing to see the semblable coherence of his men's spirits and his . . . Their spirits are so married in conjunction, with the participation of society, that they flock together in consent, like so many wild geese" (5.1.64–6, 68–71).

This envious, satiric speech, along with Falstaff's later pun on Davy's husbandry (5.3.11), highlights the quasi-erotic nature of male intimacy, rarely suggested by chivalric or Petrarchan compliment in *Part 2* but possibly a powerful motive, given the indifference of most characters toward women and marriage. (And, for that matter, men seem appealing to women only when dead or likely to die.) But whether Falstaff's mockeries of daily routine in Gloucestershire can be taken as evidence of literal sexual conduct is far more doubtful. As Eve Kosofsky Sedgewick observes *apropos* of the eroticism in Shakespeare's twentieth Sonnet, "the sexual context of that period is too far irrecoverable for us to be able to disentangle boasts, confessions, undertones, overtones, jokes, the unthinkable, the taken-for-granted, the unmentionable-but-often-done-anyway, etc."[32] We will see that when Antony idealistically addresses "mine honest friends" and describes himself as "a master / Married to your good service" (4.2.31), he and the members of his entourage are being pulled apart by the violent changes in his political fortunes. A strong tension between altruism and self-interest is, David Konstan speculates, "irreducible" as an "antinomy in the nature of friendship."[33] And if Renaissance friendships between men functioned, according to Alan Bray, through a convention or "code" which "individuals were still free to manipulate," then the norms, let alone the disorders, of assured friendship or friendly service become all but impossible to pin down.[34]

What does seem relatively clear, both from courtesy books and from the reported conduct of masters and servants, is that bodily closeness functioned as a sign of this privileged and protected love. Richard Gough reports that the wife of a neighbourhood gentleman killed a young female servant because she saw her husband flick water in the servant's face while this servant held water for him to wash his hands, the wife "conceiveing it too famillier an action."[35] Sir Walter Raleigh valued physical closeness to Queen Elizabeth.[36] Generations of noblemen, including the Earl of Essex, rebelled because, they asserted, they had literally been denied access to the monarch.[37] "I do allow this wen to be as familiar with me as my dog," says the Prince disdainfully, showing Poins Falstaff's letter (2.2.106–7). Perhaps because of the blatant calculation involved (Falstaff also calls the Prince *his* dog, 1.2.146), Laurens Joseph Mills thought it "doubtful" in *One Soul in Bodies Twain* that the friendship tradition he was tracing had any influence on the creation of Falstaff.[38] I believe, however, that Shakespeare understood just how blissful a mix of security with companionship might prove. The "lords and owners of their faces" (Sonnet 94), countenancing others through their use of inherited "heaven's graces" (and "nature's riches") could be worshipped for the happiness and safety they provided. As his sonnets to the Young Man repeatedly suggest, countenancing would bring together urgent needs and satisfactions, troped through acutely personal or familial language, with the expansiveness of mutual self-fashioning. "Our friends do not keep us on edge but they do keep our edge on us," writes Ronald A. Sharp, celebrating the creativity and comfort of friendship.[39] Few friendships have ever been as creative as the relation between Falstaff and Prince Hal. But when the balance of unequal reciprocity suddenly shifts, a convergence between service and friendship can become a dangerous border country. As the new King Henry V tips Falstaff over a precipitous edge, he says, "I have turn'd away my former self" (5.5.58), thereby confounding a formula for dismissing servants ("turn'd away") with the classical, humanistic ideal of male friendship as a union of selves.

Henry V sustains a connection between the selves of Henry and Falstaff by associating the King's "wildness, mortified," his "reformation in a flood" (1.1.26, 33) with the death of Falstaff "at the turning o' th' tide"

(2.3.13). The rejection of Falstaff appears to have had the broad public impact which Niccolò Machiavelli desired when he mentioned several methods of gaining a proverbial reputation with the public: saving a father, killing a son, or returning captured women.[40] For Fluellen who epitomizes a straightforward military fraternalism uncomplicated by intimate associations, this rejection is already a legend: "As Alexander kill'd his friend Clytus, being in his ales and his cups; so also Harry Monmouth, being in his right wits and his good judgments, turn'd away the fat knight with the great belly doublet" (4.7.44–8). The reported impact on Falstaff, the feelings that shatter his heart ("fracted and corroborate" 2.1.124) and make his body "as cold as any stone" (2.3.24) can perhaps be imagined through dramatized analogies: the King's later sadness and rage at the treachery of his bed-fellow, Scroop, and the utter abjection of Falstaff's old friends Bardolph, Pistol, Mistress Quickly, and Doll Tearsheet. When Nim remarks that "the King hath run bad humors on the knight" (2.1.121–2), he suggests that being turned away has caused the fatal fever that seems to both dissolve and harden Falstaff's body.

As a figure for broad civil disorder, this body has become such a commonplace of Shakespeare criticism that we may not take its ordinary social dimensions seriously. When Jean-Louis Flandrin reconstructs the fragile helplessness of servants who foresaw the collapse of their households, he assumes a passivity much like that evoked in the writings of Basse, Darell, Howell, or I. M., and not the vitality of a Falstaff who can gallop from Gloucestershire to London in the confidence of receiving total gratification: "I know the young king is sick for me" (5.3.135).[41] Falstaff has aged in *Part 2* but his sudden illness and death is still a terrible measure of the damage which a lord and master could do to a dependent friend by putting him ten miles beyond the pale of intimate contact and partial trust.

Whenever friendship or marriage converge with service we are apt to be emphatically reminded of bodies and their conditions. In a passage cited in chapter 3, I. M. makes his case for having masters served by men of similar status by comparing the gentle servingman to Adam's rib, Eve.[42] Francis Bacon describes the helpfulness of friends as supplements to or extensions of a body's life: "A man hath a body, and that body is confined to a place, but where friendship is, all offices of life are as it were granted to him and his deputy. For he may exercise them by his friend."[43] The language of feasting, drunkenness, sexual intercourse and disease, so pervasive in the *Henriad*, may gesture toward a set of customary practices. For assured friendship has many properties of the susceptible, incontinent bodies studied by Gail Kern Paster as cultural archetypes.[44] If such friendship had ever possessed a literal body, it would probably have been perceived as old-fashioned and corrupt, like Falstaff's; Shakespeare's contemporaries were well aware that, as Linda Levy Peck writes, the "mentality of service and courtesy limited changes in policy and practice."[45]

Were we to visualize this type of subsumption as a body, it might look like a baggy and chaotic relative of Plato's fish-trap, rather than like a neat hierarchy or ladder. Upper orders would bulge around and encompass lower ones loosely accommodated within them in a mobile system of mutual support, while the whole would be connected by a haphazard array of arterial passages and quite shot through with apertures opening it up to nurture, invasion and collapse. This corporeal fantasy might also have a face like that of the "Titan" kissing or melting "a dish of butter" with which Prince Hal mocks Falstaff's pretensions (*Part 1*: 2.4.120–2). Because the Prince misleads and turns away the friend he has countenanced (his joke on Falstaff helps the fat knight's "tallow" to dissolve (2.4.111–12), he himself could be the rebellious son/sun "Titan." It is no accident that the two plays where assured friendship is most functional are also haunted by vivid images of colossal figures or that the contradictions of fluidity and stone, so notable in the tidal death of Falstaff, should recur in the deaths of Enobarbus and Cleopatra. Such deaths seem to be implicated in the confusing fates of vast social formations. They are made partly intelligible through figures of hidden or inward transformation proper to physical bodies.

I have suggested that one disorder especially incident to fusions of childhood and service is the instrumentalizing or enslavement of the agent, sometimes signified by hands and feet. The disorder associated with fusions of wife and servant roles is an alienated agency or will, troped as a monstrous creature somehow generated from oneself. Where service overlaps with friendship, metaphors of insidious debility and base infection spring up, along with the gigantic shapes mentioned above. Most prevalent among the occupational maladies afflicting assured friendship is flattery, often compared to a poison, an aggressive parasite, or a cancer ("this great wen"). So chronic is flattery that any attempt to analyze it might seem to trivialize those histories and tragedies where it flourishes. It becomes much more interesting as social poetry when one bears in mind the perspective on ethics supplied by status: flatterers, favorites, and parasites tend to be criticized by people placed higher in the social hierarchy and looking down. Giants, on the other hand, seem to be imagined by those who are looking up from positions of greater dependency.

Such visions, colored by myths and by ardent personifications of strength and weakness, are no more reliable than the peculiarly facial "smile of safety" which "Rumour" initially fixes to the fissured system of countenancing in *Part 2*. Prince Hal probably gives Falstaff a small page (later "my tall fellow" to Shallow, 5.1.58) so as to inflate Falstaff in the minds of Englishmen. Thus perceived, he may conform to the popular stereotype with which Prince John berates the Archbishop: that of the "false favorite" who abuses "countenance" when he swells and ripens in the "shadow" of royal greatness (4.2.24–6.11–15).

But Falstaff mocks the tendentiousness of such myths by caricaturing himself as "a sow that hath overwhelm'd all her litter but one" (1.2.11–12); he describes the red face of an addicted sack-drinker as a "beacon" "warning . . . all the rest of this little kingdom, man, to arm" (4.3.108–9). Symbolic giants do not die when turned away. Falstaff also appears to regard himself as Diana's forester, as a moon-man who, instead of hiding in shadows, casts reflected light when he steals under her "countenance" (*Part 1*, 1.2.25–9). There is something tragically lunatic about his trust in Hal's countenancing and about the association between his death at the "turning of the tide" and the King's abrupt reformation. The physical presence of an older, whiter, waning Falstaff on stage might well contradict that image of titanic disorder "so surfeit swelled" which the new King produces for consumption by underlings.

FRIENDLY FLATTERY IN *ANTONY AND CLEOPATRA*

Enobarbus in *Antony and Cleopatra* has few illusions about the mighty rulers of his world. Yet he dies, by moonlight, of a broken heart because he has left Antony and has then been forgiven by him. Were Enobarbus as cynical or independent as he appears earlier in the play, this kind of tragic lunacy would be meaningless. I have linked him with Falstaff because he too seems to be destroyed by an assured friendship. Countenancing has made him acutely vulnerable to a rupture with his lord. The "place" of Enobarbus in the stories of Antony and Cleopatra is in fact where this study began. More than other followers, his career brings into the foreground the slipperiness of an ethos best practiced, a Della Casa would say, by those who do not take themselves too seriously (modesty being a crime in a courtesan!)[46] During a crisis such an ethos could promote survival through imitating enemies and abandoning friends. No gentle servingman such as Basse describes, Enobarbus nevertheless epitomizes a role whose "privileges," Basse writes, "upon doubts consist."[47] As suggested in the Introduction, this role closely associates Enobarbus with Cleopatra and her women; it features at the same time a resilient bond with Antony, a friendship conditioned by the play's near-fusion of domestic and military retinues, its extraordinary development of subordinate agents.

Both Antony and Cleopatra refer to their many household servants and political supporters as "friends." As in 2 *Henry IV*, assured friendship breaks down distinctions between personal and professional needs so that servants and allies can become trusted intimates. Octavia laments her situation when her husband and brother make war by saying that her heart is "parted betwixt two friends" (3.6.77). When Cleopatra tells Thidias that she can listen to Caesar's message in the company of Charmian, Iras, and Enobarbus, all trusted "friends," Thidias replies, "So haply are they friends to Antony" (3.13.48). Thereupon, Enobarbus tries to erase this suspicious distinction between personal virtue and professional interest by flattering Thidias and Caesar: "If Caesar please, our master / Will leap to be his friend; for us, you know / Whose he is we are, and that is Caesar's" (3.13.50–2).

Further complicating the nature of friendship here is the fact that even Caesar has been in some sense a follower of Antony's, inspired by the very model he is trying to wreck. Antony recalls Caesar's mere "lieutenantry" at Phillipi (3.11.39); Caesar recalls that the man he has "followed" or hunted down (5.1.36) was

> my brother, my competitor
> In top of all design, my mate in empire,
> Friend and companion in the front of war,
> The arm of mine own body, and the heart
> Where mine his thoughts did kindle . . . (5.1.42–6)

The ambitious officers caught up in an agonizing power struggle are petty versions of the rising Caesar; they behave opportunistically and unpredictably as they juggle the demands of loyalty and self-interest. Ventidius judiciously protects himself by conquering less of Parthia on Antony's behalf, while Menas proposes to support Pompey by slaughtering Pompey's guests, Antony, Caesar and Lepidus. A third officer later cuts Pompey's throat to oblige Antony, much to Antony's distress.

Such "friends" become the "dogs of war" first unleashed by Antony in *Julius Caesar* (3.1.273). The formalistic critical tradition of treating them as foils or choral figures obscures their dynamic influence. Emrys Jones indicates the importance of "innumerable others" when he writes that they "helped to make up the political force known to history as 'Antony'.

It is no part of Shakespeare's conception to insulate his hero's fall from the fates of his nameless dependants."[48] Throughout the play, the stories of friends continually distract our attention from the protagonists and explain the tidal rhythms of historical change. Those who are closest to an ebbing leader become the most exposed and vulnerable; when Enobarbus revolts from Antony, he discovers that Caesar is killing such inconstant followers, often by placing them in the "van" of battle so that "Antony may seem to spend his fury / Upon himself" (4.6.9–10). However desperately characters (and some readers) may wish to believe that the outcome of this tragedy is fated (as Plutarch maintains), it is also significant that Hercules, that hard-working patron of heroes, apparently leaves Antony when Enobarbus does.[49] The play invites us to imagine, with those he has led and protected, that Antony is himself a Herculean guardian, a "pillar of the world" (1.1.12) or, in Cleopatra's more mythical vein, "The demi-Atlas of this earth, the arm / And burgonet of men" (1.5.23–4). But without the agencies of his friends Antony is scarcely capable of dying, let alone winning his final battle. Assured friendship is the social body in which leaders and their followers survive, but a lethal trap during a crisis of obligation and loyalty.

Unlike the confidants and advisors in plays about Antony and Cleopatra by Cinthio, Garnier, and Daniel, Shakespeare's friends help to shape a tragic plot. Their participation in Antony's fortunes transmutes in fascinating ways the very nature of the flattery by which they influence him. Plutarch has no doubt that such flattery, in which he includes all of Cleopatra's wiles, is entirely self-interested in motive and deadly in effect. Because of his moralistic stance and antipathy to Cleopatra, the subtlety of the social analysis with which he furnished Shakespeare may have been overlooked. To understand how Shakespeare actually changed the function of flattery, it is necessary to look more closely at what Plutarch says.

According to Plutarch, Antony, with his "Asian" proclivities, is especially susceptible to flatterers whom Plutarch regards as Cleopatra's agents. Both in his "Life" of Antony and in his *Moralia* essay, "How a Man May Discern a Flatterer from a Friend," Plutarch emphasizes the great sophistication of these flatterers, especially evident in their strategic, self-protective foolishness and in the perverse rhetoric of their praise and blame. Because Antony believes that men who exchange mocks with him, who speak to him "so plainly and truly in mirth would never flatter him in good earnest in any matter of weight," they can fool him. According to the "Life," they make him think that "when they would give him place in any matter of weight" they are merely "ignorant," rather than being flatterers who have "handled him finely thereby" (199). Plutarch's flatterers gain their selfish ends by telling the truth about trivial matters while pretending not to understand serious ones; Antony's appetite for speciously egalitarian companionship damages his judgment, and in North's translation, drives away his own "faithful servants and friends" (248). Excoriating a jester's disguise, an unprincipled use of frankness to simulate "the proper voice of friendship," Plutarch shows in *Moralia* essay how the flatterer tries to "frame and accommodate himself wholly to all those things that he taketh in hand; yea, and to resemble those persons just by way of imitation whom he meaneth to set upon and deceive."[50] Convinced that such a "covert" flatterer attacks the capacity for self-knowledge and justice, Plutarch compares his deep and insidious mode of operation to that of lice, "deadly poisons," and tumours (39, 65).

Particularly dangerous, according to Plutarch, are those flatterers who know how to vilify attitudes contrary to those their victims actually have. This technique is more destructive than simply calling someone's vice a virtue (i.e., saying that Antony's luxuriousness is generosity). In his *Moralia*, he refers to the "friends of Antonius" who, "when he burned in love of the Egyptian queen Cleopatra, would persuade and make him believe that she it was who was enamoured upon him, and by way of opprobrious imputation they would tell him to his face that he was proud, disdainful, hard-hearted, and void of all kind affection. This noble queen (would they say) . . . for the love of you pineth away, and consumeth herself" (67). In the "Life," Cleopatra's flatterers use the likelihood of her suicide to work upon "Antonius' effeminate mind" (241).[51] Plutarch's *Moralia* essay waxes metaphorical on the difficulties of detecting such subtle, devious flattery. He compares it to removing wild seeds from good wheat or writes that like water, the flatterer is "variable and changing always from one form to another, much like as water which is poured out of one vessel into another, even as it runneth forth, taketh the form and fashion of that vessel which receiveth it" (42, 45). The best way, therefore, to detect a flatterer is to use a pretense of change, luring the flatterer into improbable agreement with new attitudes or actions: "Make him believe once that you will change your copy, and that you are about to shake off this idle life . . . you shall have him to soothe you up and second your song" (47–8).

By relocating Plutarch's "variable and changing flattery" in the social context of assured friendship, Shakespeare alters it in two ways. He uses Plutarch's figures of volatility to characterize the superior viewpoint of his rulers and he produces versions of flattery which can be termed friendly in a more positive sense. Both Antony and Caesar distrust their followers. Antony refers to "Our slippery people" (1.2.185) and Caesar speaks of them as "a vagabond flag upon the stream . . . [lackeying] the varying tide," that is, servile in their allegiance to the leader of the moment (1.4.45–6). "Lackeying" has a powerful early modern resonance, chiming with the suspicions of patriarchs who warned against "glowworms" (Burghley), "cuppeflyes" (Humfrey), and other treacherous "hyrelings" (Wentworth), preparing young men to manage followers who quickly discover how the "tyde runneth" (Percy).[52] *Antony and Cleopatra* is steeped in an awareness that the extraordinary imitativeness which equipped servants and followers of all sorts to satisfy elastic and unpredictable demands could also equip them to exploit flaws of character or, as Plutarch complained, to criticize minor failings while keeping silent about major ones.

But this play also foregrounds the awareness that when moved by affection and good will, cunning flatterers can provide constructive counsel. Even if they lack the openness often considered a prerequisite for friendship, they perform an office described in Guazzo's *Conversations* as using "an honest kinde of deceite" in reprehension.[53] Guazzo, who like Plutarch, identifies flattery with poison, is here concerned with the problem of managing friends rather than with the problem of detecting of flatterers. Guazzo's interlocutor says of courtiers that it is impossible to be a "friende of Caesars" and still "utter his minde freely."[54] The wonder is that Antony's friends do keep trying.

How astonished Enobarbus would be to learn that Shakespeare had modelled him in part upon sinister flatterers who served Cleopatra, and not merely upon passing references to two of Antony's military subordinates.[55] But whereas Plutarch's flatterers blame Antony for his "Hard-hearted" treatment of the queen who "for the love of you pineth away," Enobarbus responds to Antony's "I must with haste from hence," with

> Why then we kill all our women. We see how mortal
> an unkindness it to them; if they suffer our
> departure, death's the word. (1.2.133–5)

> Under a compelling occasion, let women die. It were
> pity to cast them away for nothing, though between them
> and a great cause, they should be esteem'd
> nothing. Cleopatra, catching but the least noise
> of this, dies instantly. (1.2.137–41)

An attempt to inflame Antony's passion has become, through an ironic shift, a critique of emotionally dishonest postures as conquering war-lord and seductive temptress. Equally barbed are his joke about Roman orientalism (what a good thing that Antony has managed to take in the sight of Cleopatra during his travels!) or his comment on Antony's attitude toward the death of his wife, Fulvia: "the tears live in an onion that should water this sorrow" (1.2.169–70). Enobarbus does speak "plainly and truly in mirth" during this crucial passage, as Antony decides to return to Rome; but he also addresses a "matter of weight." His wit engages Roman attitudes in a kind of dialogue, keeping open the possibilities of recognition and self-criticism. His reply to Antony's concern for the "business" "broached" in the state by Fulvia – that the "business" of Cleopatra "broach'd" in Egypt "wholly depends on your abode" – gets brushed aside by Antony with "No more light answers" (1.2.171–6). Such answers can indeed be taken lightly by the listener, but they concern one of the weightier matters in the play: Antony's attachment to Cleopatra.

It is illuminating to notice that the "light" speech of Enobarbus resembles that of Charmian and Cleopatra, the "women" from whom he distinguishes himself ("Why then we kill our women"). To mock Cleopatra's adulation of Antony, Charmian remembers and mimics the voice of another, younger Cleopatra. Their amiable argument, including Cleopatra's request for reassurance ("Did I, Charmian, / Ever love Caesar so?"), Charmian's taunting echoes ("O that brave Caesar!" "The Valiant Caesar!") and Cleopatra's fervent denials, produces Charmian's remarkable apology: "By your most gracious pardon, / I sing but after you" (1.5.66–73). Here Shakespeare rewrites Plutarch's advice on distinguishing a friend from a flatterer who tries to "soothe you up and . . . second your song." Charmian's song entertains the idle queen who could "take no pleasure" in a eunuch's singing (1.5.9–10) by imitating the queen's own voice. Cleopatra had responded to Charmian's more obvious rebuke, "You think of him too much" with "O, 'tis treason!" (1.5.6–7). Instead of merely soothing Cleopatra, Charmian suggests how repetitive the pattern of her love affairs has been.

We can ask, thanks to feminist and materialist studies, whether mimicry by changeable men and women weakens and relaxes an oppressive social structure or whether the structure recuperates and expends mimicry.[56] It is evident, too, that both Enobarbus and Charmian practice a type of "cosmesis," described by Frank Whigham as a strategy for camouflaging one's own vulnerability by trivializing oneself.[57] Yet self-protection by protected figures coexists in these passages with active criticism. These two servants are potentially liberating and creative flatterers. They evade full responsibility for insights which befit their master and mistress, leaving them free to grasp their implications. This calculated openness, crafted by loyal, affectionate followers, bears directly upon the unpredictable, suspended nature of the crisis still to come.

Enobarbus is equipped to understand Cleopatra so well because within the great-house ménage they seem to share, they must employ similar skills. Like the servants described by Della Casa, they know how to walk "betwixt two precipices," avoiding either servile flattery or clownish moroseness.[58] Noblewomen and chief officers, as we have seen in chapter 3, often competed for influence and power. Although a queen, Cleopatra has long depended upon Roman protectors. Janet Adelman observes that "the fathers of Cleopatra's harshest critics were her lovers."[59] Her methods of flattering Antony transfigure those decried by Plutarch. Where Plutarch stigmatizes the jesting mirth of parasitic flatterers as "a fine device to make difference of meats with sharp and tart sauce," ("Life," 199) Enobarbus celebrates Cleopatra's ability to make "hungry / Where most she satisfies" (2.2.236–7); "He will to his Egyptian dish again" (2.6.126).

Far more daring than either Enobarbus or Charmian, Cleopatra persistently wrangles with Antony in their early public interviews, mocking his romantic pretensions and challenging his motives for returning to Rome. She responds to the "falsehood" of his hyperbolic love with "Why did he marry Fulvia, and not love her? / I'll seem the fool I am not" (1.1.40–2). Cleopatra initiates a strategy in which she cosmetically risks being perceived as a jealous woman in order to challenge the good faith of Antony's Roman marriage and of his vows to her. From the outset, she exercises in a much more provocative fashion the skills Walter Darell commended to gentle servingmen: "Did not Antonius the lustie gallant preferre Cleopatra the black Aegyptian for her incomparable courtesie before all the blasing starres in the citie of Rome?"[60] She is too provocative for Charmian who counsels, "cross him in nothing" and "Tempt him not so too far." "Thou teachest like a fool: the way to lose him," Cleopatra replies (1.3.9–11).

In the opening scenes, Cleopatra mocks her protecting lord for his self-deception. In Baldesar Castiglione's words, she exercises the courtesan's privilege to "sting men for their faults more freely than men may sting them."[61] This privilege was thought to compensate women for their lack of sexual and political freedom. She exposes the politics of Roman love and marriage with her question, "Can Fulvia die?" (1.3.58), a question which will be pertinent whenever Roman men employ women, dead or alive, as ideological weapons in their civil wars. She may be trying to distract Antony from hearing the messengers from Rome, if hearing them means being governed by a scolding wife and a "scarce-bearded youth." "Grow up and decide for yourself," she could be implying when she mimics Fulvia's voice. Such flattery could be a means of keeping Antony by stretching his options and enabling, not coercing, his choices. Indeed, she may prepare him to hear the messengers one scene later.

As do Enobarbus and Charmian, Cleopatra places herself at the mercy of her listener who is free to take her words in jest and generally does so. Flattery may lie with the listener's expectations as well as with the speaker's designs. Responses to Cleopatra have often imitated Antony's wonder and delight: "Fie, wrangling queen! / Whom everything becomes" (1.1.48–9). But to regard Cleopatra as infinitely capable of seductive, theatrical charm is to become a Roman orientalist, to share Antony's condescension toward his Eastern entertainer. Her wrangling is skilled work, friendly flattery which serves his interests and her own. She needs a protector and champion as well as a lover. Especially in Act 1, Scene 3, the dialogue between the lovers betrays the strain on Cleopatra of both mirroring and mocking the attitudes of her "courteous lord." Untroubled by his own ability to play both the pious Roman widower and the hero serving a courtly mistress, Antony surely cannot hear Cleopatra's reply after he has accused her of mere idleness in opposing his departure: "'Tis sweating labor / To bear such idleness so near the heart / As Cleopatra this" (1.3.93–5). But the audience may, and with her words, a sense of creativity that (to sustain her metaphor) is pregnant but never entirely fulfilled. Irena Makaryk takes her cue for observing that Cleopatra chafes at her role as mistress from a production in which Cleopatra was exhausted by the tensions of this scene.[62] Plutarch's *Moralia* essay attributes to Cleopatra and her followers a talent for flattery which swells and effeminizes a victim; flattering speech is like "the soft bed pillows that women lie on" (63).[63] Shakespeare, however, shows that she can use this talent to challenge Roman policies. As Guazzo's *The Civile Conversation* puts it, Cleopatra can "play the Foxe with Foxes, and delude art with art."[64]

I am suggesting, then, that friendly flattery becomes damaging when its deliberately limited nature prompts the listener to limit its purposes. Within assured friendship, good lords and dependents enjoyed the three benefits of classical friendship, use, virtue, and pleasure, but in ever-shifting balance and proportion. The dependent friendly flatterer juggles these benefits but can easily be understood from above as knavishly self-serving or superficially light, and certainly far from virtuous. "They fool me to the top of my bent," Hamlet concludes, once he has pretended to change his mind, that ruse to detect subtle flatterers, and Polonius has agreed that the same cloud resembles a camel, a weasel, and a whale (3.2.384). But what if Polonius is being cautiously deferential? Early in *Antony and Cleopatra*, Antony reveals his own simplistic and binary view of flattery as being both pleasant and deceptive when he reassures Caesar's messenger by saying, "Who tells me true, though in his tale lie death, / I hear him as he flatter'd" (1.2.98–9). The susceptibility to flattery which Plutarch had treated as a great flaw in Antony's temper now takes the form of selective hearing. It is as if the very geniality which makes him deaf to the prudential element in sarcasm is rooted in his willingness to accept folly at face value. His condescending pride offers Enobarbus and Cleopatra a cover for duplicity, should they ever decide to use it. While his refusal to take them seriously protects them, it also insulates him from the full strength of their wisdom when they speak "plainly and truly in mirth."

Hence Antony can ignore Enobarbus when he does finally give straightforward advice with other officers and urges Antony not to fight Caesar on the sea (3.7.34ff.) Yet the sea appropriately tropes the social element of assured friendship in which both Antony and Cleopatra have flourished, supported by and supporting friends. The schoolmaster sent as an ambassador to Caesar reveals his sense of Antony's scope through his apology, "I was of late as petty to his ends / As is the morn-dew on the myrtle leaf / To his grand sea" (3.12.8–10).[65] After Antony dies, Agrippa says that "a rarer spirit never / Did steer humanity" (5.1.31–2). The nautical metaphor, "steer," is well suited to a character who has risen to power by navigating through the turbulent waters of personalized Roman politics. These waters become particularly treacherous when the greatest of his dependents suddenly acts upon the ever-present fear suffered by those who need protection, and saves herself by abandoning Antony at Actium. Other friends soon follow her example. As Antony recognizes after his ultimate defeat at sea, the "dogs of war" now seek new leashes: "The hearts / That [spannell'd] me at heels, to whom I gave / Their wishes, do discandy, melt their sweets / On blossoming Caesar" (4.12.20–3). After Actium, the tensions negotiated by assured friendship become the contradictions which pull Antony apart, as he eddies wildly between love and scorn for his allies, household, and Cleopatra herself.

Not surprisingly, Antony's understanding of the dilemma faced by his attendants and officers is far superior to his understanding of Cleopatra and her circumstances. He believes that his household servants are part of him ("all of you clapp'd up together in / An Antony" 4.2.17–18), and speaks of his relation to those he is about to leave as a marriage (4.2.31).[66] Unlike Henry V, he turns no one away, and they all weep, says Enobarbus, like women (4.2.36). As we have seen, Caesar exploits Antony's feelings by putting deserted officers in the van of battle. Antony's bond to his men remains powerful in the scene of Antony's attempted suicide when Eros, the freed but protected servant, gets Antony to turn away his worshipped "countenance" so that Eros can slay himself, not his "dear master" (4.14.85–6,89), or when one of the nameless guards ("good friends") who bear Antony to Cleopatra exclaims, "Woe, woe are we, sir, you may not live to wear / All your true followers out" (4.14.133–4). If his followers do leave, they are heeding counsel which Antony gives right after Actium when he urges a group of "friends" to take his treasure and "fly" to Caesar (3.11.2–6).

Yet he never understands how much Cleopatra and his followers have in common. I mentioned above her reply that honor and safety "do not go together" after Antony, dying, urges her to seek both from Caesar (4.15.47). Antony hates to send "humble treaties" to Caesar, to "dodge / And palter in the shifts of lowness" (3.11.62–3); Cleopatra, however, is willing to treat such shifts as opportunistic and necessary ruses. It becomes clear after Actium that Antony's apparent affinity for the ordinary slaves and knaves of Egypt, so disgusting to Caesar, has been a kind of slumming which satisfies his appetite for exotic pleasures. Cleopatra, on the other hand, never speaks contemptuously of her people or servants, with the exception of Seleucus, her treasurer, who embarrasses her before Caesar by revealing that she has "kept back" half of her wealth (5.2.147–8). It is significant that she takes responsibility here for the conduct of "one that I have bred" by articulating a basic principle of good lordship, mentioned by the ever-pragmatic Guazzo: that "the faults of the servant belong in a maner to the Maister."[67] Caesar blames his sister Octavia for returning to Rome like a "market-maid" (3.6.51); after Antony dies and the "odds is gone" (4.15.66), Cleopatra tells her women that she is "No more but [e'en] a woman, and commanded / By such poor passion as the maid that milks / And does the meanest chares" (4.15.73–5). Both Antony and Caesar would find her dialogue with the "rural fellow" who brings her the fatal asps distasteful, not because they are both Roman but because they are both incapable of imagining what it would be like to inhabit the places of those they lead.

All the strains in assured friendship become evident during the scene where Thidias, sent by Caesar to win Cleopatra through deceptive flattery, seems to be succeeding. Enobarbus has obsequiously flattered

Thidias himself, but disturbed by Cleopatra's responses to Thidias, he projects his own wavering loyalty upon her and runs off to fetch Antony. Seeing Thidias kiss Cleopatra's hand, Antony explodes into the first of two great rages. And when his servants do not immediately heed his summons to deal with "this Jack," he cries out,

> Authority melts from me. Of late, when I cried "Ho!"
> Like boys unto a muss, kings would start forth
> And cry, "Your will?" – Have you no ears? – I am
> Antony yet. (3.13.90–3)

Had Antony made better use of his own ears, had he noted the prudence of his friendly flatterers or the wisdom of his officers, he might never have had to ask Cleopatra, "To flatter Caesar, would you mingle eyes / With one that ties his points?" (3.13. 156–7) By whipping Thidias, he shows how thoroughly his suspicion of slippery subordinates has now become the solvent of his own self-esteem. The effect of his fury upon Enobarbus is contagious; by deciding to leave Antony at this point, Enobarbus initiates his own dissolution. For her part, Cleopatra does not argue with a contempt for dependents that is beginning to include herself:

> To let a fellow that will take rewards
> And say "God quit you" be familiar with
> My playfellow, your hand, this kingly seal,
> And plighter of high hearts! (3.13.123–6)

Instead, she patiently asks a question, "Not know me yet?" (158) which will haunt their remaining time together.

What this particular tragedy seems to know well is that countenancing works through loyalty based on security. If security weakens, the unequal bonds maintained through continual accommodation seem to both stiffen and melt. We can be relatively certain, both about this social process and about Antony's motivation within it, even though we can never know, while Antony is alive, how passion and self-preservation combine to move the Queen of Egypt. When Antony rages at Cleopatra, blaming her for his final defeat, he confounds the agencies of his followers with that of his mistress:

> My fleet hath yielded to the foe, and yonder
> They cast their caps up, and carouse together
> Like friends long lost. Triple-turn'd whore! (4.12.11–13)

The virulent Roman prejudice reported by Enobarbus to Cleopatra, "That Photinus an eunuch and your maids / Manage this war" (3.7.14–15), proves true but only as consequences of Antony's flight from Actium and later, of his intense fury.

Thoroughly frightened by his threat to "blemish Caesar's triumph" by killing her first (she does not hear him compare her to Lichas, the friend and servant slain by Hercules), Cleopatra now heeds Charmian's advice to play safe: "To th' monument! / There lock yourself, and send him word you are dead" (4.13.3–4). Because Antony has already resolved on suicide before he hears Mardian the eunuch deliver Cleopatra's message, fulsomely obeying her orders to report "that the last I spoke was 'Antony,' / And word it, prithee, piteously" (4.13.8–9), Cleopatra is not responsible for his death. But it does seem fair to suggest that such selfish, deceitful flattery is what Antony has often expected and rarely received. A servile collusion such as he has mistakenly identified on earlier occasions now plays a symbolic role in his final destruction.

On the reading I have presented here, Cleopatra's great speech praising the dead Antony to Dolabella (5.2.79–92) is both myth and social description. It celebrates her personal vision of Antony, but it also imagines a colossal, protecting figure as seen from below. The legs that "bestrid the ocean" belong to a genius of good lordship and have been walking on the volatile, oceanic agencies of alliance. The arm that "[c]rested the world" sheltered and guarded his "friends." The voice, "propertied / As all the tuned spheres" to these "friends," was an instrument for precise social accommodations. The "livery" bestowed on kings, along with the "realms and islands . . . / As plates dropped from his pocket," describes him in terms suited to a magnanimous, hospitable, early modern prince. These details are preceded by a remarkable account of the "countenance" in which, Eros had said, "the worship of the whole world lies" (4.14. 85–6). Cleopatra's version is more apocalyptic and cosmic:

> His face was as the heav'ns, and therein stuck
> A sun and moon, which kept their course, and lighted
> The little O, th' earth. (5.2.79–81)

Here, as throughout the play, Cleopatra speaks both as a lover and as an assured friend.

If the social values of countenancing were not so materially substantial in the world of this play, neither Enobarbus nor Cleopatra and her maids would exhibit "such celerity in dying." Upon learning that Antony has sent his treasure after him, Enobarbus immediately expects "swift thought" to break his heart (4.6.34). Like Falstaff, Enobarbus suffers the loss of bliss, a pain so complete that only the "blessed" moon can bear witness to it (4.9.7). His moon, like Falstaff's, tropes the mimicry and lunacy in his conduct toward his master, but it is overcast by his discovery that he has exchanged a good lord for a bad, a "mine of bounty" (4.6.31) for a vindictive machiavel who will distrust, even execute him. Hence the "poisonous damp of night" which he begs the moon to "dispunge" upon him is a poison of his own making, his "fault" in leaving Antony through self-interest (4.9.13, 16). Only when cut off from Antony and in despair does Enobarbus fully express the supposedly normative ethos of aristocratic service which, writes Mervyn James, required from the servant "an unqualified and exclusive devotion to his master, and implicit obedience to his commands."[68] Without Antony, Enobarbus has no self to serve. His ending foreshadows Antony's, his "damp" corresponding to Antony's acute sense of self-loss as an indistinct "vapor," his flinty fault on which he breaks his heart to Antony's sword, and his foul "ditch" to the humiliating mess of Antony's suicide.

After Antony dies, Cleopatra and her women have "no friend / But resolution, and the briefest end" (4.15.90–1). Although she, too, acts with "dispatch," her death prevents humiliation. As if to proclaim her new autonomy and an end to the contradictions of assured friendship (so disastrous for Enobarbus), she announces that the "fleeting moon / No planet is of mine" (5.2.240–1). Both Cleopatra and Enobarbus have been faulty in the great crisis of obligation following Actium; both have resorted to deceitful, unfriendly flattery. But in another striking revision of Plutarch, Shakespeare emphatically turns the insidious poison associated with flattery into the method by which Cleopatra enacts her courageous resolution.

Cleopatra has easily decoded Caesar's courtly promises, his advice to "Feed, and sleep" (5.2.187) as flattery meant to inflate and damage its victim. "He words me, girls, he words me, that I should not / Be noble to my self" (5.2.191–2). The country clown who arrives bringing hidden vipers becomes the "instrument" of her "liberty" (5.2.237–8). This liberator helps us to see why Antony can't understand Cleopatra or women like her. "He that will believe all that they say, shall never be saved by half that they do," says the clown (5.2.255–6); he refers to a "very honest woman, but something given to lie," who, having died of the worm, gives it a "good report." How well he describes, without condescension or illusion, the role of the friendly flatterers in this play. Unless Antony accepts their mockery as entertainment, they cannot use it to test and strengthen his judgment. His errors destroy them all.

Plutarch's *Moralia* essay compares the effects of hidden flattery both to poison and to the "wanton pinches and bitings of luxurious women." Because those who catch their victims through counterfeit frankness complain of merely minor vices, their criticism tends to "tickle and stir up the lust and pleasure of men by that which might seem to cause their pain" (67). In another of those extraordinary concentrations of language which synthesize death and life, yet distinguish the toils of grace from the sterile traps of empire, Shakespeare transfigures Plutarch's "luxurious women." Cleopatra compares the fatal effect of her kiss on Iras to "a lover's pinch, / Which hurts, and is desir'd" (5.2.295–6). "O, couldst thou speak," says Cleopatra to her snake, "That I might hear thee call great Caesar ass / Unpolicied!" (5.2.306–8) If a wise serpent could hiss in English syllables, this is how it might sound. In her final and most startling act of imitation, Cleopatra flatters no one. She sings for herself.

CHAPTER 5

Tragic dependencies in King Lear

Chapters 5 and 6 will focus upon two tragedies, *King Lear* and *Macbeth*. These plays are closely linked through their transformations of native legend and their representations of warlike, aristocratic societies. Both raise haunting problems about the agency of spirits, invite us to imagine evil on a demonic scale, and take us well over the edge of civilization into barbarism and savagery. In Naomi Conn Liebler's view, both "interrogate virtually every kind of human interrelatedness and definition of identity: feudal, familial, spousal, national."[1] Shakespeare has created tragic plots in which specific interactions by specific individuals prove terribly destructive precisely because they seem always to have worked, to have been validated by customary wisdom and tradition. Hence these plays can rend the hearts and minds of spectators who expect either confirmation or subversion of social arrangements.

But *King Lear* and *Macbeth* also differ profoundly in respects which a study of dependent relations may attempt to clarify. *King Lear* features outcasts who need and respect civilized order. A succession of characters who follow Cordelia in being thrust from place and position also follow her when they value appropriate bonds and obligations. Moreover, they do not venture far from their collective life or the physical structures which protect it. Even Edgar, proclaimed an "outlaw" to his father's "blood" and prepared for dangerous exposure in the wild, quickly joins the group of characters shut out of Gloucester's house and follows his father back into a more domestic space. Soon, clad in the garb of a household servant, he leads his father toward Dover on a path which seems almost well-travelled, thanks to the appearances of Lear and Oswald and to Edgar's vocal shifts in status.

Macbeth, on the other hand, features isolation and brutality in the dark: violent soliloquies by Macbeth and his wife, the murders of Duncan and Banquo, and the eventual suicide of Lady Macbeth. Great strongholds like the castle where assassins kill Macduff's family seem porous by comparison with the hovel and the room where Lear and his friends find shelter. Macbeth himself is neither outcast nor outlaw, for outlaws, too, often operate by codes which reflect or oppose established law.[2] Macbeth destroys all familial and civil bonds by slaughtering children, wives, friends and allies. His surviving enemies are not cast out; they voluntarily choose exile and freedom beyond the borders of a Scotland they will liberate.

In his film of *King Lear*, Grigori Kosintsev evoked the profoundly social nature of the play, not only by filming crowds of beggars in Edgar's hovel or on the move toward a center of power, but also by returning the action to the primitive stockade where it begins. One dimension of this social nature appears in the interest which the play has held for lawyers.[3] Even the villains care about such matters as inheritance, household regimen, and the rules of chivalric combat. Cornwall admits that he and Regan can torture Gloucester, but "we may not pass upon his life / Without the form of justice" (3.7.24–5). At his maddest, Lear stages the trial of Goneril and Regan (3.6., quarto text) and furiously satirizes abuses of law. Extreme suffering in some scenes and barbaric language in many may have caused us to exaggerate the alienation actually experienced by the characters.[4] But it would be difficult to exaggerate the alienation of Macbeth. In his filmed adaptation, *Throne of Blood*, Akiro Kurosawa virtually replaced Scotland's open moorland heath with dense thickets, suggesting that Macbeth carries a bewitched and rooky wood within him wherever he goes. Such isolation would be intolerable for outcasts like Edgar and Lear, social beings who are hurt to the quick by the treatment they receive.

The following chapter on *King Lear* reconfigures the three approaches developed in Part I. It augments current studies of service in the play by emphasizing unpredictable interactions and unsettled normative attitudes.[5] Tragedies can make audiences and critics doubt what they know and how. The final chapter on *Macbeth* departs from those that precede it by placing issues of service and bondage in a more political context. It associates *Macbeth* with *Hamlet*, *Coriolanus*, and *Othello*, tragedies which explore the relation of service to slavery and freedom. Although my argument often relies on political concepts, it also tries to address a particular social practice recognized as slavery by the characters themselves. When Lear terms Cordelia's murderer a "slave," he indicates, together with moral and social baseness, the loss of freedom afflicting so dehumanized an instrument. The Captain eager to carry out the "great employment" of killing Lear and Cordelia prefigures the desperadoes hired by Macbeth to assassinate potential enemies. Like the servant used by a vicious wife to plot against the Paphlagonian prince in Sir Philip Sidney's *Arcadia* (a source for Gloucester's story), such predators can "make a ladder of any mischiefe."[6] *King Lear* dramatizes such behavior through a series of servants and employers, but *Macbeth* treats it more extensively: the slaves of *Macbeth* come to include Macbeth and Lady Macbeth.

The proliferation of slaves in *Macbeth* makes possible, I will argue, a more sustained critique of the dependent relations which prevent or enable political freedom. In *King Lear*, most political acts are inseparable from strong loyalties which animate characters whether they are clearly good or evil or, like Edgar and Lear himself, somewhere in between. The resistance of Cordelia, Kent, and Gloucester's servant arises with spontaneity from common quasi-familial attitudes. Edgar prepares for revenge and kingship by serving his father in the persons of a bedlam beggar (once an ordinary servingman who loved his mistress all too well) and a peasant. Even Edmund, feeling beloved when Goneril and Regan die for him, tries to save their father and sister from assassination. In *Macbeth*, love and friendship, however flawed or ambiguous, eventually vanish from Scotland; stark bondage to terror helps to produce a much broader comprehension of attitudes which support tyranny and inhibit freedom.

REASONING LEAR'S NEEDS

Montaigne admits in his essay "Of Husbanding Your Will" that because our lives can be maintained so cheaply, we should think of our own "habits and condition" as if they were a "second nature."[7] He confesses, "What my habit lacks, I hold that I lack. And I would almost as soon be deprived of life as have it reduced and cut down very far from the state in which I have lived it for so long."[8] These reflections parallel King Lear's reasoning to his daughter, Regan: "Allow not nature more than nature needs, / Man's life is cheap as beast's" (2.4.266–7). Any discussion or production of *King Lear* must engage with questions about what Lear's needs are and whether they are justified. How we define or resolve these questions will influence how we approach Shakespeare's most comprehensive representation of social bonding. I begin with Montaigne and his sense of needs relative to an accustomed "state" because Montaigne also argues that the responsible magistrate only attains "freedom of soul" by befriending himself, limiting his obligations to others, and, in a figurative sense, remaining at home: "You have quite enough to do at home; don't go away."[9] It may be worth taking a chance on Montaigne's domestic wisdom: that disorderly human "souls" are best judged "by their settled state, when they are at home, if ever they are; or at least when they are closest to repose and their natural position."[10]

If ever Lear is "at home" in Montaigne's sense, or "closest to repose," it would be as his retirement begins, immediately before his furious quarrels with Goneril and Regan, and again, after his reconciliation with Cordelia.[11] His essential "habit" of life is to depend upon the devotion of his followers, an attitude which we can fairly describe as feudal or aristocratic as long as we understand both its currency and force in the early seventeenth century. Chapter 4 has argued for the contemporary resonance and seductive appeal of protected friendship in *2 Henry IV* and in *Antony and Cleopatra*. When one of his hundred knights observes to Lear that Goneril's household entertains him with much less "ceremonious affection" or "kindness" (1.4.58–60), this knight is identifying a division between the service and friendship which together knit up a web of alliances.[12] It is a mistake, I believe, to imagine that Lear avoids love as understood by Stanley Cavell: an acute personal and private recognition of one's dependence upon others.[13] For Lear often asserts or implies his need for his knightly following. He seems to assume that love is inseparable from mutual support. Indeed, he regards his own children and Edgar as assured friends, making few distinctions between the duties owed him by daughters, noblemen, and body servants.[14] Nor is he necessarily wrong in doing so; we have seen how service readily converged with other types of dependent relationship. Albany is attempting to recreate the bonds of assured friendship through his final appeal to Edgar and Kent: "Friends of my soul, you twain, / Rule in this realm, and the gor'd state sustain" (5.3.320–1).

With King Henry's rejection of Falstaff in mind, his violent splitting of friendship from service, it may become more apparent that *King Lear* also explores the surprising vulnerability of the cast-off follower. Only now it is the hearts of outcast masters which break as well. The figure of the giant endemic to countenancing, a figure caricatured in Falstaff or elegized in Antony, comes terribly to life in Lear's titanic rages against his daughters and the storm. Edgar probably alludes to his own father's desire to destroy him when he re-enters Gloucester's house with giant-the-Jack killer's words, "'Fie, foh and fum, / I smell the blood of a British man'" (3.4.182–4). Edgar may imagine that he is himself the knight "Child Rowland" approaching "the dark tower" of his father's tyranny. But his archaic term, "Child," also implies criticism of his own passivity, while his jargon suggests that childishly innocent sons collude with the blood-thirsty passions attributed to fathers and leaders. At the same time, Edgar adopts the part of a crazed servingman who has been too intimate with his mistress and lost his place, falling prey to an acute form of invasive disorder, possession by diabolic spirits.

These examples suggest the wide range of role reversals in *King Lear*. They also suggest something of the chaos and extremity with which this play dramatizes types of inter-relationship emphasized in earlier chapters. Those who become outcasts behave unpredictably, even outrageously, complicating the junctures of service with childhood, marriage, and friendship. This wild storm in and among systems of subordination resembles the active upsurge of underlings in the later scenes of *Antony and Cleopatra*. But in *King Lear*, such chaos begins in the first scene and continues to the last when Lear enters bearing Cordelia's body. Specific interactions of service with other forms of dependency are difficult to define when Lear himself confounds these dependencies through his attitudes toward his daughters and followers. The demands which he makes on characters who owe him "subscription" are at first unlimited. He has little of Hamlet's finely tuned awareness of distinctions in status, or of those "differences" which Kent proposes to teach Oswald by beating him.

Two of the sections below emphasize a peculiar but powerful confusion of roles and values evident in Lear's relationships with subordinate figures. The third focuses on Edgar's possession by demons in order to show why the collapse of friendly alliance or service creates an unbearable sense of vulnerability. Although these sections correspond to the major topics and concerns of earlier chapters, they have also been designed to set forth three broad varieties of paradox, featured (and simplified) in the subtitles which precede them. These are crucial ambiguities which a study of multiple subordinations may hope to illuminate, not contradictions which may be altogether explained.

INNOCENCE AND SERVILITY

When Kent returns from exile disguised as Caius, an all-purpose servant, he embodies Lear's need of an entirely dependable following, young or old. But as Bradley pointed out, Lear's devoted supporters often manage to make things worse.[15] Moreover, if we can be certain that by any strict and orthodox standard Cordelia and Kent have at first behaved disobedi-ently, we still cannot be confident of a norm by which to assess their later obedience. They tend to be brash or forceful when caution seems wise, passive (like Edgar) when brashness might be expected. None of these characters receive a training in service such as the one planned by Pisano when he advises Imogen to wait upon Lucius in *Cymbeline*. As cherished daughter, royal advisor and eldest son forced to become helping hands, all misfit their roles and play them at times with evident strain. In suggesting that they manage to seem both innocent and servile, I wish not only to emphasize the degradation they suffer voluntarily but also to question the nature of their self-sacrificing behavior.

When characters are as brave as Kent or Cordelia, they cease to be fair game for critical suspicion. As Nicole Loraux maintains with regard to Antigone who gives her life in order to bury her brothers, "She bears witness to the limits beyond which the thinkable cannot be subverted."[16] Presumably this means that criticism is silenced by Antigone's courage when she dies for her beliefs: in the immediate aftermath of a tragic sacrifice, thought often seems petty. But what kind of thought and for how long? Tragic endings may be crafted to overwhelm audiences, but they also provoke resistance and lingering discomfort. Successive performances or readings generate even more questions, as we shift from feeling that characters might have acted otherwise to asking whether and at what points they could have done so. If final sacrifices are rarely in question, events preparing for them should be.

One question that might be stimulated by the ending of this tragedy bears directly on the conduct of Kent and Cordelia. We see that Albany, well-disposed toward Lear, temporarily forgets him, that Lear is unable to save Cordelia, and that he is beyond help by well-meaning supporters. Does this not create a sense that the mutual reciprocities glimpsed by Lear in his madness have never been achieved? Throughout the play, Lear's bonds to subordinate characters remain disturbingly unbalanced. Despite the brave selflessness of Kent and Cordelia in helping Lear, they are touched by servility through their one-sided relations with him.

A group of anecdotes from the life of Endymion Porter, gentleman attendant upon Prince Charles, may be used to comment on this issue. Porter relates a true castaway tale in which he suffers a broken shoulder escaping from a wrecked vessel near Calais; his loyal servant either drowns or is crushed when he follows his master by jumping after him.[17] At the time (October, 1622), Porter was en route to Spain on a mission concerning a possible Spanish match for the Prince. In a second castaway episode, crying out that he is the King's servant does not save him, together with his Spanish companions, from being stripped by Dorset natives when his ship breaks up just off the English coast.[18] Later, when he is exiled in France, he writes in a letter that he has lost his estates through loyalty to his "master," King Charles, and that he would have starved if "an Irish barber that was once my servant" had not lent him money.[19] He also protests that he will study the King's good "all the days of my life."[20] As if continuing Porter's creed, his youngest son, devoted to James II, protests, "My duty and loyalty have taught me to follow the King my master, and by the grace of God, nothing shall divert me from it."[21]

These anecdotes suggest that Kent is not particularly old-fashioned in his attitude toward Lear. Dire accidents and political crises expose Porter to humiliating abjections, while his own servant, coming second, loses his life at Calais. But the docility of Cordelia and Kent differs from that of Porter or his unfortunate servant in one significant respect. Both characters initially resist a total identification with Lear. After Cordelia has vigorously distinguished attachments to fathers and husbands ("Sure I shall never marry like my sisters, / To love my father all" 1.1.103–4), it becomes ironic that she does marry "to love my father all" when she tries to rescue him. After Kent has opened his attack on Lear's susceptibility to flatterers with a calculated address to "king," "father," "master," and "patron" (1.1.140–2), it becomes harder to accept his subsequent uncritical posture. In effect, Lear learns to detect the flattery of those who "told me I was everything" (4.6.104–5), while Kent and Cordelia learn to behave as if he really were "everything" and they were whole-hearted pawns (to use Kent's term for himself, 1.1.155).

Cordelia and Kent play out the terrible consequences of Lear's failure to recognize differences between daughters and followers, a failure which persists during his changes of fortune. As we have seen, the roles of children and other dependents must often have overlapped in the early modern era. This does not mean that contemporaries saw no differences between these roles.[22] It does mean that a fusion negotiable in one set of circumstances might become a destructive confusion in others. Lear probably expects his daughters to respond to his initial challenge as if they were assured friends, adopted sons such as Edgar might have been had Lear offered to "entertain" him (3.6.78–9) in saner and earlier times. For their parts, his daughters understand their relation to Lear more narrowly or selectively than would be the case with a Kent or an Endymion Porter. Cordelia claims to love Lear only as a father, while her sisters, so fluent in the hyperboles of assured friendship, must have regarded him primarily as an incompetent master.[23] Like Hamlet, aristocratic children were often well placed to sense or resist a power which might excessively instrumentalize them. Leo Salingar observes that in referring to her "bond" with Lear, Cordelia might have "conveyed the sense of subjection as well as constraint."[24] Even as Lear divides his kingdom, his daughters fragment his comprehensive role. Their divisions make his disastrous.

"At home" during Act 1, Scene 4, Lear offers "love" after Kent serves him by tripping Oswald (1.4.86). Like other princes, (especially Richard the Second and Prince Hal), he may well prefer the followers he has chosen to his kinfolk. It is arguable that Lear only begins to notice his daughters when they hurt him or to appreciate his strong bond to Cordelia when he is treated as he had treated her and cast off like an unruly dependent. Rather than avoiding family love because he feels unworthy or ashamed of a personal need, Lear desires the predominantly homosocial love bonding the *famiglia* he has led for much of his life. This capacity both bespeaks and inspires powerful emotional needs, even as it condemns Lear's followers to shocking treatment. Edgar probably refers to the humiliation of Caius, forced to sit in the stocks, when he describes his meeting with the banished Kent who "did him service / Improper for a slave" (Q 5.3.221–2).

I doubt then that there is much difference between the "love" which Lear offers to Caius in Act 1 and to Cordelia in Act 5. As they go off to prison, Lear treats his daughter as if they were both rusticated and modishly disaffected young knights, hiding from their fellows, gossiping about ambitions and venereal diseases (the mysterious "good-years" 5.3.24). Cordelia has finally been welcomed into companionate service and entertained as one of his cherished hundred. Her rescue mission has begun when thirty-six of Lear's knights carry him off to Dover. If we recognize these knights in the "century" (4.4.6) which she sends after her runaway father, we may also sense that their activity partly redefines Cordelia herself as an ally or assured friend. How firmly she distinguishes her purposes as a military leader from those of "blown ambition" (4.4.27) which is a menace to the unbalanced reciprocities of such friendship and, of course, Edmund's primary motive. It is interesting to observe that Edmund swells to fit gaps opened up when Cordelia is sent away. He quickly sheds the servility of a bastard who "came somewhat saucily to the world before he was sent for" (1.1.21–2) and has, through "service to custom," been packed off regularly ever since. Edmund would no doubt see Cordelia's new deference to Lear as a wholly servile "bondage" to "aged tyranny" (1.2.49–50). Edgar would probably have urged her to confront her enemies ("Shall we not see these daughters and these sisters?") instead of yielding to Lear's extraordinary vision of life behind bars.

What should Cordelia do after she returns to England as a queen and a general? Does she honor Lear so passively when he begins to recover because she still identifies herself primarily as a daughter or because, as his knight, she wants to exalt the confidence of her leader?[25] Or is she really deferring to Lear's attendant, the Gentleman (Quarto "Doctor") to whom she has said (in both texts) "Be govern'd by your knowledge, and proceed / I' th' sway of your own will" (4.7.18–19)?[26] In refusing to blame her father ("No cause, no cause"), she may primarily obey good medical wisdom, explicit in the Quarto Doctor's advice to avoid making Lear "even o'er the time he has lost" (Q 4.7.79).[27] The play engages audiences with the perplexities of intensely personalized politics, inviting us to share Cordelia's embarrassment when Lear kneels to her, and to surmise that the relation which he imagines between himself and his daughter is premised on a continuing exchange of childlike subjections: "We two alone will sing like birds i' th' cage; / When thou dost ask me blessing, I'll kneel down/And ask of thee forgiveness" (5.3.9–11).

In the chronicle play of *King Leir*, the King and Cordelia compete in their reconciliation scene by trying to out-kneel one another, popping up and down and reducing a precarious, one-sided balance of attachments to farce. Shakespeare's troubling reconciliation and indeed his play as a whole lack the relatively clear sense of how obligations are defined or limited which distinguishes *King Leir*. For example, Perillus (corresponding to Kent) emphatically denies any hope of reward when he first befriends Leir.[28] After he has left "his friends, his country, and his goods" (1707) to join Leir, the two old men become such good friends that each protests his willingness to die for the other, when threatened by an assassin in Scene 19. Leir refers to Perillus as "my Damion" (1562) and as "truest friend, that ever man possest" (1786). Kent, on the other hand, may retain his disguise to avoid imposing obligations on a master who never recognizes firm social distinctions. After Lear casts off Cordelia, he repeatedly terms his Fool "boy," an intimate address which fuses childhood with humble service, preparing us for the horrific confounding of innocence with utter abjection in "my poor Fool is hang'd" (5.3.306).[29]

"At home" with the hundred knights who replace Cordelia, providing Lear with an interim "nursery" of sorts, the old king is at first surprisingly youthful and energetic, a style to which Kent apparently adjusts himself in playing the bumptious forty-eight-year-old "Caius." Consequently it may be easy to forget why the hundred have come into being. As if he anticipated Kent's warning, "Reserve thy state" (1.1.149), Lear quickly banishes Kent, invests his royal power in Albany and Cornwall, and then proclaims,

> Ourself, by monthly course,
> With reservation of an hundred knights
> By you to be sustain'd, shall our abode
> Make with you by due turn. (1.1.132–5)

Whether the hundred are themselves young and rowdy are questions best decided by directors.[30] Lear, many critics have thought, merely needs these knights as conspicuous symbols of his rank. It is probable though that Lear also acts at some level through a concern, like Kent's, for his own "safety" (1.1.157) as well as responding to the loss of Cordelia's expected care. A. C. Bradley rightly felt that Cordelia had an obligation to "preserve" her father as well as her sense of truth.[31] The hundred, as Goneril and Regan clearly perceive, could easily function as a body-guard.[32] Rosalie L. Colie has emphasized Lear's civility in refraining from using this group for his self-defence.[33] But if Lear has been enjoying their familial companionship, he may not have surmised that he even needs defending until it is too late. Because the key issue of protection will be examined more fully in the final section of this chapter I will only point out now that some guarantee of safety is what Lear may have been hoping to hear in his daughter's pledges of loving allegiance.

That Lear is too innocent about danger, too preoccupied with the pleasures of assured friendship may be implied by the Fool's jokes offering Lear's new follower, Kent, a coxcomb as his badge of service or in advising Lear to "Ride more than thou goest" (1.4.121). He seems to mean that a riding household of followers needs support from landed wealth if they are to support Lear. ("When thou clovest thy crown i' th' middle and gav'st away both parts, thou bor'st thine ass on thy back o'er the dirt" 1.4.160–2.) Not to recognize this fact is to join the world of fools and children. (LEAR "Be my horses ready?" FOOL "Thy asses are gone about 'em" 1.5.32–4.) The Fool's mock prophecy, "That going shall be us'd with feet" (3.2.94) may also glance at the absurdity of having mounted sup-porters who are fragmented in power and purpose, a condition earlier anticipated in Edmund's professed alarm at the "dissipation of cohorts" (Q 1.2.148).

Despite the Fool's persistence in yoking Lear's innocent expectations with his increasingly servile treatment, Lear is slow to understand that his own status has altered. Kent may hint at this change when he exclaims to himself, sitting in the stocks,

> Good King, that must approve the common saw
> Thou out of heaven's benediction com'st
> To the warm sun! (2.2.160–2)

In imagining the plight of a cast-off servingman, William Basse complains that Lords and Ladies "turne us walking in the Summers Sunne."[34] Lear, however, would find any similarity between his condition and that of a cast-off servant inconceivable. When he kneels as if to Goneril before Regan, he intends to show her that acknowledging his dependency would disgrace them all:

> Do you but mark how this becomes the house!
> "Dear daughter, I confess that I am old; [Kneeling]
> Age is unnecessary. On my knees I beg
> That you'll vouchsafe me raiment, bed and food." (2.4.153–6)

He will blame the titanic elements for collaborating with his daughters like "servile ministers" (3.2.21), but he never has to become such a minister himself. He does not have to suffer Hamlet's acute sense of being used as an instrument, much less turn into one as Macbeth does.

This account of innocence and servility in *King Lear* has linked subordinate children with assured friends, roles considered separately in chapters 2 and 4. It suggests that Lear is overly dependent on the followers he loves; he confounds his children with his assured friends when he trusts them to confirm his division of the kingdom. Lear eventually blames himself for believing Goneril and Regan when they tell him he has been "everything" to them. Yet the play also indicates that his own significant attachments are more narrowly and positively defined. And he does become "everything" to Kent and then Cordelia, characters who with his devoted knights embody his abiding faith in loyal and loving supporters. Their innocence might have seemed less foolish had Cordelia's army triumphed in battle.

The next section approaches another kind of love in a different way; it refracts the play's treatment of female sexuality through the arguments of chapter 3 concerning the appropriation of a master's will. As that chapter demonstrated, the labors of women and servants could contaminate one another in a diseased imagination. I am much in debt to the work of feminists who have been disturbed by what they see as a patriarchal representation of women in *King Lear*. From this perspective, Cordelia's eventual assimilation to a male ménage seems, like Kate's, to reinforce male power.[35] In order to suggest that the play does evoke a feminine presence that is potentially creative, I rely less on explicit dramatic events

and more on patterns of images. Other critics who have glimpsed such a
feminine presence have responded to a shadow conjured up through
riddles, jokes and songs as well as crazed or furious outbursts. Her
existence becomes even more probable if we take into consideration social
histories, sources and analogues, parallels with other plays and revisions of
King Lear by feminist writers.

GENERATION AND MONSTROSITY

King Lear abounds in references to sexuality and procreation but dramatizes the marriage bond as tenuous. It also displaces the nurturing functions of maternity onto daughters and men. Coppélia Kahn attributes the
absence of mothers in the play to Lear's repression of his feminine side.[36] I
believe that we can recognize a maternal presence through its inter-
figurations with service. By killing the "slave" who hangs Cordelia, Lear
reasserts his mastery. But one of the most painful moments in all of drama
occurs as he enters bearing Cordelia's dead body. A tragic sense of this
moment as a secular male *pietà* probably includes the awareness that Lear
has created it, ultimately giving monstrous birth to Cordelia's death.[37] At
the same time an audience may see that he has joined the company of
supportive, faithful servants, of those who have born and guided others
throughout the play.

   Shakespeare prepares for this shocking fusion of service with maternity
in several ways. First, as has long been known, he fashions Lear's madness
with the help of Samuel Harsnett who, in his *A Declaration of Egregious
Popish Impostures* (1603), attacked as fraudulent the claims of Catholic
priests to have exorcized members of a household possessed by spirits in
the late 1580s. Harsnett mentioned a male victim, Richard Mainy,
afflicted with the "Moother" and referred to the exorcism of a young
female servant, Sara Williams, as being "delivered" of the devil.[38] F. W.
Brownlow comments that because the young people treated by Harsnett's
priests were socially inferior to the men they trusted, "they had no defense
against the diagnosis."[39] Harsnett had pointed out that the priests focused
on and seemed to have special power over people who felt obligated.[40]

   From a "conception" of "neglect" (1.4.67–8) and a sorrow experienced
as a "mother" which "swells up toward my heart!" (2.4.56), Lear develops
an hysterical madness or extreme melancholy. Like Harsnet's "Moother,"
Lear's need not be gender-specific.[41] Moreover, it arises during a conflict
of obligations as both the Fool and his daughters remind Lear how
helpless he has become.[42] His attack coincides with his discovery of his

messenger, Caius, thrust into the stocks. While Lear goes off-stage to find Regan, Kent asks, "How chance the King comes with so small a number?" The Fool replies with a jaundiced wisdom closer to that of Della Casa than to that of the naive Rosencrantz, fearing the "cess of majesty:" "We'll set thee to school to an ant, to teach thee there's no laboring i' th' winter . . . Let go thy hold when a great wheel runs down a hill, lest it break thy neck with following; but the great one that goes upward, let him draw thee after" (2.4.67–74) Then, in a simple song, he equates such wisdom with knavery and forecasts the storm sequence: Lear shut out in the rain with two "laboring" servants who repudiate service "for gain" and "for form" (2.4.78–85).

Another kind of preparation for the harrowing *pietà* in which Lear carries and attends to Cordelia occurs when Lear accuses Goneril (and more hesitantly, Regan) of being bastards (1.4.254, 2.4.132), or wishes sterility upon them. These attacks have been understood as an intensely personal aversion to female sexuality. But it is possible that Lear is also using a shared discourse in which an extreme use of sexual analogy describes a total collapse of dependable support. That is, he is accusing his daughters of desiring to exercise an agency independent of his own. For the jealous masters of chapter 3, the very process involving such agencies becomes monstrous. Patricia Parker has pointed out that puns on "bearing" are associated with a proliferation of agents in *Richard II*.[43] It could be their runaway power that Lear is getting at when he seems to associate his unkind daughters, dependants who owe him "subscription," with "luxury, pell-mell" and with "Centaurs" (4.6.117, 124). Psychological and social motives need not exclude one another. But when he hits upon the centaur analogy, Lear still needs his hundred horsemen ("I lack soldiers" 117) and is contemplating revenge ("It were a delicate stratagem, to shoe / A troop of horse with felt. I'll put't in proof, / And when I have stol'n upon these son-in-laws, / Then kill, kill, kill, kill, kill, kill!" (4.6.184–7). In any case, he does not know that Goneril and Regan have literally lived down to his earlier insults by lusting after Edmund.

Lear's insults also function within a more general pattern of social images. Throughout the play characters compare good service to fruitful, legitimate pregnancy and bad service or serviceability to lust and bastardy. Like Camillo in *The Winter's Tale*, both Kent and Edgar are wifely. Kent is "full of labors" and Edgar is "pregnant to good pity," while Edmund and Oswald are associated with sexual viciousness.[44] A sense of perverted pregnancy saturates the punning language with which Edmund fashions himself ("I grow, I prosper" 1.2.21). It is almost predictable that after

Kent assaults Oswald with "you whoreson cullionly barber-monger, draw!" (2.2.33), Edmund should be the first character who enters to Oswald's rescue. Edmund thinks he is escaping servile subjection by reporting to his father the very words (his own) with which Edgar is prepared to blame Edmund for "damned practice:" "'thou must make a dullard of the world / If they not thought the profits of my death / Were very pregnant and potential spirits / To make thee seek it'" (2.1.74–7). But when Goneril encourages Edmund, she shares his language: "this kiss, if it durst speak, / Would stretch thy spirits up into the air. / Conceive, and fare thee well"(4.2.22–4). She probably puns on "Conceive," insinuating that she will both fashion and reward extraordinary ambitions. When both sexes manipulate the erotic vocabulary of Renaissance courtship and will-power, the significance of actual sexual drives becomes hard to gauge.

A third kind of preparation for the final tableau is created by the figurative presence mentioned above. This presence haunting the social borders of several Shakespearean tragedies is that of a pregnant or rejected servant girl or daughter. Ophelia and Desdemona both sing songs which reflect their plights, often directly treated in ballads but not, it would seem, on the stage. To be sure, the pregnant ballad singer, forsaken by friends and family or abandoned in the wild may not be so dramatic a subject as the well-born wife or daughter threatened with her situation. And as John Kerrigan observes, "All voluble distress is hard to sustain in performance."[45] In any case, we won't learn from Shakespeare what would have happened to a Juliet had her father actually carried out his furious warning: "hang, beg, starve, die in the streets, / For, by my soul, I'll ne'er acknowledge thee, / Nor what is mine shall never do thee good" (3.5.192–4). We do learn, however, that people must have dreaded such exposure. When Caesar wants to vent his outrage at the way Antony has dishonored Octavia by abandoning her for Cleopatra, he tells his sister that she has returned to Rome as a "market-maid" (3.6.51). "That ever I should call thee castaway!" he exclaims (40). At the other end of the social spectrum, *Macbeth*'s third witch adds to her cauldron a "Finger of birth-strangled babe / Ditch-deliver'd by a drab" (4.1.30–1).

For young people who depended on service occupations, the danger of losing places and protectors could have been reduction to a slavishly instrumental, dubiously human status, to life as a thing (Parolles), creature, or parasite, laboring for a pittance, bearing bastards (if a woman), joining the company of vagabonds and beggars, dying in a ditch. The evidence provided by social historians does not suggest that householders cast out their own children, hurling them into the "staggers," as the King of France threatens Bertram (2.3.163). It was other peoples' children, employed as their servants, whom they sent away. Historians agree that social tolerance for pregnant brides ended abruptly when bastards were born. According to Keith Wrightson, "Dismissal of pregnant girls from service and callous hustling from parish to parish of those whose place of settlement was questionable were not uncommon."[46] Similarly, Martin Ingram writes that it was a "stock practice" for masters to dismiss pregnant servants.[47] Without a doubt, the master–servant system was, in Anthony Fletcher's words, "open to wide abuse," even if fellow servants as well as masters were often responsible for pregnancies.[48] The positions of young female servants could be precarious, especially if they were employed in larger houses with many attendants and officers.[49]

But except in ballads or in specific horror stories recovered by historians, the figure of the pregnant, cast-off servant girl rarely emerges with much vividness from the literature of the past.[50] She swells statistical counts for bastard-bearing and infanticide, but the motives of her woe remain shadowy; she could have been a casualty of a deferred marriage rather than a sex victim, or have killed her baby inadvertently by delivering it herself in a cold barn.[51] Peter Laslett once reflected that an historian "can only feel himself to be in the position of the scientist in his bathyscope, miles beneath the surface of the sea, concentrating his gaze for a moment or two on the few strange creatures who happen to stray out of the total darkness into his beam of light. Where have they come from, and what will happen to them? he cannot help asking himself."[52]

The feminine presence imagined in *King Lear* is just such a "strange creature." She owes her existence to the profound disturbance of relationships in the play, and she helps to express the King's derangement. At the same time she can be associated with a more inclusive dimension of Lear's madness. Fruitfully dilating the figure of the "mother" in this play, Adrian Poole calls it "a lurking, shadowy figure for the power of others to come to life within the realm he [Lear] had thought entirely his own to rule and dispose of as he pleased, his kingdom."[53] The cast-off servant almost comes to life through a number of references and through her proximity to Lear himself.

She is latent, for example, in an important exchange near the beginning of the play. The King of France provokes Cordelia into defending herself when he asks Lear to explain his sudden rejection: "Sure her offense / Must be of such unnatural degree / That monsters it, or your fore-vouch'd affection / Fall into taint" (1.1.218–21). His words have prompted some readers to suspect that the monsters lie in Lear's affection, not in Cordelia's behavior, and that they surge to the surface of his mind when Cordelia refuses to love her father "all."[54] But Cordelia herself seems to know exactly what France is getting at: a secret offense like that with which Hero can be charged in *Much Ado About Nothing* through the agency of her maid, Margaret. And so Cordelia forcefully denies any wrong-doing with "It is no vicious blot, murther, or foulness, / No unchaste action, or dishonored step, / That hath depriv'd me of your grace and favor" (1.1.227–9). Shakespeare's Cordelia need not go "wand'r-ing up and down / Unhelped, unpitied, gentle maid, / Through many an English town," as in the Lear ballad (62–4) or as in *King Leir* where she is "turnd into the world" (602) before France finds and weds her.[55] Shake-speare's France quickly takes Cordelia to wife, with words which begin to suggest both the wild chaos of dependencies in this play and the miserable exposure it causes: "Thee and thy virtues here I seize upon, / Be it lawful I take up what's cast away"(1.1.252–3). The laws to which he refers probably concern the claims on goods lost at sea and/or washed ashore.[56]

She appears too in equivocal allusions to the condition of a cast-off servant/daughter. One of these is the Fool's aside addressed to young women in the audience: "She that's a maid now, and laughs at my departure, / Shall not be a maid long, unless things be cut shorter" (1.5.51–3). The Fool has been hinting that bad house-keepers, imagined as inept servants and wasteful cooks, with their discarded seeds or eggs and left-over scraps of food, somehow account for Lear's homelessness. He mocks both Lear's expectations and his daughter's conduct, possibly helping to inspire Lear's ferocious curses against fertility. By taunting maids he is using the analogy between lust and bad service mentioned above. But he may also be warning "she that's a maid" against an absurdly tumescent world in which she could suddenly find herself unemployed and cast out like an unshelled oyster, snail, or king (1.5.25, 27–31). Other such allusions are Edmund's reference (1.2.130) to his illegitimate nativity under Ursa Major (named for the unhappily pregnant nymph, Calisto, who served Diana) and the Fool's riddling allusion (1.5.35) to the seven stars or Pleiades; there was a tradition that one of these daughters of Atlas had gone missing. Another young woman at risk appears in the Quarto version of the mock-trial sequence, when the Fool picks up on Edgar's song, "Come o'er the bourn, Bessy to me," with "Her boat hath a leak" (Q 3.6.25–6). This scrap of song introduces a figure who has been linked to Cordelia, but who could also be the feminine counterpart of Tom o' Bedlam, a servingman ruined through an illicit affair with his mistress.[57]

These feminine figures are joined, I think, by Lear himself when he encounters Gloucester (who has probably seduced his own Calisto) and uncannily identifies him as a "blind Cupid" (4.6.137). It is as if (like Ophelia) Lear knows what seduced women discover, that "good sport" with a master can turn them into whores (or the mothers of "whoresons" as Gloucester says earlier). Lear also seems to share in the rage and pain of such a woman when he blames an imagined "rascal beadle" for lashing the very whore he desires. G. R. Quaife maintains that "to be whipped through the market and back again for an hour during its busiest period was the norm." A number of unwed mothers, forced to keep moving from town to town, "were delivered in the open street."[58] As Lear reaches his most radical and expansive sense of our collective capacity for injustice, he wants his listeners to hear the sounds of a new-born child: "we came crying hither. / Thou know'st, the first time that we smell the air / We wawl and cry" (4.6.178–80).

In dramatic terms there is nothing particularly far-fetched about Lear's eventual identification with a woman who has been shamed and cast away. What happens to him is a consequence of his error in disowning Cordelia. Kneeling to Regan, Lear implies that she treats him as a servant, a role he finds unthinkable. But in his madness he bears witness to the suffering that an "unhelped, unpitied gentle maid" might have experienced. When he meets Gloucester near Dover, he has reached an imagined social space where he can speak for cast-off women, crying infants, and hypocritical beadles. The "absent mother" in *King Lear* is less a psychological cause than a social result of his great error, an awareness he will wander into *after* he so badly misjudges the loves of his children.

This development corresponds to father–daughter relationships in two other Shakespearean plays. Both Calchas in *Troilus and Cressida* and Leonato in *Much Ado About Nothing* are fathers who experience an acute social displacement when they apparently lose themselves within a daughter's degradation. Before he asks the Greeks to exchange Cressida for Antenor in "recompense" for his "services," Calchas laments:

> I have abandon'd Troy, left my possession,
> Incurr'd a traitor's name, expos'd myself,
> From certain and possess'd conveniences
> To doubtful fortunes, sequest'ring from me all
> That time, acquaintance, custom, and condition
> Made tame and most familiar to my nature;
> And here, to do you service, am become
> As new into the world, strange, unacquainted. (3.3.5–12)

He seems to prefigure his daughter's experience as an outcast in her later literary history. Leonato responds to allegations that his daughter is a whore by wishing he had "with charitable hand / Took up a beggar's issue at my gates, / Who smirched thus and mir'd with infamy, / I might have said, 'No part of it is mine'" (4.1.131–4). By coupling sexual with social disaster in the image of a "beggar's issue," he conjures up a maternal figure which careless and uncharitable masters helped to produce. After all, Leonato's lax supervision of someone else's daughter placed in his care may have made it easier for Margaret to simulate Hero's liason with Borachio. Comparison with these examples suggests that Lear reaches a more generous attitude. His shadowy affiliation with a cast-off servant girl swerves across the play's almost systemic opposition between chaste good servants and lusty bad ones. It reminds us that such oppositions often serve the interests of masters indifferent to social justice.

Revisions of *King Lear* have confirmed the textual presence of a vagrant daughter in Shakespeare's play. In a particularly sentimental version described by R. A. Foakes, Amelia Opie's *Father and Daughter* (1806), a seduced girl "elopes from home and returns to find her father mad; she nurses him, but on the day when he recovers his senses, he dies."[59] Virginia Woolf's feminist parable about Shakespeare's sister in *A Room of One's Own* gives a daughter who never returns to her coercive father both a fatal pregnancy and a creative talent like her brother's. Woolf was almost certainly thinking of Edgar's servile misery, which she would also recall in *Between the Acts*, when she wrote that a gifted woman might have "mopped and mowed about the highways," or "ended her days in some lonely cottage outside the village, half witch, half wizard, feared and mocked at."[60] In *Questions i asked my mother* (1987), Di Brandt alludes to *King Lear* when she writes about her ambivalence toward her father and her struggle with Mennonite patriarchy. Brandt characterizes herself as a "missing Mennonite peasant girl" who has battled over biblical interpretation ("i'll weep i'll not weep we glare at each other with bright fierce eyes my father and i") and begged her lover, "let / me weep one last time / for old kings."[61] Ironically it is the father who becomes servant-like:

> his forty years dominion over
> every living thing comes only to this playing
> cook's helper in my mother's kitchen his
> mighty furrowed thousand acres contracted so
> suddenly to her modest garden plot . . . [62]

Jane Smiley works into a dark corner of her own *Lear* story, *A Thousand Acres* (1991), the probable suicide of a Canadian girl-friend from Manitoba, cast out by her religious parents and killed when she drove her car in front of a large truck.[63]

In concluding this chapter, I will be looking at matters made notorious in early modern England by investigations of witchcraft and demonic possession. The extent to which witchcraft and possession shape the language of cruelty and suffering in *King Lear* has not been widely recognized. They have this impact because the tragedy is often concerned with the breaking of bonds which guaranteed protection. The following section builds upon the argument of chapter 4. It indicates that when Edgar takes cover in his disguise as mad Tom, a servant seemingly broken by a damaging relationship, he not only enacts the madness of his own father in attacking a defenceless son. He also tells a story accounting for his situation which illuminates the worst abuse of assured friendship.

ACCOMMODATION AND POSSESSION

Edgar pretends that he has lost his place and been possessed by fiends because he made love to his employer. This tale of knavish lust exemplifies bad service of a type so petty that it seems to require little comment. Like the pervasive flattery in *Antony and Cleopatra*, it has never been regarded as an issue of crucial importance where the play as a whole is concerned. No one doubts that Edgar, playing many roles, has what Harry Berger, Jr. terms "complicity" with a broad perplex of attitudes in *King Lear*.[64] But his fictive biography has attracted little notice other than as a reflection of his family ties and personal character. For example, William Carroll, who situates Edgar in the contexts of early modern vagabondage and beggary, calls him a "grotesque version of what it must be like to be Edmund."[65] His simulated possession does interest Stephen Greenblatt, but by stressing a theatricality which empties Edgar's case of any psychological or religious meaning ("Edgar is no more possessed than the sanest of us"), Greenblatt also empties possession of much substance as a symptom of a general social disorder.[66] What is it about fusions of friendship with service in this play which might help to explain why five fiends torment an outcast servingman?

When characters in *King Lear* refer to friends or friendship, they generally imply expectations, courtly or military, of clientage and alliance.

Gloucester prompts Edmund to "remember" Kent as an honorable "friend" (1.1.28) or blames on "late eclipses" his fear that "Love cools, friendship falls off, brothers divide" (1.2.106–7). Cornwall and Regan treat Gloucester as a "noble friend" and a "good old friend" when they first enter his house. This instrumental dimension of friendship also appears as Lear rewards "my friendly knave" for tripping Oswald and as Gloucester lets go the hand of his "friend," Edgar, offers him a purse, and prepares to jump from the cliff (4.6.28). Planning to seek out Albany, Edgar wants to "bestow" Gloucester "with a friend" (4.6.286). Friends like Kent and Edgar are primarily protectors. Kent tries to usher Lear into the hovel with "Some friendship will it lend you 'gainst the tempest" (3.2.62); Edgar finally bestows his father under a tree.

So impersonal a sense of friendship could help to explain why these characters have been linked with the chilly individuals described in Lawrence Stone's study of the English family or judged to be avoiding love.[67] Even Kent is identified by Edgar as "noble Kent, your friend" (5.3.269) when Lear rejects his services in Act 5. Assured friendship in *King Lear* has less of the congeniality so evident in *2 Henry IV* or in *Antony and Cleopatra*. With none of the characters "at home" or secure for very long, what becomes primary in such friendship is trustworthy alliance and active protection. One source for the play, *The Mirror for Magistrates*, stresses the great danger to which Lear is exposed from "meaner upstarte gentiles" when stripped of "halfe his garde."[68] In William Warner's version of the story, Lear himself discovers "Nor are they ever surest frends, on whom we most do spend."[69] In Shakespeare's tragedy, he is the first to imagine what an absence of friends might mean when he treats Cordelia herself as a disloyal follower and casts her off to be "Unfriended," meaning "(un) neighbor'd, pitied, and reliev'd" (1.1.203, 119). The hundred knights who replace Cordelia are to some extent a body-guard. (Cf. pp. 113–14 above.)

To be "unfriended," then, is to be "unaccommodated." As I have shown in chapter 4, an unaccommodated man or woman loses the patronage of those who "countenance" followers and attendants, often providing quasi-parental supervision but also the sustaining personal connection troped by Kent's suit to Lear: "You have that in your countenance which I would fain call master" (1.4.27–8). It would reduce the significance of Lear's encounter with naked Edgar to insist that "unprotected" is the only meaning expressed by Lear's great speech: "Thou art the thing itself: unaccommodated man is no more but such a poor, bare, fork'd animal as thou art" (3.4.106–8). But I also think that too abstract a philosophical or cultural interpretation of "unaccommodated" here can carry modern readers away from an important critique of assured friendship which Edgar, with his lively fictive biography, is well prepared to make.[70]

This critique applies to the intimacies which make assured friendships work rather than to the customs of countenancing as a whole. Although his horrific disguise tempts us to blame masters for the oppression of beggars and vagabonds, it is important to remember both that Edgar also blames himself and that weaker servants often needed protecting. This play, writes Liebler, "exposes the structures of civilization *per se* as system, articulated in relationships that require careful, consistent protection by *some* structure of hierarchy and communitas."[71] When physical danger makes protection especially urgent, it also exposes masters to the ambitions of parasites. The very intimacy or personalism characteristic of assured friendship gives followers who can simulate loyal obedience an enormous advantage. Like an unfriendly flatterer, such a parasite is lethal. In effect, by attaching him (or her) self to the power of a superior victim, the parasite ultimately can drain the host's life of all value save power and power alone. Earlier chapters have considered the serious abuses of agency which arise from fusions of service with other subordinations: becoming the instrument or slave of another's will; alienating that will through independent action; weakening it through insidious flattery. All of these abuses converge in *King Lear*; none of them is fully equivalent to a 'demonic' possession which can turn agency against itself. Such possession is probably, to quote Edgar, "the worst" of these disorders. The hangman termed by Lear a "slave" is no mere tool of another's will; he is a predatory parasite, deriving his agency from Edmund and potentially capable (like Edmund) of possessing anyone powerful enough to trust him with "work" (5.3.39).

When mad Tom swipes at a vexing fiend (3.4.61–2), he is engaged in his new occupation or "study": "How to prevent the fiend, and to kill vermin" (3.4.159). His story indicates that Edgar may not need to know his father's personal reasons for casting him out; he thoroughly understands the social system he inhabits. He pretends to have been one of the "vermin" who infest the seams between friendship and service as thoroughly as fleas infest Tom's blanket. Unlike the chambermaids and waiting women in Harsnett's accounts, this victim has himself been an active possessor, a gallant member of a riding household (he refers to his horse, Dolphin, at 3.4.56 and 99–100) intent on seducing his mistress and others; he "serv'd the lust of my mistress' heart" or "slept in the contriving of lust, and wak'd to do it" (3.4.86–7, 88–9). The five fiends who now follow and possess "Tom" are, therefore, figures for his own strong predatory ambitions. His fall from well-accommodated follower to crazed outcast tortured by devils and fleas suggests once again how precarious the status of a servant could be, and how wasteful the expense of agency in the lusts caused by parasitism. In the discourses of possession and witchcraft, demons who frequently afflict servants, preventing them from work or ruining their productive labor, are themselves regarded as servants of the devil.[72]

Because he blames himself for parasitism and emphasizes its devastating consequences, it is hard to believe that Edgar is merely adopting a metaphor commonly projected, as Carroll observes, by masters upon beggars and vagabonds.[73] For this disorder requires that master and servant collude, as if engaged in a dire parody of reciprocal dependency. It may become impossible to judge who is serving whom: Edgar pretends to be vexed by fiends whom he twice thinks of as 'following' him (3.4.46, 140), but he also claims that "the foul fiend" has led him through fire and water and tempted him with suicide (3.4.51–5). When he says that it is better to be poor Tom "and known to be contemn'd / Than still contemn'd and flatter'd" (4.1.1–2), he fuses parasite with host (both contemptible) and stresses the destructiveness of human parasites. Those who support the outrageous desires of some powerful heart are like the fiend Flibbertigibbet who "mildews the white wheat, and hurts the poor creature of the earth" (3.4.118–19).

Whether Edgar has ever been literally complicit with an abuse of assured friendship, or whether his autobiography is a vermin-killing antidote, his own cure seems to develop through service to a "poor creature of the earth" in the person of his own creator, Gloucester, who has come to believe "Our flesh and blood . . . doth hate what gets it" (3.4.145–6). Regan's cruel question, "What need one" (attendant or follower, 2.4.263) is answered when Edgar defeats Regan's agent Oswald and saves Gloucester's life. He seems to have killed his own persona at the same time: "I know thee well; a serviceable villain, / As duteous to the vices of thy mistress / As badness would desire" (4.6.252–4). The effect is ghostly, as if Edgar, still under sentence of death, were a vengeful wraith forced to regain his own life by taking the lives of two domestic "familiars": Oswald and the "unpossessing bastard" of a brother (2.1.67) who virtually conjured up his demonic possession in the first place.

POSSESSION AND WITCHCRAFT

Given the activities of Edmund and Oswald, it is appropriate that Edgar turns parasites, conventionally superficial hangers-on, into demonic fiends. Edgar speaks as if his fiends have penetrated him deeply ("made him proud of heart" 3.4.55–6). "Five fiends have been in Poor Tom at once," beginning with "lust, as Obidicut" (Q 4.1.58–9). Tom's demons are overwhelmingly invasive as well as banal, intimate as well as alien. The language of possession offers Edgar a means of imagining an inscrutable malice that lurks in ordinary social arrangements. For the same reason, Edgar and Lear resort to the language of witchcraft: Lear asks whether there is "any cause in nature that make these hard hearts?" (3.6.77–8) Like references to possession, those to witchcraft are often associated with "lust," meaning primarily a sterile reduction of an agent's will to act conscientiously rather than a sexual desire or deed. Both discourses belong to the nexus of images that pierce or rend, singled out by Carolyn Spurgeon.[74] Both reflect a consciousness of being helplessly exposed and acutely injured or "cut to th'brains" (4.6.192–3). They tell us how it might feel to be wholly cast out of the social safety net forged by customs of countenancing and assured friendship. In this context, it is relevant to mention the theory proposed by Keith Thomas concerning the growth of witch beliefs in England after the Reformation. Fear of witches was intensified, he believes, by the Protestant practice of relying exclusively on prayer for protection or spiritual shelter against witches and other evil spirits.[75] Thomas points out that while "Strictly speaking, the belief in demonianism was distinct from that in witchcraft," "it was frequently believed that an evil spirit had entered into a victim because a witch had sent him there." Consequently, "the notions were in practice intertwined."[76]

Just as there are literally no giants, centaurs, pregnant waifs or demons in *King Lear*, so there are no witches.[77] Yet Lear alludes to witchcraft very early in the play when he swears by the "mysteries of Hecat and the night" in casting off Cordelia (1.1.110). Soon he terms Goneril a fiend and curses the "unnatural hags" Goneril and Regan with sterility, blasting, and fogs (2.4.278). The ferocity of his battles over household authority prepare us for his meeting with Tom who, in the words of Janet Adelman, inhabits "witch's turf."[78] This crazed servingman fends off the menace of witchcraft by exclaiming to Lear, "Bless thee from whirlwinds, star-blasting, and taking!" (3.4.59–60) and by pronouncing a spell, "aroint thee, witch, aroint thee" (3.4.124). When Lear arraigns his daughters as if they were witches (in the Quarto text), he briefly joins Tom in a world of invisible domestic malevolence where spirits take the form of stools or pass through doors.[79]

Associations between witchcraft and servility become more prominent in *Macbeth*. But at least briefly and at one of his darkest moments, Lear himself seems like a servant of the devil as he desires to have "a thousand with red burning spits / Come hizzing in upon 'em" (Goneril and Regan, 3.6.15–16). Hubert called for spits in order to blind Arthur. Is Lear imagining an exorcism or, instead, a branding which would impose a definitive sign of subjection, a witchmark or infernal badge of livery?[80] During the quasi-witch trial that follows, Edgar reacts to Lear by commenting "Look where he stands and glares!" (Q 3.6.23); he reports, probably in an aside, on the uncanny rage in Lear's eyes.[81] At his most furious, Lear is "child-changed" in the sense that his daughters have made him into something far worse than an old child: a changeling or monster.

Goneril and Regan both detest their father's weakness and wish to exploit it. This mentality is expressed by Regan's brutal line, "I pray you, father, being weak, seem so" (2.4.201). Most characters in their society would fear the complete vulnerability which may go with being "unaccommodated," although Lear himself does not. The experience of seeing Tom in the storm, Gloucester says, "made me think a man a worm" (4.1.33), but Gloucester reluctantly takes this creature into his house and later gives him clothing and a job. The other castaways in *King Lear* find shelter and relief, however temporary. In *Macbeth* no one who needs it can find a refuge within Scotland. Through their aversion to weakness and intolerance of need, Goneril and Regan anticipate a hero whose response to human worms of any kind would surely be to smash them.

CHAPTER 6

Freedom, service, and slavery in Macbeth

Macbeth is an appropriate play with which to conclude an exploration of service and dependency in Shakespeare. Almost every scene contains suggestions of servitude and bondage. Almost all the characters are preoccupied with security. The hero, who has been a warrior-guardian like Coriolanus or Othello, behaves much as do Edgar's parasitic fiends and engages desperate supporters who are lethal extensions of his own will to violence. With the help of the weird sisters, a ghost, and various "cruel ministers," he drains labor and agency of value. His play evokes absence and emptiness, whether we stress analogies between Scotland and the traditional deprivations of Hell or concentrate on the political and social dimensions of tyranny. Macbeth himself convinces many spectators and readers that he is hopelessly bound either by a commitment to serve the devil or by his own disposition. Barbara Everett, for example, writes that "however free we call his choice to destroy himself and others, he can never get out of it." "It is a play of extreme economy; everything is there, and there is no way out."[1]

Side by side with Everett's testimony to the terrifying effect of *Macbeth*, I would like to set an observation made by William Arrowsmith. In his "Introduction to *Hecuba*," he comments that "just because necessity is hard and because the justification it gives – in politics, in love, in war – is unanswerable, it is the justification most frequently debased."[2] Arrowsmith is thinking of characters who abuse their power when they use arguments from necessity. I am thinking more about critics who have been overly persuaded by such characters or by systems which apparently determine their behavior. Tragedies tempt us to accept necessities while suggesting that some of them may be answerable after all. They challenge us to find ways out. My argument below, that *Macbeth* evokes freedom through a representation of bondage, is premised, then, on an assumption about the nature of tragedy. As with *Othello*, it is important to observe, following Nicole Loraux, that the "effect of constraint . . . is all the more powerful because it shows up in words rather than in institutions."[3]

For most inhabitants of Scotland, freedom comes to mean the destruction of Macbeth and his tyranny. But when Macduff proclaims, just after killing Macbeth, that "the time is free" (5.9.21), critics who have emphasized the baleful powers of monarchy and patriarchy will probably doubt that regicide offers an effective way out of political necessities. A rivalrous and violent custom of succession through primogeniture will go on and on. Perhaps we should pay more attention to the sweeping sense of relief expressed in Macduff's proclamation. No one could have hoped to live freely under Macbeth because his tyranny converts the normal mechanisms for assuring safety into death traps. Hecate's view applies to all inhabitants of Macbeth's Scotland: "security / Is mortals' chiefest enemy" (3.5.32–3). Like the irresponsible deities in a tragedy by Euripides, Hecate is, as Nicholas Brooke says, "a goddess from a machine."[4] She has too many ways out ("I am for th'air," 3.5.20), too little concern for human obligations and needs. She may have been a late addition to the text, yet she seems appropriately antithetical to characters who do make hard choices for freedom of some kind: Malcolm and Donalbain, who quickly perceive that they cannot be safe in Scotland or together (2.3.135–46); Banquo, who remains in Scotland but struggles to keep his "bosom franchis'd and allegiance clear" (2.1.28) when solicited by Macbeth; Macduff, who endangers his family to save his country; and Young Siward who holds his "unshrinking station" (5.9.8) and dies fighting Macbeth as if he were the "devil himself" (5.7.8). The Lord who reports the flight of Macduff to Ross hopes that

> we may again
> Give to our tables meat, sleep to our nights;
> Free from our feasts and banquets bloody knives;
> Do faithful homage, and receive free honors;
> All which we pine for now. (3.6.33–7)

Malcolm later cheers on his "cousins" with "I hope the days are near at hand / That chambers will be safe" (5.4.1–2). Far below the thanes in status are the "constrained things" (5.4.13) who "move only in command" (5.2.19), represented on stage by the young servant or "cream-fac'd loon" who heralds the arrival of the "English force" (5.3.18). At the beginning of the play, the "skipping kerns" or mercenaries who support the rebellion of Macdonwald "trust their heels" and save themselves (1.2.30). But at the end, many of the "wretched kerns, whose arms / Are hir'd to bear their staves" (5.7.18) choose to turn upon Macbeth and to fight on the side of his opponents (5.7.25).

These examples associate freedom with safety as well as with widespread resistance to oppression. None of the political systems or orders seemingly operative in *Macbeth* (Michael Hawkins has found four) would have valued freedom in terms of individual liberties protected by the due process of law.[5] Therefore, a reader with strong democratic sympathies may well be inclined to underestimate the appeal of "safe" chambers and to recall that the line of "Banquo kings" would end in the absolutism of James the First and his son, Charles. Or, if we accept the significance in *Macbeth* of the "Buchanan disturbance," as Alan Sinfield terms it, the fact that the "kingdom's pearl" or elite surrounding Malcolm (5.9.22) have just brought off a quasi-republican tyrannicide, we may still regard the final absence of women or the populace as ominous. Strong doubts like these can quickly reduce freedom in *Macbeth* to a spasmodic outburst caused by ongoing contradictions which the "pearl" normally manage in their own interest.[6] Even David Norbrook's thoughtful discussion of republicanism in *Macbeth* tends to close out the significance of freedom in this tragedy by settling it back into a conservative and traditional framework.[7]

In order to suggest that *Macbeth* evokes freedom through representations of bondage, I could indicate, as Orlando Patterson has done, that slavery nurtures a consciousness of freedom.[8] At the very least, bondage fosters resourceful negotiations within strict limits, for even in the isolating prison of Scotland, characters meet to consider their options, advise one another, or simply bear witness to events. But I am also going to proceed by questioning a cherished belief among many modern libertarians and democrats: that being in or under the will of another person, a condition often used to define servants, is incompatible with freedom. Instead, I will argue that one means by which the Macbeth and Lady Macbeth create virtual slavery in themselves and others is by perverting service. Service in this play can be consistent with freedom; it is opposed to slavery, not identified with it.

One writer who might have agreed with this position is Étienne de La Boétie (1530–63), still better known as Michel de Montaigne's exemplary friend than as the author of a provocative political treatise on *Voluntary Servitude*. La Boétie thought that people get the rulers they deserve. Through indifference and the force of custom, they cooperate with their tyrants, enslaving themselves. Were they to withdraw their consent, their "Colossus" would quickly fall of his own weight and shatter.[9]

Murray N. Rothbard attributes this astonishing "juridical idealism" to a firm belief in universal natural rights, anticipating eighteenth century views (and, one might add, those of seventeenth century English Levellers, who were the first to propose a written constitution based on such rights.)[10] "We are all naturally free, inasmuch as we are all comrades," La Boétie writes; a new-born would always choose freedom, but this "native endowment, no matter how good, is dissipated unless encouraged, whereas environment always shapes us in its own way . . . in spite of nature's gifts."[11]

By proclaiming that "the time is free," Macduff universalizes a freedom achieved by "comrades" who are in many cases young. His words contrast with Macbeth's order measuring the deadly interval in which Banquo will be murdered: "Let every man be master of his time / Till seven at night" (3.1.40–1). I am not suggesting that the play explicitly champions a natural, inborn freedom like La Boétie's, although the emergence of similar ideas among religious independents makes it likely that a few spectators may have been starting to think in such terms. And Macbeth's image for retribution from peers and contemporaries, his comparison of their pity to a "naked, new-born babe, / Striding the blast," does visualize something like La Boétie's "native endowment." La Boétie is concerned with a long-term tyranny supported by a group he colorfully describes as "dregs," "notorious robbers and famous pirates," and "man-eaters."[12] These people have been corrupted by ambition and avarice; they put up with evil in their ruler so that they can commit evil against more helpless persons. Ironically, they also torture and exhaust themselves in order to succeed, accepting servility without belonging to themselves.[13] Presumably he calls them "dregs" because it has taken the ruler and his guard a while to sink down and drain out. Macbeth speeds up this process by employing desperadoes. The most overt resemblance between treatise and play lies in their sense of how a tyrant, estranged from an interactive network of connections, weakens himself. "It is because he does not know how to love that he ultimately impoverishes his own spirit and destroys his own empire," writes La Boétie.[14] Macbeth, who has betrayed kinsmen and comrades (and abandoned his wife), falls into "the sear, the yellow leaf," forfeiting "honor, love, obedience, troops of friends" (5.3.23, 25).[15]

Voluntary Servitude and *Macbeth* may share a moment in history when personal relations have not yet been firmly discriminated from political ones and when a sense of free agency, of belonging to oneself, might still coexist with subordinate social status. Because of developments in seventeenth century history and in political theory, women, children, and many servants would be excluded from a class of persons deemed capable of free citizenship. In *Liberty Before Liberalism*, Quentin Skinner traces what he prefers to call a "neo-Roman" rather than a "republican" strand in seventeenth-century thought back to the *Digest* of Roman law where liberty is always defined in relation to slavery. The essence of slavery is to be "*in potestate*, within the power of someone else."[16] This dependency is thought to be crucial, as opposed to other components in the definition of the slave: a liability to violence or death at any time, or being a material property. The early modern thinkers who derived this idea from moralists and historians (especially Livy as mediated by Niccolò Machiavelli), an idea reinforced by critiques of court favoritism like Sir Thomas More's, used it to assert that the threat as well as the fact of coercion on the part of a ruler constituted enslavement.[17] Skinner opposes to the classical liberal view that will is free if not directly coerced the neo-Roman view that the will is only autonomous if free from the danger of coercion. Although this neo-Roman tradition declines with the decline of courts and intimate courtship, it may be recognized, he suggests, in John Stuart Mill's analysis of how women are subjected. It has been overlooked by those who emphasize either the absence of obvious impediments to freedom or the exercise of individual rights.[18]

Skinner's argument is illuminating. It has clear relevance to anyone living in a supposedly democratic society where the state has been given arbitrary powers.[19] Whenever people need to distinguish between a rule of law which enables liberty and a discretionary prerogative which destroys it, they may find the neo-Roman conception of slavery particularly useful.[20] The thinkers with whom Skinner is concerned understand very well the blighting consequences of privilege and precedent. On the other hand, they also adopt a legalistic definition of slavery which conflates it with early modern dependency and probably helps to prolong the subordination of women, children, and inferior servants. Customary dependent relationships were consistent with the popular liberties which clashed against the new legalism working to define a political establishment based on rights.[21] Moreover, as I have indicated above, contemporaries could distinguish between service and slavery, between selling their labor and selling themselves.[22]

One legacy of this neo-Roman approach may be a readiness to surmise that an un-rationalized, customary dependency mystifies authority. For example, Norbrook ends his exploration of republican themes in *Macbeth* by observing that according to the more classical standards of a George Buchanan or John Milton, Shakespeare's tragedies are disorganized: they lack "clear divisions" between genres, stages of the action, and social levels of diction. "The effect is that the social order, like the play, seems to be bound together not just by some abstract plan but also by a host of intricate only semiconscious symbolic interactions."[23] This is a fine description, but need it follow, as Norbrook believes, that Shakespeare must have idealized a more traditional political unity premised on the "mystical cohesion" of the body politic?[24] Perhaps he is reflecting the strong animus of his republican theorists against kings who exploited personal or familial analogies to support absolutism. (Kings, for their part, were intent on dismantling the personal powers of aristocratic kinship.) This animus, born of passionate struggles among the seventeenth century elite, apparently survives in Orlando Patterson's superb analysis of chattel slavery as primarily defined by social death and degradation. Near the end of *Slavery and Social Death*, Patterson insists, "It is an abuse of language to refer to membership and belonging as a kind of freedom; freedom is not a faculty or a power to do something."[25]

In preceding chapters I have tried to show how different kinds of "belonging" in plays can empower dependants through an interplay of subordinate roles. Unbalanced or thoroughly unequal reciprocities between or among distinct persons often produce dynamic, surprising actions. Characters constrained by subject positions may nevertheless resist or transform the purposes which try to turn them into instruments or things. In the following discussion I will draw upon the neo-Roman equation between slavery and latent forms of coercion to describe the role of the weird sisters, but I will also pay particular attention to the agencies of supporting figures whom Macbeth uses as props for his tyranny. For all of their charisma and complexity, the leading players become servile by enslaving others.

THE POINTLESS AGENCY OF THE WEIRD SISTERS

Shakespeare developed the three weird (Folio "weyward") sisters as characters who can juggle with every dimension of the dependencies considered in earlier chapters. They employ two babes as "servile ministers" who, appearing to Macbeth as prophetic spirits, "palter" with his hopes. Both in person and in action they represent a monstrous maternity which is thoroughly sterile and destructive. They seem to possess their victims in an invasive and corrupting manner. Rather than repeat chapter 5 by detailing confusions within major categories of relationship, I would like to use these confusions to emphasize once again a fundamental difference between *King Lear* and *Macbeth*. In *Lear* the innocence of children and supporters can be compromised or sullied; it rarely seems like a complete alternative to evil as is often the case in *Macbeth*. Monstrous maternities help to generate some of Lear's profoundest insights. Exposure and vulnerability do not become so acute, or terror so great that they remove all sources of physical and spiritual shelter. Because the weird sisters erase most moral ambiguities, there can be little to say about them from the perspectives adopted in chapter 5. This, I will suggest, may be the most important attribute of their agency in an early modern context. As most critics have acknowledged, their powers and motives remain obscure.

Throughout the play, Macbeth attempts to obfuscate his own agency and deny responsibility for his actions, an attitude epitomized by his outburst on seeing Banquo's ghost: "Thou canst not say I did it" (3.4.49). One way of approaching the opacity of the sisters might be to suggest that they not only encourage this trait in Macbeth; they also behave as if they were servants themselves, but servants whose duties and obligations are impossible to define. With the First Sister ("like a rat without a tail, / I'll do, I'll do, and I'll do"), they are furiously active, but what are they actually doing? "A deed without a name," is their answer to Macbeth's question, "What is't you do?" (4.1.49). When they first meet Macbeth upon the heath, offering predictions in the form of salutations and messages, they behave as if they were ambitious attendants in-waiting, a meager crowd cheering on a royal progress-to-be. Their strange appearance aside, they recall the three poor men who try to hook on to Gaveston's rising star at the beginning of Christopher Marlowe's *Edward the Second*. This activity is pre-supposed by Hecate, "the mistress of your charms" (3.5.6) when she berates them for daring to "trade and traffic with Macbeth," a "wayward son / Spiteful and wrathful, who (as others do) / Loves for his own ends, not for you" (3.5.11–13). But if the sisters are free to ape aspiring followers on the heath, why are they also subordinate to their familiars, apparently going off when sent for ("I come Graymalkin," "Paddock calls")? Hecate too leaves when her spirit calls her to "come away." And what is the relation of the weird sisters to their masters (4.1.63), the apparitions who answer Macbeth's other questions? Are these spirits who supervise the sisters, or does "masters" simply mean inferior ministers or instruments as in *The Tempest*?[26]

For an audience still dependent on reliable service of many kinds, the opaque nature of the sisters might seem like a fundamental corruption of agency. The discourse of early modern service oscillates between criticism of servants whose persons and doings are either much too visible or are not visible enough. Those who competed with or criticized retainers tended to notice crowds of uniforms clustering at wealthy doorways or waiting about the entries to royal courts.[27] "Vallentine," the courtly speaker in a dialogue called *The English Courtier, and the Countrey-gentleman* (1586), considers that, with the exception of those few who do necessary household jobs, servingmen in livery are mere "furnishings."[28] Complaining about the apprenticeship of aristocratic sons, Edward Chamberlayne (1669) refers to their servile condition, including the need to "eat and wear what their master pleaseth" as "Marks of Slavery."[29] On the other hand, wearers of livery may have regarded such marks as a sign of secure position, as well as a means of making mutual obligations more evident. Marlowe's *Doctor Faustus* exposes the age-old fantasy of being served by invisible workers as a desire to play god.[30] Not that wearing livery protected William Basse, who complained that the hardest working servant might appear to be the most slothful, just as the fastest plummet or lead ball, no longer visible, has required the "most paines" in first swinging it round and round.[31]

Implicit in many discussions of service is the extent to which beings supposedly subject to the will of their employers actually enjoy some freedom of choice in how they behave. The difficulty of detecting a servant's personal motives from his or her observed behavior helps to explain the constant resort to prohibitions against "eye service," which may mean out-right duplicity to an employer or simply going through the motions of a task, wasting goods and energy. God, the prescribers promise such servants, can judge your motives and performance even if your master or mistress cannot.[32] But what is God supposed to think of a servant who covers the "infirmities" of a master, as William Gouge advises?[33] Basse stoically considers the situation of a servant who must hide his gentle birth because "greater states" can't "abide / Ambition" in lower ones.[34] And most prescribers also advise servants to obey in "out-ward" matters only. This obedience of the flesh, not the spirit, is consist-ent, Matthew Griffith maintains, with a refusal to "sooth up those they serve, in their wicked courses" and with self-justification when unfairly accused.[35]

It might seem impertinent to cite these guides to service in connection with the weird sisters if Macbeth's self-appointed helpers did not preface their first encounter with him by reporting their attacks upon two archetypal guides: a captain and a pilot. Removing a pilot's thumb could crucially affect his manual ability to turn a wheel and steer a course. Keith Thomas and Emmanuel Le Roy Ladurie point out that rural witchcraft was regarded as especially threatening when it attacked the capacity to work. It afflicted cows and crops, to be sure, but its power was most maleficent through its effects on arms and tools.[36] What the witches do, I suggest, is to render service non-functional. They are too visible; they are not visible enough, together and not together, manipulative and feckless, here and nowhere. They make agency pointless, not so much by inverting or parodying authority (as witch-hunters liked to believe) but by confusing it so that the vital activity of practical discernment, of freely judging one's complex obligations or, indeed, of working with or through dependent relations, breaks down.[37] The weird sisters help Macbeth to run away from "the pauser, reason" in the broadest practical sense, so that he isolates himself from all the carefully negotiated interdependencies of ordinary existence.[38] If any words can describe the function of the sisters in this regard, it is their tendency to "Hover through the fog and filthy air" (I.I.I2). Here, I believe, we may find some equivalent to the ever-present threat which Romans who lived under tyrants characterized as "slavery," a threat experienced both as fear for one's life and (what could be worse) as an awareness of stupefying damage to one's own resourcefulness and initiative.[39]

Approached through a distinction between service and slavery, the weird sisters seem to behave like mad Tom's vermin. Their doings suggest that they are possessors possessed. The clearest thing about their agency may be its nonsensical incoherence. John Turner, who calls their ideology "parasitic" and gives a splendid account of their inscrutable nastiness, tries to locate them in a feudal economy. He sets their "gnomic gobbets" of prophecy against the "reciprocities of love and trust" exemplified in Duncan's artful courtesy.[40] But unlike the parasites identified in *King Lear*, the sisters show no desire to gain from an assured friendship with Macbeth.[41] Although their influence has been described with metaphors of nursing and inseminating as well as biting and sucking, it may be the very absence of normal mediation in their relationships which makes one reach for some basic sense of biological exchange in defining them. Slavery can at least help us to grasp the effects of their activity. Afflicted by their hovering, Macbeth and his wife give up freedom of will and sound the depths of abjection.

In one of the best critical responses to *Macbeth*, Paul Jorgensen begins with Shakespeare's power to disturb audiences as well as characters "throughout our nervous system" by using the symptoms of witchcraft and possession to create terror.[42] He shows that *Macbeth* is "tense and alive with images of labored gesture, of stress, climbing, leaping, running, and straining," all suggesting the futility of action. Witchcraft in particular is associated with useless toil, and even Duncan seems to regard service as a painful activity.[43]

I doubt that Duncan's view has been much influenced by the sisters; his words seem to be informed by the "positive politeness" which Lynne Magnusson has explored as an art of social dialogue.[44] Duncan anticipates resentment for the work done on his behalf by his subjects when he greets Lady Macbeth with

> The love that follows us sometime is our trouble,
> Which still we thank as love. Herein I teach you
> How you shall bid God 'ield us for your pains,
> And thank us for your trouble. (1.6.11–14)

His elaborately reflexive speech implies that this king may be more attentive than God to the incommensurate credits and benefits garnered, thanks to his subjects, by God's representative: their "love" can never be taken for granted. Macduff speaks the same language of reciprocal obligation when he apologizes to his host for causing Macbeth "joyful trouble" (2.3.48) immediately before he goes in to arouse Duncan and discovers his murder:

MACBETH The labor we delight in physics pain.   This is the door.
MACDUFF I'll make so bold to call,   For 'tis my limited service. (2.3.50–2)

Macduff is freely if inconveniently serving his master.

THE WAR ON SERVANTS AND DEPENDENTS

When she first persuades Macbeth, the actions of Lady Macbeth make some sense in contexts, feudal or early modern, where the roles of wives and male officers overlapped. Deborah Willis has treated her both as a "gender hybrid" like Queen Margaret and as a flattering attendant.[45] If Macbeth reneges on his oath to kill Duncan, his wife maintains, he becomes her inferior and her child. How then can Lady Macbeth also be regarded as a flattering follower? Because, I think, she resembles the Duke of Buckingham as well as Queen Margaret; Buckingham attempts to act as Richard's "other self," intuiting Richard's desires and easing his way. It might be supposed that Lady Macbeth loves Macbeth too much, but it might also be supposed that she has merged her will in her husband's. She can be identified, therefore, as one of those all too loyal servants or favorites (loving or not) who, according to Richard Strier, "aid and abet a rebellion 'in the natures of their lords.'"[46] Having fashioned herself as the perfect hand-maid, a one-way mirror for Macbeth's mind, she can indeed articulate his hopes and fears. But she also has no defense against his terrible visions, which cause her to faint and drive her mad. If she is indeed open to Macbeth's "inner man," as John Bayley has proposed, her ultimate fate may recall that of Doctor Faustus, enslaved and destroyed by exposure to an over-powering lover (as Semele was by Jove).[47]

Her madness also recalls, more immediately, the fates of Duncan's attendants, suggesting a significant association of Lady Macbeth with actual servants in the play. During the first two Acts, Lady Macbeth tries to become an instrument or tool. Upon reading Macbeth's letter about his encounter with the sisters, she hardens herself into the equivalent of a military fortress ("The raven himself is hoarse / That croaks the fatal entrance of Duncan / Under my battlements" 1.5.38–40), into something filled "topful / Of direst cruelty" and proof, through her thickened blood, against "th' access and passage to remorse" (42–4). Her violent language anticipates Macbeth's in conflating herself with "my keen knife," unable to see "the wound it makes" beneath "the blanket of the dark" (52–3). To assure Macbeth of success, she compares his courage to a mechanism which can be screwed into a "sticking place" where it will function as a reliable weapon (1.7.60).[48] Macbeth compliments her on her "undaunted mettle" (1.7.73), which may be understood as punning upon un-dented metal or armor. And there is something of the same inhuman superficiality about her own bizarre pun on Duncan's blood as a gilding with which to smear the faces of the grooms, "For it must seem their guilt" (2.2.53–4). Contemplating a murder she speaks and feels like a castle-keep or an armament room: she facilitates her crime by thinking of the grooms or officers she plans to incriminate as living limbecks and sponges to be filled in effect "topful"' or "drenched" with wine, wassail, and sleep (1.7.64–71). These instrumentalizing images are less notorious than those with which she denies her gender, but they are ultimately important in connecting Lady Macbeth to Duncan's grooms under the signs of servitude and witchcraft.

Ever attentive to relations between or among dependents, Shakespeare forges a particularly ironic link between the agencies of Lady Macbeth and the young grooms she has regarded merely as means to her brutal end. In one possible source for his play, William Stewart's *Buik of the Croniclis of Scotland*, a "chalmer child" who "la be syde the king all nycht" is himself murdered by the assassin, Donewald.[49] After a second regicide, to which one Makobey's wife incites her spouse, Stewart blames her by exclaiming, "so foull ane blek to put in his gloir / Quhilk haldin wes of sic honour befoir."[50] This tiny "blek" or bit of soot (*OED*) corresponds to the blood on the grooms, marked up by Lady Macbeth herself and reported when Lennox says, "Their hands and faces were all badg'd with blood; / So were their daggers" (2.3.102–3). Macbeth promptly degrades the status of the youths he has just killed by replacing livery badges with "the colors of their trade" (115). Hence, "the damned spot" which Lady Macbeth later tries to wash from her "little hand" already connotes a servility she has helped to create. Gary Wills suggests that the spot can be linked with the mark left when a familiar has sucked upon a witch: "Spots were evidence of the devil's ownership, a brand, a seal that could not be disowned."[51] I would emphasize that Lady Macbeth has earlier welcomed Duncan to her castle with protestations about "our service" (1.6.14) and "Your servants ever" (1.6.25). Psychological readings of her madness emphasize her guilty sense of the blood as belonging to Duncan, a king who resembled her father, and ignore the social dimensions of her crime. To understand that Lady Macbeth is indelibly "badg'd" like Duncan's dead guardians may be to glimpse once again the activities of the sisters as they "hover" over the play. She has enslaved herself to an endless, repetitive, and inconsequential labor of doing as she strives to clean herself.

Like his wife, Macbeth perverts the language of service, spoken so precisely by Duncan and Macduff. Just before Macbeth murders Duncan, Banquo praises him for his hospitality to the King, now "shut up / In measureless content" (2.1.16–17). Macbeth replies, "Being unprepar'd, / Our will became the servant to defect, / Which else should free have wrought" (2.1.17–8). "Servant to defect" means "we did what we could, under the circumstances," but it also means, all too accurately, "we have worked as the agents of nothingness." Again like his wife, Macbeth becomes a virtual slave; he labors more furiously and of course far more destructively than she does, but with the same sense of repetitive futility. Unlike his wife, he remains conscious about his own horror and pain as he becomes a thing or instrument, mutually dependent on other de-humanized things or assassins. His war upon children, in particular, acquires wider significance when seen in terms of an association between service and freedom.

"War on children" is Cleanth Brooks' phrase in his justly famous essay on a salient pattern of images in *Macbeth*, "The Naked Babe and the Cloak of Manliness." Brooks argues that the many babes in the play are its "most powerful symbol" and that they signify "the future which Macbeth would control and cannot control."[52] By noticing, as Willis has done, that Macbeth is obsessed about his rivalry with first-born sons, one may supplement Brooks' babes with a significant group of older children or youths while locating this poetic pattern in a more historical context. Willis emphasizes the vulnerability of young men as "cause and effect of the feudal order's problematic construction of masculinity;" the "tragic mechanism" in patriarchy, she suggests, is "regularly returning males to the vulnerable position of the infant."[53] Macbeth's protestation of loyalty to Duncan, "our duties / Are to your throne and state children and servants" (1.4.24–5), suggests that patriarchy is not inevitably "tragic" and that dependencies can converge or fuse in productive ways. Macbeth's rhetoric alerts Willis to a personal motive: he wishes he were Duncan's own son and first-born, just a few lines before Duncan names Malcolm as his successor. I think it could also prepare us for the way he will soon make war on children and servants at one and the same time, beginning with the murder of Duncan's grooms.

Stewart's "chalmer child," mentioned above, would probably have been a young man and, like Duncan's chamberlains, a knight and future thane, chief of a clan, and one of the king's barons and land-holders. "Thane" originally meant a servant, minister or attendant; it apparently derives from an old and pre-Teutonic term meaning child, boy, or lad. "Child," of course, had once meant "knight" and "knight," too, had once meant "lad or servant." When Malcolm praises Macduff's "noble passion" as a "Child of integrity" (4.3.114–15), he is commending Macduff for both knightly *virtu* and moral authenticity. John Boswell's observation that words for children have often been used to identify servants or slaves was noted in chapter 2. Especially relevant to *Macbeth* is his observation that "during most of western history only a minority of grown-ups ever achieved . . . independence: the rest of the population remained throughout their lives, in a juridical status more comparable to 'childhood,' in the sense that they remained under some else's control."[54] Comparable to but not identical to; we should blame the peculiar nature of Macbeth's tyranny rather than patriarchy in general for infantilizing Scotland's young men. When Lady Macbeth refers to Duncan's guards as "grooms," she may well be deliberately demoting their status, even as she empties these "spungy officers" of human value.[55] Macbeth's later reference to their daggers as "Unmannerly breech'd with gore" (2.3.116) reduces the chamberlains, Nicholas Brooke comments, "to flogged criminals, or possibly small boys."[56] It would be thoroughly in character for Macbeth to confound a child or son with a deadly weapon.

Weapons altogether replace children when Macbeth plans a Herod-like slaughter: "From this moment / The very firstlings of my heart shall be / The firstlings of my hand" (4.1.146–8). Here he transfers his rage against an endless succession of Banquo kings or first-borns, which he cannot halt, to Macduff's lineage, which he can exterminate. It is significant that these "firstlings" have so servile or instrumental a character, not only because of Macbeth's human weapons whom I will consider below, but also because the slaughter he intends will encompass Macduff's "wife, his babes, and all unfortunate souls / That trace him in his line" (4.1.152–3). Ross reports to Macduff the murders of "Wife, children, servants, all / That could be found" (4.3.211–12). Macbeth's war on children has become a war upon kinship and ménage, upon dependent relations in the broadest sense, upon "that great bond / Which keeps me pale!" (3.2.49–50). How appropriate it seems, therefore, that young men who are sons of all sorts eventually fight against this tyrant. Malcolm's victorious army will include "Siward's son / And many unrough youths that even now / Protest their first of manhood" (5.2.9–11). Macbeth's "naked babe" could be a figure for their collective stewardship of Scotland.

MACBETH AS A SERVILE MINISTER

As Macduff prepares to fight Macbeth, he shatters Macbeth's trust in the prophecy made to him by the Second Apparition:

> . . . let the angel whom thou still hast serv'd
> Tell thee, Macduff was from his mother's womb
> Untimely ripp'd. (5.8.14–16)

From the beginning Macbeth's will-to-power has had an oddly dependent, servile nature. Lady Macbeth introduces this dependency when she considers that "valor's minion" and "Duncan's harbinger" wants

> That which cries, "Thus thou must do," if thou have it;
> And that which rather thou dost fear to do,
> Than wishest should be undone. (1.5.23–5)

Her packed and cryptic assessment can be taken at this point in the play as an assertion of Macbeth's courage in responding to unavoidable challenges. Only later do we discover that he needs to create necessities. She indicates too that he is motivated by fear or dread but whether fear is an incidental or a primary cause she doesn't say. And what might this extraordinary warrior be afraid of? Even if she knows, we have to infer his motives from his actions much later in the play. Meanwhile, her role as one who in effect cries "thus thou must do" when she enforces the necessity of the oath which Macbeth has sworn (1.7.56–9) confirms her preliminary understanding of Macbeth's desires.

The incipient servility of Macbeth's disposition becomes much more evident when he begins to behave as a serial killer by proxy.[57] Once he has been persuaded to "bend up / Each corporal agent" (1.7.79–80) and murder Duncan, he readily pretends that he is compelled to kill Duncan's chamberlains ("who could refrain?" 2.3.116). When Malcolm and Donalbain flee, the unfortunate officers are regarded (in what, Macduff implies, is the received but inadequate explanation, 2.4.23–7) as assassins who have been suborned. This mockery of truth becomes the model on which Macbeth then fashions the killers of Banquo. "I am reckless what I do to spite the world," says the second killer (3.1.109–10). Because these hirelings are already desperate, Macbeth plies them with unnecessary persuasions:

> This I made good to you
> In our last conference, pass'd in probation with you:
> How you were borne in hand, how cross'd, the instruments,
> Who wrought with them, and all things else that might
> To half a soul and to a notion craz'd
> Say, "Thus did Banquo." (3.1.78–83)

Here Macbeth describes his own crazed sense of himself as an instrument, forced to hold a "barren sceptre" and serve as a conduit for Banquo's dynasty. Moreover, when he asks, "Are you so gospell'd / To pray for this good man, and for his issue, / Whose heavy hand hath bow'd you to the grave, / And beggar'd yours for ever?" (3.1.87–90), he begins to forge the next link in a deadly chain, his plan to eradicate Macduff's family "and all unfortunate souls / That trace him in his line" (4.1.152–3).[58] The two poor murderers are not much concerned about their lineages. Macbeth's excuse for having to kill Duncan's chamberlains is clearly wearing thin by the time that Lennox recalls how Macbeth tore the "two delinquents" who were "the slaves of drink and thralls of sleep" (3.6.12–13).

Macbeth's motive for preferring actions which "thou dost fear to do" remains hidden. It is possible, however, that the play brings on Banquo's ghost, both so that an audience sees what Macbeth is doing to his victims and so that they may glimpse his secret fears. I suggested earlier that Macbeth would want to smash a human "worm" like the bedlam beggar, mad Tom. He regards dependency as equivalent to a sickening helplessness. His wife probably intuits this attitude when she incites him to violence by identifying the compelling power of the oath they have sworn with the act of dashing out an infant's brains (1.7.56–9). What should have been more helpless and abject than a bloody corpse? And who could be better qualified than Banquo, his former companion and councillor, to exemplify Macbeth's madness: terror at vulnerability and tyranny in order to suppress it? Like the ghost of Julius Caesar, Banquo's gives agency to the possibilities which his murder had been designed to prevent. He illustrates an impossible contradiction between weakness and strength, but behaves in a distressingly normal manner, taking a stool at the banquet and later ushering in a succession of royal descendents with malicious paternal pride. This is not the wary and conscientious Banquo who was presented earlier but a servile minister with a vengeance, a spectral tyrant or "colossus" (La Boétie) and a figure for Macbeth's personal and political terrors. Theater audiences need to behold this "[u]nreal mock'ry" on stage because it serves as a hideous instrument for seeing into Macbeth himself.

At the risk of being taken for a proponent of alarum systems and police surveillance, I have insisted through-out this study that early modern service was knit up with customary protection; servants needed it when younger and often provided it when older and stronger. Particularly in considering the precarious workings of assured friendship, I have tried to bear in mind the shiftiness of subject positions and the potential distortions of a top-down or bottom-up perspective on a play. For Macbeth to desire total security ("I'll make assurance double sure / And take a bond of fate," (4.1.83–4) is indeed desperate, as George Hunter argues in pointing out that "security" could mean "a culpable absence of anxiety."[59] There is nothing culpable, however, in the acute desire for security expressed by Lady Macduff or felt by an audience expecting an attack on her unprotected household. Macbeth has assassinated Banquo in order to become "whole as the rock," only to feel "cabin'd, cribb'd, confin'd, bound in/To saucy doubts and fears" (3.4.23–4) after Fleance escapes. "But Banquo's safe?" he asks (24). Banquo's ghost gives a hideous form to these alternatives of servile fear and monolithic safety. He acts out the hopelessness of "security" as both Macbeth and jaunty Hecate understand it. Security enforced by tyranny is indeed "mortals' chiefest enemy" (3.5.33). When a king hires murderers to destroy those who protect and perpetuate his kingdom, he creates one of the harshest tragic necessities. Macduff's flight is more like that of Malcolm or Fleance than that of Hecate; his actions are intended not to escape from the ghastly securities of Scotland but to eliminate their cause, Macbeth. If he could not bear an almost intolerable anxiety and loss, there might be no way out whatsoever.

In spite of Macbeth's success in corrupting the servants of his thanes ("There's not a one of them but in his house / I keep a servant fee'd," 3.4.130–1) and in employing assassins, the "constrained things" who finally serve him in Dunsinane come across as surprisingly fresh, distinctive, and numerous. These newly visible and reluctant dependents, including a waiting gentlewoman, messengers, a doctor and Seyton, mark a change from the spies and "shag-ear'd" murderers who have been Macbeth's associates.[60] They help to enhance the irony of Macbeth's judgments on himself:

> that which should accompany old age,
> As honor, love, obedience, troops of friends,
> I must not look to have; but in their stead,
> Curses, not loud but deep, mouth-honor, breath,
> Which the poor heart would fain deny, and dare not. (5.3.24–8)

Like La Boétie's tyrant, he has moved "beyond the pale of friendship."[61] But when he feels most alienated, he is surrounded by a rapidly shifting cast of attendants. In dramatic terms they qualify the sense of his soliloquies. To Macbeth, "Life's but a walking shadow, a poor player, / That struts and frets his hour upon the stage, / And then is heard no more" (5.5.24–6). He denigrates professional players, who were of course the servants of a lord, along with those "shadow[s]" who were friendly followers of many kinds. When he lashes out at the "cream-fac'd loon" and at the "Liar and slave" who bring him bad news (5.3.11, 5.5.34) he is still talking to himself.

In the final speech of the play, Malcolm promises, as a part of future business, that he will produce "forth the cruel ministers / Of this dead butcher, and his fiend-like Queen" (5.9.34–5). What the characters on stage actually see is an unforgettable image of a tyrant. "Behold," says Macduff, "where stands / Th' usurper's cursed head" (5.9.20–1). Whether Macduff has positioned the head on a lance, a pike, or a pole, it is obvious that the severed head could not stand at all without some kind of instrument to hold it up. Given a chance by directors, who sometimes choose to omit the head, audiences can recognize what Macbeth has managed to become while still alive: a maddened intellect born along by bodies, his own and others, which he has reduced to inhuman props. This image all too literally fulfills the premonition created earlier by the *armed Head* that warned him to "beware Macduff" (4.1.71). How differently Lear dies, supporting his daughter and supported by a small troop of loyal friends. This emblem of a tool wearing a head makes visible the horror of becoming a human thing in a world where service and clientage were still facts of life. If I were directing a production of *Macbeth*, I would try to include Doctor, Gentlewoman, "cream-fac'd loon," and many "wretched kerns" in the final celebration of a freer time to come.

Epilogue: Some reflections on the Porter

Unless the actor doubles in another role, one of Shakespeare's most memorable servants would not be theatrically visible when Dunsinane falls. What does the Porter have to do with questions of freedom, service and slavery in *Macbeth*? Unlike the numerous domestic messengers, attendants, torch-bearers, and servers who have already appeared at Inverness, engaged in their tasks, the Porter has the stage wholly to himself and can prevent us from taking his work for granted. Will he ever get around to opening that door? Will he exercise his role of watchful guardian and find out who is eager to come in? How long will he "stop up th' access and passage to remorse," the imminent public discovery, by way of another door, that Duncan lies murdered? As far as the Porter himself is concerned, he is invisible and can therefore turn his occupation into a game for his own enjoyment. This simply does not happen in other plays where comic receptionists please themselves by wittily delaying the access of one character to another. Characters like Launcelot Gobbo in *The Merchant of Venice* or Margaret in *Much Ado About Nothing* try to get attention by showing off, but until the Porter grows cold and opens the door, such conventional responses to a comedy of obstruction need not develop.

Because he is alone while he entertains himself and the audience, the Porter seems like an exception to one of the rules proposed in this study: service generally functions in relation to other dependent roles. His perspective and conduct do not interact immediately with those of children, wives, or friends. He does not belong to a particular society or group in some restrictive or enabling way. His scene requires no special settings, props, or stage business which might encourage an audience to think about modern equivalents for service or to criticize a current abuse of subordinates. He needs no guns or police dogs when it is often all a drunken Porter can do to get his key into the door. What might be gained by taking this figure seriously as a servant?

It would be easy to treat the Porter as an example of wasteful "eye-service," as a symbol of how the two Macbeths corrupt service and dependency. Because they have hired him, he could be assumed to share their guilt through dramatic proximity and formal design. He resembles both Lady Macbeth, who also greets real and imagined visitors, and the grooms so bound by drink and sleep that they perforce admit Duncan's killers. His complicity seems even more probable if we consider that early modern audiences regarded porters as highly responsible officers. Their duties required a continual exercise of discretion in deciding who should enter or leave the gates of a large establishment. Busily unlocking and locking the gates for meals and prayers and shutting them up every night, such a porter would have had much "turning the key" (2.3.2–3). He should have been (like the Thane of Cawdor), absolutely reliable, for the safety of the house often depended on his diligence. Sobriety would have been part of his job description.

Luckily Shakespeare had other plans for figures like the Porter and Malvolio. So evocative is the language of his game, as the Porter pretends to be a Hell-porter and fiend, that his performance becomes, in many interpretations, a turning point in the action of *Macbeth*. He can also be regarded as a fulcrum for critical attitudes in a more general sense. Do we emphasize what he keeps in or lets in, confinement or release, the closed or the open door? Throughout this study I have pushed against several doors by trying to show that interdependency can empower subordinates, that tragedies have ways out and that rules for porters or anyone else may have limited value as historical evidence. This is not to remove doors and throw them away. Some sense of his normal responsibilities can make us more aware of how thoroughly this apparently isolated Porter knows the world. His hospitable catalogue of those who "go the primrose way to th' everlasting bonfire" (2.3.18–19) should remind any critic that literature helps us to imagine and possibly confront hell on earth.

One implication of this study has been that service worked as a school for theater as well as a school for ethics. Observing another's inclination in oneself, imitating a role and changing people or perceptions through interaction: these are theatrical as well as social arts. The Porter charms audiences because he identifies so generously with a range of sinners. He could have been taking tickets at the Globe. Most of his imagined criminals pale in comparison with his employers. When Macbeth and Lady Macbeth attack service, they attack the capacity to work in response to needs and obligations. But their influence has obviously not yet reached the Porter. Drunk as he is, he can do what no other servant in

Shakespeare's plays can do: recreate a particularly demanding occupation as sheer play. This devil is more of an actor than a servile dependent or slave. His performance breathes freedom into the theater – before he finally chooses to open the door, apologizes, and asks for his reward.

Notes

INTRODUCTION: "SLIPPERY PEOPLE"

1 I have relied on Marvin Spevack ed., *The Harvard Concordance to Shakespeare* (Cambridge, Mass.: Harvard University Press, 1973) in reaching these estimates.

2 Marc Bloch, *Feudal Society*, trans. L. A. Manyon (Chicago: University of Chicago Press, 1961), vol. 1, 219.

3 See Edmund S. Morgan, *The Puritan Family: Religion and Domestic Relations in Seventeenth-Century New England* (New York: Harper and Row, 1966), 109; compare Dorothy Marshall, *The English Domestic Servant in History* (London: Historical Association, 1949), 3, John Hajnal, "Two Kinds of Pre-Industrial Household Formation System," in *Family Forms in Historic Europe*, ed. Richard Wall *et al.* (Cambridge: Cambridge University Press, 1983), 93, and Robert J. Steinfeld, *The Invention of Free Labor: The Employment Relation in English and American Law and Culture, 1350–1870* (Chapel Hill: The University of North Carolina Press, 1991), 17–22.

4 Peter Laslett, "Mean Household Size in England since the Sixteenth Century," in *Household and Family in Past Time*, ed. Peter Laslett (Cambridge: Cambridge University Press, 1972), 151; *The World We Have Lost* (London, Methuen, 1965). Two fine studies of drama which address the significance of service are Mark Thornton Burnett, *Masters and Servants in English Renaissance Drama and Culture: Authority and Obedience* (London: Macmillan, 1997), focused on non-Shakespearean plays, and Michael Neill, "Servant Obedience and Master Sins: Shakespeare and the Bonds of Service," in *Putting History to the Question: Power, Politics and Society in English Renaissance Drama* (New York: Columbia University Press, 2000), 13–48. Neill has also edited a collection of new essays on service, forthcoming in *The International Shakespeare Yearbook* 5 (2005).

5 Laslett, *The World We Have Lost: Further Explored* (London: Methuen, 1983),2.

6 Laslett, *Family Life and Illicit Love in Earlier Generations: Essays in Historical Sociology* (Cambridge: Cambridge University Press, 1977), 13. Historians estimate that servants constituted 10 percent of the population from 1574 to 1821; 40 percent of all children became servants in their adolescence. See Laslett, "Mean Household Size" 151–2; *Family Life*, 32, 43; compare Gordon

J. Schochet, *Patriarchalism in Political Thought: The Authoritarian Family and Political Speculation and Attitudes Especially in Seventeenth Century England* (Oxford: Basil Blackwell, 1975), 68–70. Ann Kussmaul, *Servants in Husbandry in Early Modern England* (Cambridge: Cambridge University Press, 1981), 3, believes that servants "constituted around 60 percent of the population aged fifteen to twenty-four" or a majority of all young people; compare Alan MacFarlane, *Marriage and Love in England: Modes of Reproduction 1399–1840* (Oxford: Basil Blackwell, 1986), 86.

7 Kate Mertes, *The English Noble Household 1250–1600: Good Governance and Politic Rule* (Oxford: Basil Blackwell, 1988), 55.

8 Richard C. Barnett, *Place, Profit, and Power: A Study of the Servants of William Cecil, Elizabethan Statesman* (Chapel Hill: University of North Carolina Press, 1969), 5; compare 9. According to David Cressy, "Kinship and Kin Interaction in Early Modern England," *Past and Present* 113 (1986), 66, people used "basic relational terms" "without precision or consistency."

9 Richard Gough, *Human Nature Displayed in the History of Myddle* (1701), intro. W. G. Hoskins (Fontwell: Centaur Press, 1968).

10 Laslett, *The World We Have Lost*, 20–1.

11 Except where otherwise noted, all references to Shakespeare's texts are based on G. Blakemore Evans ed., *The Riverside Shakespeare*, second edition (Boston: Houghton Mifflin, 1997).

12 Ann Rosalind Jones and Peter Stallybrass emphasize the impersonality of current market relationships in *Renaissance Clothing and the Materials of Memory* (Cambridge: Cambridge University Press, 2000), 20.

13 See Thomas Platter, *Thomas Platter's Travels in England* (1599), trans. Clare Williams (London: Jonathan Cape, 1937), 164.

14 In an innovative study, Maurice Hunt, *Shakespeare's Labored Art: Stir, Work, and the Late Plays* (New York: Peter Lang, 1995), traces the dichotomy between labor as admirable diligence (in a more Protestant view) and as contemptible humiliation (in a more aristocratic and courtly view).

15 See Bruce Robbins, *The Servant's Hand: English Fiction from Below* (New York: Columbia University Press, 1986), 20, 25–7, 32.

16 I agree with Michael D. Bristol that laughter at foolish servants may reveal "structural ambiguity in the social system" but question the immediate relevance of an emphasis on "collective" life or popular experience where servants are concerned. See *Carnival and Theater: Plebeian Culture and the Structure of Authority in Renaissance England* (London: Methuen, 1985), 129, 9, 23–5.

17 Raymond Williams, *The Country and the City* (London: Hogarth Press, 1985), 197.

18 Orlando Patterson, *Slavery and Social Death: A Comparative Study* (Cambridge, Mass.: Harvard University Press, 1982), 13. Compare Moses I. Finley, *Ancient Slavery and Modern Ideology*, (Harmondsworth: Penguin Books, 1980), 116, pointing out that because slaves often survived through compromise and accommodation, any understanding of their lives will be stultified by "rigid behavioural alternatives."

19 Williams, *Marxism and Literature* (Oxford: Oxford University Press, 1977), 40. Williams is here following the theories of V. N. Volosinov on linguistic communication.

20 M. M. Mahood, *Bit Parts in Shakespeare's Plays* (Cambridge: Cambridge University Press, 1992) emphasizes the roles of servants in chs. 3 and 8. In "'Flatcaps and Bluecoats': Visual Signals on the Elizabethan Stage," *Essays and Studies* ns.33 (1980), 25, G. K. Hunter questions editorial assumptions behind individualized cast-lists; such lists may discourage readers from recognizing how "social tensions that 'explain' the character arise from the social ambiguity or insecurity of his role."

21 This aspect of my approach is particularly in debt to several scholars who have analyzed cultural discourses influential for conceptions of status: Catherine Belsey, *The Subject of Tragedy: Identity and Difference in Renaissance Drama* (London: Methuen, 1985), Lynne Magnusson, *Shakespeare and Social Dialogue: Dramatic Language and Elizabethan Letters* (Cambridge: Cambridge University Press, 1999) and Frank Whigham, *Seizures of the Will in Early Modern English Drama* (Cambridge: Cambridge University Press, 1996).

22 Marshall, *The English Domestic Servant in History*, 27.

23 Sarah C. Maza, *Servants and Masters in Eighteenth-Century France: The Uses of Loyalty* (Princeton: Princeton University Press, 1983), 6.

24 Mervyn James, *Society, Politics and Culture: Studies in Early Modern England* (Cambridge: Cambridge University Press, 1986), 284; compare James, *Family, Lineage, and Civil Society: A Study of Society, Politics, and Mentality in the Durham Region, 1500–1640* (Oxford: Clarendon Press, 1974), 32–3.

25 Keith Wrightson and David Levine, *Poverty and Piety in an English Village: Terling, 1525–1700* (New York: Academic Press, 1979), 177–8.

26 Ronald F. E. Weisman, "Reconstructing Renaissance Sociology: The 'Chicago School' and the Study of Renaissance Society," in *Persons in Groups: Social Behavior as Identity Formation in Medieval and Renaissance Europe*, ed. Richard C. Trexler (Binghampton: Center for Medieval and Early Renaissance Studies, 1985), 40, 43. Compare the approach to reciprocal relations within specific historical communities of David Aers in *Community, Gender, and Individual Identity: English Writing 1360–1430* (London: Routledge, 1988), 4.

27 Judith Newton and Deborah Rosenfelt, eds., "Introduction" to *Feminist Criticism and Social Change: Sex, Class and Race in Literature and Culture* (New York: Methuen, 1985), xxvi.

28 Walter Darell, "A Pretie and Shorte Discourse of the Duetie of a Servingman" (1578), reprinted in "A Conduct Book for Malvolio," ed. Louis B. Wright, *Studies in Philology* 31 (1934), 115–32. Other contemporary complaints include William Basse, *Sword and Buckler: Or, Servingmans Defence* (London, 1602) and I. M., *A Health to the Gentlemanly Profession of Servingmen* (1598), in *Shakespeare Association Facsimiles* 3 (Oxford: Oxford University Press, 1931).

29 Darell, "A Pretie and Shorte Discourse," 122–4.

30 Ibid., 129.

31 Annibal Guasco's letter is paraphrased by Ruth Kelso in *Doctrine for the Lady of the Renaissance* (Urbana: University of Illinois Press, 1956), 222. Living "at hand," writes Basse in *Sword and Buckler,* sig. A4v, stanza 3, the servingman abandons will.

32 Platter, *Travels in England,* 164.

33 Thomas Fossett, *The Servants Dutie or the Calling and Condition of Servants* (London, 1613), 18–19.

34 William Gouge, *Of Domesticall Duties: Eight Treatises* (London, 1622), 604.

35 William Whately, *A Care-Cloth: Or a Treatise of the Cumbers and Troubles of Marriage* (London, 1624), sig. A4r–v.

36 For the English positions see David Wootton, "Leveller Democracy and the Puritan Revolution," in *The Cambridge History of Political Thought 1450–1700,* ed. J. H. Burns (Cambridge: Cambridge University Press, 1991), 428–32, C. B. Macpherson, "Servants and Labourers in Seventeenth Century England," in *Democratic Theory: Essays in Retrieval* (Oxford: Clarendon Press, 1973), 214–19 and Christopher Hill, "Pottage for Freeborn Englishmen: Attitudes to Wage Labour in the Sixteenth and Seventeenth Centuries," in *Change and Continuity in Seventeenth Century England* (London: Secker and Warburg, 1974), 223–35. On the attitudes of French thinkers, see Maza, *Servants and Masters in Eighteenth-Century France* 312.

37 Thomas Howell, *Howell's Devises* (1581), intro. Walter Raleigh (Oxford: Clarendon Press, 1906), 30.

38 See Judith Rollins, *Between Women: Domestics and Their Employers* (Philadelphia: Temple University Press, 1985), 37 and Theresa McBride, *The Domestic Revolution: The Modernization of Household Service in England and France, 1820–1920* (New York: Holmes and Meier, 1976), 116; compare Leonore Davidoff, "Mastered for Life: Servant and Wife in Victorian and Edwardian England," *Journal of Social History* 7 (1974), 416–17.

39 Jonas A. Barish and Marshall Waingrow, "'Service' in *King Lear*," *Shakespeare Quarterly* 9 (1958), 348.

40 Finley, *Ancient Slavery and Modern Ideology,* 122.

41 Davidoff, "Mastered for Life," 407.

42 Especially when they closely identify service with slavery. See Fossett, *The Servants Dutie* 46, William Perkins, *[Christian] Oeconomie: Or, Houshold-Government,* in *Works* (London, 1631), vol. 3, 697–8, Francis Dillingham, *Christian Oeconomy or Houshold Government* (London, 1609), sig. O4r–v, and Torquato Tasso, *The Housholders Philosophie,* trans. T. K. (London, 1588), sig. D3v. In "'Servile Ministers': *Othello, King Lear* and the Sacralization of Service," Neill suggests that some apologists for service made it more acceptable by evoking distinctions from slavery. See the 2003 Garnett Sedgwick Memorial Lecture at the University of British Columbia (Vancouver: Ronsdale Press, 2003). I am grateful to Neill for sending me this thought-provoking essay.

43 Steinfeld, *The Invention of Free Labor,* 101.

44 According to Diana Fuss, *Essentially Speaking: Feminism, Nature and Difference* (London: Routledge, 1989), 18, "'Contradiction' emerges as the 'always already' of deconstruction, its irreducible inner core without which it could not do its work."

45 Mertes, *The English Noble Household 1250–1600*, 137.

46 See Laslett, *Family Life*, 4–5 and Schochet, *Patriarchalism in Political Thought*, 71. Compare Paul Griffiths, *Youth and Authority: Formative Experiences in England 1560–1640* (Oxford: Clarendon Press, 1996), 319–20.

47 Jean-Louis Flandrin, *Families in Former Times: Kinship, Household and Sexuality* (Cambridge: Cambridge University Press, 1979), 148–9, drawing on the evidence of French catechisms.

48 I. M., *A Health to the Gentlemanly Profession of Serving-men*, sig. J3r.

49 See in particular *The Merry Wives of Windsor*, 1.3. I consider the rejection of Falstaff in chapter 4 and the disguises of Kent and Edgar in ch. 5. Plays by other dramatists include *Sir Thomas More*, *When You See Me You Know Me*, and *The White Devil*.

50 Howell, *Devises*, 51.

51 Basse, *Sword and Buckler*, sig. B1r, stanza 8.

52 Morris Palmer Tilley, *A Dictionary of Proverbs in England in the Sixteenth and Seventeenth Centuries* (Ann Arbor: University of Michigan Press, 1950), 593, no.S239. Proverbs no.S230–56 concern servants and service.

53 This is a summary of Michael Walzer's argument in *Just and Unjust Wars: A Moral Argument with Historical Illustrations* (New York: Basic Books, 1977), 22–8, questioning views of war as absolutely criminal.

54 Walzer, *Just and Unjust Wars*, 4.

55 Susan Dwyer Amussen, *An Ordered Society: Gender and Class in Early Modern England* (Oxford: Basil Blackwell, 1988), 6. Other historians have been careful not to distort evidence obtained primarily from police records and death statistics.

56 In Xenophon, *Xenophon's Treatise of Housholde*, trans. Gentian Hervet (London, 1534), sigs. D2v–D3r, a disorderly household corps is compared to a theatrical troupe where players speak "what so ever fell into theyr braynes" and to an army where all ranks are "in a plumpe."

57 Compare Emrys Jones ed., "Introduction" to *Antony and Cleopatra* (Harmondsworth: Penguin Books, 1977), 39 and Neill, "Servant Obedience and Master Sins," 27–8.

58 Anon., *The English Courtier, and the Countrey-gentleman* (1586), in *Inedited Tracts: Illustrating the Manners, Opinions, and Occupations of Englishmen During the Sixteenth and Seventeenth Centuries*, ed. W. Hazlitt (London: Roxburgh Library, 1868; rpt. New York: Burt Franklin, 1964), 1–93.

59 Laurence Humfrey, *The Nobles or of Nobilitye* (London, 1563), sig. U6r. Richard Brathwaite regrets this change in preference. See *Some Rules and Orders for the Government of the House of an Earle* (1630) in *Miscellanea Antiqua Anglicana* (London: R. Triphook, 1821), 11–12.

60 See Hill, "Pottage for Freeborn Englishmen," 220 and *Liberty Against the Law: Some Seventeenth-Century Controversies* (London: Penguin Books, 1996), 26.

61 For persuasive criticism of an emphasis on crises in current thinking see Cressy, "Foucault, Stone, Shakespeare and Social History," *English Literary Renaissance* 21 (1991), 128–30: "pattern-making is not necessarily good history" (130).

62 In his wide-ranging essay, "Servant Obedience and Master Sins" Neill observes that the "recognizably modern subjectivity" in Diderot's *Rameau's Nephew* has been produced in part by hypocritical servants who prefigure a "world of competitive individuals" (45).

63 David Harris Sacks, "Searching for 'Culture' in the English Renaissance," *Shakespeare Quarterly* 39 (1988), 472–3, 488, objects to approaches which either dichotomize society or impose on it a "mythology of cultural unity."

64 E. P. Thompson, "Eighteenth-Century English Society: Class Struggle Without Class?," *Social History* 3 (1978), 149.

65 See Thompson, "The Grid of Inheritance: A Comment," in *Family and Inheritance: Rural Society in Western Europe, 1200–1800*, ed. Jack Goody *et al.* (Cambridge: Cambridge University Press, 1976), 341.

66 See Wrightson, "Estates, Degrees and Sorts in Tudor and Stuart England," *History Today* 37 (1987), 20.

67 Wrightson, *English Society 1580–1680* (New Brunswick: Rutgers University Press, 1992), 92; his quotation is from Chilton Powell's *English Domestic Relations, 1487–1653*, 169. For similar scepticism about moralistic advice, thought to be often ignored in practice, see Linda A. Pollock, *Forgotten Children: Parent-Child Relations from 1500–1900* (Cambridge: Cambridge University Press, 1983), 45, 89, Margaret J. M. Ezell, *The Patriarch's Wife: Literary Evidence and the History of the Family* (Chapel Hill: University of North Carolina Press, 1987), 61, Amussen, *An Ordered Society* 111, and Ralph A. Houlbrooke, *The English Family 1450–1700* (London: Longman, 1984), 145.

68 Alice T. Friedman, *House and Household in Elizabethan England: Wollaton Hall and the Willoughby Family* (Chicago: University of Chicago Press, 1989), 43.

69 Griffiths, *Youth and Authority* 110.

70 For a summary and critique of three major emphases, demographic, sentimental, and economic, see Michael Anderson, *Approaches to the History of the Western Family, 1500–1914* (London: Macmillan, 1980). Adrian Wilson surveys major trends, including suspicion of literature as evidence; see "A Critical Portrait of Social History," in *Rethinking Social History: English Society 1570–1920 and its Interpretation*, ed. Adrian Wilson (Manchester: Manchester University Press, 1993), 29–30. A. L. Beier criticizes Laslett for treating service too positively in *Masterless Men: The Vagrancy Problem in England, 1560–1640* (New York: Methuen, 1985), 24–5. Ilana Krausman Ben-Amos generally stresses "experience, skills and independence" (85) rather than extremes of passivity and rebelliousness in *Adolescence and Youth in Early*

Modern England (New Haven: Yale University Press, 1994), while Griffiths, *Youth and Authority*, questions over-emphasis on the house-bound quality of youth culture (113–16); he maintains that "there were many different ways of growing up" (6).

71 For his definition of literary evidence see "The Wrong Way through the Telescope: A Note on Literary Evidence in Sociology and in Historical Sociology," *British Journal of Sociology* 27 (1976), 319–20. Laslett sets out seven theoretical concerns for the guidance of practicing historians, 324–5.

72 Patterson asserts, *Slavery and Social Death* 11, that "it is the height of arrogance, not to mention intellectual irresponsibility, to generalize about the inner psychology of any group." Laslett, "The Wrong Way through the Telescope," 330 and Griffiths, *Youth and Authority*, 10 warn against depending heavily on literate, privileged sources.

73 Anthony Fletcher's frequent citation of plays in *Gender, Sex and Subordination in England 1500–1800* (New Haven: Yale University Press, 1995) in order to illustrate widely received mentalities and discourses seems to derive from this principle.

74 See Jonathan Barry, "Introduction: Keith Thomas and the Problem of Witchcraft," in *Witchcraft in Early Modern Europe: Studies in Culture and Belief*, ed. Jonathan Barry *et al.* (Cambridge: Cambridge University Press, 1996), 10.

75 Griffiths, *Youth and Authority*, 174.

76 Aristotle, *Aristotle's Poetics: Translation and Analysis*, trans. Kenneth A. Telford (Chicago: Henry Regnery Company, 1961), 5. Subsequent references are to this text.

77 Laura Caroline Stevenson, *Praise and Paradox: Merchants and Craftsmen in Elizabethan Popular Literature* (Cambridge: Cambridge University Press, 1984), 4.

78 Froma I. Zeitlin, *Playing the Other: Gender and Society in Classical Greek Literature* (Chicago: University of Chicago Press, 1996), 353.

79 Compare Simon Goldhill, *Reading Greek Tragedy* (Cambridge: Cambridge University Press, 1986), 46, on how the characters of the *Oresteia* practice a "one-sided laying claim to evaluative and normative words."

80 Gordon Braden, *Renaissance Tragedy and the Senecan Tradition: Anger's Privilege* (New Haven: Yale University Press, 1985), 42.

81 Braden, *Renaissance Tragedy and the Senecan Tradition*, 34, 35. I argue that the grief of angry mothers shapes tragic actions through Euripidean networks in "Visible Hecubas," in *The Female Tragic Hero in English Renaissance Drama*, ed. Naomi Conn Liebler (New York: Palgrave, 2002), 51–69.

SONS, DAUGHTERS, AND SERVANTS

1 The most comprehensive recent accounts of attitudes toward youth in this period are by Linda A. Pollock, *Forgotten Children: Parent-Child Relations from 1500–1900* (Cambridge: Cambridge University Press, 1983), Paul

Griffiths, *Youth and Authority: Formative Experiences in England 1560–1640* (Oxford: Clarendon Press, 1996), and Ilana Krausman Ben-Amos, *Adolescence and Youth in Early Modern England* (New Haven: Yale University Press, 1994).

2 According to Peter Laslett, *Family Life and Illicit Love in Earlier Generations: Essays in Historical Sociology* (Cambridge: Cambridge University Press, 1977), 43, 20 percent of all children were raised in households containing servants; 40 percent became servants themselves; and only 20 percent were never either with or acted as servants.

3 Conyers Read, cited by Louis B. Wright in the "Introduction" to his edition, *Advice to a Son: Precepts of Lord Burghley, Sir Walter Raleigh, and Francis Osborne* (Ithaca: Cornell University Press, 1962), xvi.

4 See Muriel St. Clare Byrne ed., *The Lisle Letters* (Chicago: University of Chicago Press, 1981), vol. 3, 13.

5 Ivy Pinchbeck and Margaret Hewitt, *Children in English Society* (London: Routledge and Kegan Paul, 1969), vol. 1, 26–7.

6 See Nicholas Orme, *From Childhood to Chivalry: The Education of the English Kings and Aristocracy 1066–1530* (London: Methuen, 1984), 29–30, Orme, *Education and Society in Medieval and Renaissance England* (London: Hambledon Press, 1989), 277, and Grant McCracken, "The Exchange of Children in Tudor England: An Anthropological Phenomenon in Historical Context," *Journal of Family History* 8 (1983), 307.

7 Ian W. Archer, *The Pursuit of Stability: Social Relations in Elizabethan London* (Cambridge: Cambridge University Press, 1991), 88, 215, Paul Seaver, *Wallington's World: A Puritan Artisan in Seventeenth-Century London* (Stanford: Stanford University Press, 1985), 88, Griffiths, *Youth and Authority* 82–96, Christopher Hill, "The Spiritualization of the Household," in *Society and Puritanism in Pre-Revolutionary England* (London: Secker and Warburg, 1964), 443–81.

8 Mervyn James, *Family, Lineage, and Civil Society: A Study of Society, Politics, and Mentality in the Durham Region, 1500–1640* (Oxford: Clarendon Press, 1974), 140–6.

9 See Paul Van Brunt Jones, *The Household of a Tudor Nobleman,* in *University of Illinois Studies in the Social Sciences* (Urbana: University of Illinois Press, 1917), vol. 6, 12, n. 16 ("Child of his Chambre"), referring to the Derby household, and 42 (the twelve "children of honour" in the Bertie household who were closely associated with the family children).

10 Robert Crowley, *The Voyce of the Laste Trumpet, Blowen bi the Seventh Angel* (London, 1549), sig. A5r, rhymes: "For as thou didst thy master serve / So shall al thy servauntes serve the / And as thou didst hys goodes preserve / So shall thy goodes preserved be."

11 John Boswell, *The Kindness of Strangers: The Abandonment of Children in Western Europe from Late Antiquity to the Renaissance* (New York: Pantheon Books, 1988) 27–35, refers to the semantic and historical variability of these terms in "Greek, Latin, Arabic, Syriac, and many medieval languages."

12 Leah Sinanoglou Marcus, *Childhood and Cultural Despair: A Theme and Variations in Seventeenth-Century Literature* (Pittsburgh: University of Pittsburgh Press, 1978), 6, 29.

13 *The Lisle Letters*, ed. Byrne, vol. 3, 115, 118, describe how eight-year-old James, sent to study alone in Paris for a year is exposed to "so many ungracious lackeys" and "many rude and wild children."

14 Mark Girouard, *Life in the English Country House: A Social and Architectural History* (New Haven: Yale University Press, 1978), 138–43. *The Oxford English Dictionary* cites *Much Ado About Nothing* (1599), 5.2.10 for the first use of the expression "below stairs."

15 Simonds D'Ewes, *The Autobiography and Correspondance of Sir Simonds D'Ewes*, ed. James Orchard Halliwell (London: Richard Bentley, 1845), vol. 1, 35–6.

16 Jean-Louis Flandrin, *Families in Former Times: Kinship, Household and Sexuality* (Cambridge: Cambridge University Press, 1979), 144.

17 Gilbert Cousin, *Of the Office of Servauntes, A Boke Made in Latine by one Gylbertus Cognatus and newely Englysed* (1534), trans. T. Chaloner (London, 1543).

18 Thomas Whythorne, *The Autobiography of Thomas Whythorne*, ed. James M. Osborn (London: Oxford University Press, 1962), 10, 28, 46, prefers the role of music teacher and deprecates that of "serving-creature or servingman." On physical proximity as one reason for strict regulation of social behaviour see Michael Mitterauer, "Servants and Youth," *Continuity and Change* 5 (1990), 32.

19 For vivid examples of such commonplace advice see Pollock, ed., *A Lasting Relationship: Parents and Children over Three Centuries* (London: Fourth Estate Press, 1987), 178, 183, 206.

20 See Pollock, *With Faith and Physic: The Life of a Tudor Gentlewoman Lady Grace Mildmay 1552–1620* (London: Collins and Brown, 1993), 28 and Thomas Powell, *Tom of All Trades. Or the Plaine Path-Way to Preferment* (1631), ed. F. J. Furnivall, in *Shakespeare's England*, The New Shakspere Society Publications, series 6, nos. 2–3 (rpt. Vadus: Kraus Reprint Ltd., 1965), 173.

21 Michel de Montaigne, *The Complete Essays of Montaigne*, trans. Donald M. Frame (Stanford: Stanford University Press, 1958), 113.

22 Sarah C. Maza, *Servants and Masters in Eighteenth-Century France: The Uses of Loyalty* (Princeton: Princeton University Press, 1983), 289.

23 Orme, *From Childhood to Chivalry*, 28; compare Marcus, *Childhood and Cultural Despair*, 29–31.

24 Claude Desainliens, *The French Schoole-Maister* (1573), in *English Linguistics 1500–1800*, no. 315, ed. R. C. Alston (Menston: Scolar Press, 1972), 64.

25 On this common theme see Henry Percy, "Instructions by Henry Percy, Ninth Earl of Northumberland, to his Son Algernon Percy, Touching the Management of His Estate, Officers, etc." (1609), *Archaeologia* 27 (1838), 320–6. Compare Miriam Slater, *Family Life in the Seventeenth Century: The*

Verneys of Claydon House (London: Routledge and Kegan Paul, 1984), 117 on disaffected servants.

26 Matthew Griffith, *Bethel, or A Forme for Families* (London, 1634), 379.

27 Cousin, *Of the Office of Servauntes*, sig. B5v.

28 A speech made by William Lambarde in 1586, excerpted by Joel Hurstfield and Alan G. R. Smith eds., *Elizabethan People: State and Society* (London: Edward Arnold, 1972), 38.

29 J. Fit John, *A Diamonde Most Precious, Worthy to Be Marked: Instructing All Maysters and Servauntes, How They Ought to Lead Their Lyves* (London, 1577), sig. G2v. Griffith, *Bethel*, 382, recalls that in Matthew 8:5 the Centurion speaks of his sick servant to Christ "as if he had beene his only childe." See also Francis Dillingham, *Christian Oeconomy or Houshold Government* (London, 1609) sig. M3r–M5r and Joseph Hall, *Salomon's Divine Arts of Ethickes, Politickes, Oeconomicks* (London, 1609), 173.

30 Cited by Ralph A. Houlbrooke ed., *English Family Life, 1576–1716: An Anthology from Diaries* (Oxford: Basil Blackwell, 1988), 71.

31 *Plumpton Correspondence: A Series of Letters, Chiefly Domestick, Written in the Reigns of Edward IV, Richard III, Henry VII, and Henry VIII*, ed. Thomas Stapleton, Camden Society (London, 1839), vol. 4, 232.

32 Joel Hurstfield studies the functions and demise of ward-ship in *The Queen's Wards: Wardship and Marriage under Elizabeth I*, (London: Longmans, Green and Co, 1958). Compare chapter 4, "The Royal Wards" in Pinchbeck and Hewitt, *Children in English Society*, vol.1.

33 Holles is quoted by Linda Levy Peck in *Court Patronage and Corruption in Early Stuart England* (Boston: Unwin Hyman, 1990), 24.

34 Lucy Hutchinson, "The Life of Mrs. Lucy Hutchinson Written by Herself," in *Memoirs of the Life of Colonel Hutchinson* (London: J. M. Dent, 1908), 14–15.

35 Houlbrooke, *The English Family, 1450–1700* (London: Longman, 1984), 175–6, Ann Kussmaul, *Servants in Husbandry in Early Modern England* (Cambridge: Cambridge University Press, 1981), 51, 55. Compare Rosemary O'Day. *The Family and Family Relationships, 1500–1900: England, France and the United States of America* (New York: St. Martins Press, 1994), 184–8, arguing that prescribers try to create a family feeling that is in fact absent.

36 Cited by Steven R. Smith in "The Ideal and Reality: Apprentice-Master Relationships in Seventeenth Century London," *History of Education Quarterly* 21 (1981), 451. Compare Torquato Tasso, *The Housholders Philosophie*, trans. T. K. (London, 1588), sig. D2r. On the horrific abuse of some servants, see Michael MacDonald, *Mystical Bedlam: Madness, Anxiety, and Healing in Seventeenth Century England* (Cambridge: Cambridge University Press, 1984), 87–8.

37 See William Gouge, *Of Domesticall Duties: Eight Treatises* (London, 1622), 430, 442, 594–6, 615.

38 J. Jean Hecht, *The Domestic Servant Class in Eighteenth-Century England* (London: Routledge and Kegan Paul, 1956), 206. Compare Edward Berry,

Shakespeare's Comic Rites (Cambridge: Cambridge University Press, 1984), 58–67 on imitation as a method for maturation.

39 On the etymology of "minister" and its links to "master" see M. K. Flint and E. J. Dobson, "Weak Masters," *Review of English Studies* 10 (1959), 58–60.

40 On this "disposition" as a protest against court manners and ethics see David Bevington, *Action is Eloquence: Shakespeare's Language of Gesture* (Cambridge, Mass.: Harvard University Press, 1984), 181–2. The derogatory reference to "jacks" occurs in *Richard the Third* 1.3.53.

41 See Barbara Everett, *Young Hamlet: Essays on Shakespeare's Tragedies* (Oxford: Clarendon Press, 1989), 20, citing Keith Thomas, "Age and Authority in Early Modern England."

42 Having recited the many benefits of service, Cousin asks impatiently whether if "to lyve in awe" is wretched, "are nat lordes and princis sonnes then also wretched?" See *Of the Office of Servauntes* sig. C3r.

43 Everett, *Young Hamlet* 33.

44 C. L. Barber and Richard P. Wheeler, *The Whole Journey: Shakespeare's Power of Development* (Berkeley: University of California Press, 1986), 259. Compare Richard Strier, "Faithful Servants: Shakespeare's Praise of Disobedience," in *The Historical Renaissance: New Essays on Tudor and Stuart Literature and Culture*, ed. Heather Dubrow and Richard Strier (Chicago: University of Chicago Press, 1988), 111 ("merely and utterly venal and obsequious") and Bert O. States, *Hamlet and the Concept of Character* (Baltimore: The Johns Hopkins University Press, 1992), 147 ("you wonder what he ever saw in them"). More critical of Hamlet's viewpoint are Marc Shell, *Children of the Earth: Literature, Politics, and Nationhood* (Oxford: Oxford University Press, 1993), 120, Margaret W. Ferguson, "*Hamlet*: Letters and Spirits," in *Shakespeare and the Question of Theory*, ed. Patricia Parker and Geoffrey Hartman (London: Methuen, 1985), 299, 303 and Marvin Rosenberg, *The Masks of Hamlet* (Newark: University of Delaware Press, 1992), 373–4. James L. Calderwood, *To Be And Not To Be: Negation and Metadrama in Hamlet* (New York: Columbia University Press, 1983), 123–6, treats the roles of "go-between" and "get-between" primarily as formal patterns.

45 Harold Jenkins ed., *Hamlet* (London: Methuen, 1982), 462, finding an echo of the moment in Ovid's *Metamorphoses* when Orpheus loses Eurydice.

46 Compare Michael Neill: "Because all service is ultimately owed to the king, the only dependable obligations to which Hamlet can appeal are those which lie outside its hierarchy of duties." See "'He that thou knowest thine': Friendship and Service in *Hamlet*," in *A Companion to Shakespeare's Works*, vol. 1 *The Tragedies*, ed. Richard Dutton and Jean E. Howard (Oxford: Basil Blackwell, 2003), 330–1.

47 Samuel Johnson, *Samuel Johnson on Shakespeare*, ed. W. K. Wimsatt, Jr. (New York: Hill and Wang, 1960), 112.

48 That Hamlet's knavery associates him with young servingmen seems to be denied in the First Quarto (1603), 3.2.30–3, when a simpler Hamlet dissuades

the adult players from excessive foolery by citing examples of jokes which would appeal specifically to servingmen: "Cannot you stay till I eate my porrige? and, you owe me / A quarters wages: and, my coate wants a cullison: / And, your beere is sowre." See *The Three-Text Hamlet: Parallel Texts of the First and Second Quartos and First Folio*, ed. Bernice W. Kliman and Paul Bertram and intro. Eric Rasmussen (New York: AMS Press, 1991), 122, lines 1242–4.

49 William Basse, *Sword and Buckler: Or, Servingmans Defence* (London, 1602), sig. C2v, stanza 38 and sig. C3v, stanza 44, stands up for gentle servingmen who are treated with disdain. Servants are "brothers all, but very little kin," he complains, and he protests against the "rude wind-pipe" of pejorative remarks about them.

50 Stoppard is quoted by Jill L. Levenson in "'Hamlet' Andante / 'Hamlet' Allegro: Tom Stoppard's Two Versions," *Shakespeare Survey* 36 (1983), 22.

51 John Kerrigan, *On Shakespeare and Early Modern Literature: Essays* (Oxford: Oxford University Press, 2001), 7–8. See also Peter Holland, "Film Editing," in *Shakespeare Performed: Essays in Honor of R. A. Foakes*, ed. Grace Ioppolo (Newark: University of Delaware Press, 2000), 288–9.

52 This is Samuel Taylor Coleridge's suggestion. See *Coleridge's Writings on Shakespeare*, ed. Terence Hawkes (New York: G. P. Putnam's Sons, 1959), 154.

53 David Konstan, *Friendship in the Classical World* (Cambridge: Cambridge University Press, 1997), 110, cites these meanings of *opheleia* in an account of how Epicurus defined *philia* and friendship. Mutual need is implied. Jenkins ed., *Hamlet*, comments that her name "from the Greek, meaning succour, is usually thought inappropriate." See his notes on *Dramatis Personae*, 163.

54 Moses I. Finley, *Ancient Slavery and Modern Ideology* (Harmondsworth: Penguin Books, 1980), 117, 119–20. Compare Bruce Robbins, *The Servant's Hand: English Fiction from Below* (New York: Columbia University Press, 1986), 11–12. David Brion Davis, *The Problem of Slavery in Western Culture* (Ithaca: Cornell University Press, 1966), 35, observes that no "single definition has succeeded in comprehending the historical varieties of slavery or in clearly distinguishing the institution from other types of involuntary servitude."

55 For analyses of attitudes toward labor, I am indebted to Christopher Hill, "Pottage for Freeborn Englishmen: Attitudes to Wage Labour in the Sixteenth and Seventeenth Centuries," in *Change and Continuity in Seventeenth Century England* (London: Secker and Warburg, 1974), 219–38, Michael Roberts, "'Words they are women, and deeds they are men': Images of Work and Gender in Early Modern England," in *Women and Work in Pre-Industrial England*, ed. Lindsey Charles and Lorna Duffin (Dover, NH: Croom Helm, 1985), 122–80, D. C. Coleman, "Labour in the English Economy of the Seventeenth Century," *Economic History Review* ser. 2, 8 (1956), 280–95, and C. B. Macpherson, "Servants and Labourers in Seventeenth-Century England," in *Democratic Theory: Essays in Retrieval* (Oxford: Clarendon Press, 1973), 207–23. "The Regulations of Edward, Third

Earl of Derby" (1568) stipulate that "no Slaves nor boyes shall sitt in the Hall but in place therefore to be appoynted convenyent." See Edward Derby and Henry Derby, *The Household Regulations and Expenses of Edward and Henry, Third and Fourth Earls of Derby* (1561, 1568, 1586–90), ed. F. R. Raines (Manchester: Chetham Society, 1853), 9; this rule may indicate a survival of serfdom, never officially abolished and generally detested by the English. See Diarmaid MacCulloch, "Bondmen under the Tudors," in *Law and Government Under the Tudors*, ed. Claire Cross *et al.* (Cambridge: Cambridge University Press, 1988), 107, Robert J. Steinfeld, *The Invention of Free Labor: The Employment Relation in English and American Law and Culture, 1350–1870* (Chapel Hill: University of North Carolina Press, 1991), 95–6 and E. P. Cheney, "The Disappearance of English Serfdom," *English Historical Review* 15 (1900), 20–37.

56 Flandrin, *Families in Former Times*, 63. William Harrison's observation in *The Description of England* (1587), ed. George Edelen (Ithaca: Cornell University Press for The Folger Shakespeare Library, 1968), 118, that all bondmen are freed upon landing has deflected attention both from the lingering of serfdom and from the importation of black slaves stressed by James Walvin, *Black and White: The Negro and English Society, 1555–1945* (London: Penguin Press, 1973), 7–10 and by Peter Fryer, *Staying Power: The History of Black People in Britain* (London: Pluto Press, 1984), 8–13, as well as from analogous practices like ward-ship and the impressment of choir-boys.

57 Two essays that include brief comparisons are Michael Goldman, "Characterizing Coriolanus," *Shakespeare Survey* 34 (1981), 73–84 and Anthony B. Dawson, "Making a Difference? Shakespeare, Feminism, Men," *English Studies in Canada* 15 (1989), 427–40.

58 Plutarch, "The Life of Martius Coriolanus," in *Shakespeare's Plutarch*, ed. T. J. B. Spencer (Harmondsworth: Penguin Books, 1964), 297. Subsequent references are included in the text.

59 Stanley Cavell, *Disowning Knowledge in Six Plays of Shakespeare* (Cambridge: Cambridge University Press, 1987), 149. See also Cynthia Marshall, "Wound-Man: *Coriolanus*, Gender, and the Theatrical Construction of Interiority," in *Feminist Readings of Early Modern Culture: Emerging Subjects*, ed. Valerie Traub *et al.* (Cambridge: Cambridge University Press, 1996), 93–118 and Coppélia Kahn, *Roman Shakespeare: Warriors, Wounds, and Women* (London: Routledge, 1997), 144–59.

60 See Anne Barton, *The Names of Comedy* (Toronto: University of Toronto Press, 1990), 103, Cavell, *Disowning Knowledge* 157.

61 Naomi Conn Liebler, *Shakespeare's Festive Tragedy: The Ritual Foundations of Genre* (London: Routledge, 1995), 44.

62 Such fairs are vividly described in Thomas Deloney, *Thomas of Reading. Or Six Worthy Yeomen of the West* (1612) (Menston: Scolar Press Ltd., 1969), sig. B3v.

63 That female prostitutes were regularly confined through branding, brothels, and restriction to certain areas of cities may help to explain why Coriolanus

so identifies himself. See Laura Gowing's discussion of the language of insult in *Domestic Dangers: Women, Words, and Sex in Early Modern London* (Oxford: Clarendon Press, 1996), 100.

64 Ruth Nevo, *Tragic Form in Shakespeare* (Princeton: Princeton University Press, 1972), 367.

65 Barton views these servingmen ("a miniature herd") as representative of the more archaic Volscian people. See "Livy, Machiavelli, and Shakespeare's *Coriolanus*" (1985), in *Essays, Mainly Shakespearean* (Cambridge: Cambridge University Press, 1994), 154–5.

66 See the editions of *Coriolanus* by Lee Bliss (Cambridge: Cambridge University Press, 2000), Philip Brockbank (London: Methuen, 1976), and R. B. Parker (Oxford: Oxford University Press, 1994). For the meanings "release, liberation, deliverance, from captivity," *The Oxford English Dictionary* 3.b cites examples from 1582 and 1635.

67 Lambarde's criticism of this abuse is excerpted in Hurstfield and Smith eds., *Elizabethan People*, 29–30.

68 The *OED* gives "servant, slave" as the third obsolete meaning of "boy" and cites *Coriolanus* as an example of the fourth meaning, "a term of contempt."

69 Livy, *From the Founding of the City* [*Ab Urbe Condita*], trans. B. O. Foster (London: Heinemann, 1925), vol.i, 349–51. His angry mother proclaims "Had I no son I should have died a free woman, in a free land!"

70 Dennis Romano, *Housecraft and Statecraft: Domestic Service in Renaissance Venice, 1400–1600* (Baltimore: Johns Hopkins University Press, 1996), xxv, has also noticed this ambiguity: "In Italian, *servo* (*serva*) usually indicates free servants, but when employed in Latin as *servus* (It., *schiavo*) it refers to slaves."

71 Roger Manners' letter is cited by Pinchbeck and Hewitt, *Children in English Society* vol.i, 11.

72 For Annibal Guasco's letter see Ruth Kelso, *Doctrine for the Lady of the Renaissance* (Urbana: University of Illinois Press, 1956), 223, 226. Compare the advice of Christine de Pisan (still influential in the sixteenth century), cited by Kelso, 231, counselling somewhat older attendants on how to avoid flattery, yet serve a dishonest mistress.

73 Francis Osborne, "Advice to a Son," in *Advice to a Son: Precepts of Lord Burghley, Sir Walter Raleigh, and Francis Osborne*, ed. Louis B. Wright (Ithaca: Cornell University Press, 1962), 56.

74 Richard Brathwaite, *Some Rules and Orders for the Government of the House of an Earle* (1630), in *Miscellanea Antiqua Anglicana* (London: R. Triphook, 1821), 12.

75 See especially Jodi Mikalachki, ch. 3, "*Cymbeline* and the Masculine Romance of Roman Britain," in *The Legacy of Boadicea: Gender and Nation in Early Modern England* (London: Routledge, 1998) and Barbara Hodgdon, ch. 2, "Fashioning Obedience: *King John*'s 'True Inheritors'," in *The End Crowns All: Closure and Contradiction in Shakespeare's History* (Princeton: Princeton University Press, 1991).

76 Graham Holderness, *Shakespeare's History* (New York: St. Martins Press, 1985), 30–9.

77 For examples see Vivian Brodsky Elliott, "Single Women in the London Marriage Market: Age, Status and Mobility, 1598–1619," in *Marriage and Society: Studies in the Social History of Marriage*, ed. R. B. Outhwaite (New York: St. Martins Press, 1981), 93 (women serving their "near kin"); Alice T. Friedman, *House and Household in Elizabethan England: Wollaton Hall and the Willoughby Family* (Chicago: University of Chicago Press, 1989), 67, n. 58; Jones, *The Household of a Tudor Nobleman* 27; Adrian Wilson, "The Ceremony of Childbirth and its Interpretation," in *Women as Mothers in Pre-Industrial England: Essays in Memory of Dorothy McLaren*, ed. Valerie Fildes (London: Routledge, 1990), 76; Barbara A. Hanawalt, *The Ties that Bind: Peasant Families in Medieval England* (New York: Oxford University Press, 1986), 164 (medieval children listed *as* servants). The governess who warned Grace Mildmay against the company of servingmen was herself a "niece unto my father." See Pollock, *With Faith and Physic* 25. Alan MacFarlane, *The Family Life of Ralph Josselin a Seventeenth-Century Clergyman: An Essay in Historical Anthropology* (Cambridge: Cambridge University Press, 1970) 129, cites Josselin's "respect" for his sister when she served him for eight months. His daughters were probably "part-time domestic servants" before leaving home (44).

78 Christopher Hatton, *Memoirs of the Life and Times of Sir Christopher Hatton K. G.*, ed. Sir Harris Nicolas (London: Richard Bentley, 1847), 350–1.

79 Edward Gieskes, "'He is but a bastard to the time': Status and Service in *The Troublesome Reign of John* and Shakespeare's *King John*," *English Literary History* 65 (1998), 787 comments on his advancement as a "trusted royal servant." Seneca had suggested that allowing slaves free speech made them *more* loyal in Epistle 47, *The Epistles of Seneca [Epistulae Morales]*, trans. Richard M. Gummere (London: Heinemann, 1967), vol.i, 303. See also Flandrin, *Families in Former Times*, 93 on outspoken servants.

80 Emrys Jones, *The Origins of Shakespeare* (Oxford: Clarendon Press, 1977), 268–9, mentions the Senecan context of such references; see also E. A. J. Honigmann ed., "Introduction" to *King John* (London: Methuen, 1954), lx.

81 Tasso, *The Housholders Philosophie*, sig. E1v. He distinguishes the servant, who keeps other household "instruments" occupied, from the artificer and from the clerk, related to his master through friendship rather than servitude or "signiory." His insistence on the natural inferiority of servants seems to have been colored by his knowledge of ancient slavery. Katherine Rowe, *Dead Hands: Fictions of Agency, Renaissance to Modern* (Stanford: Stanford University Press, 1999), 5, traces use of the "hand" trope (the "instrument of instruments") to Aristotle, *De partibus animalium* and to Galen, *De usu partium*. Later household guides repeat Tasso's language on servants as hands or instruments.

82 Service disguises, supportive as well as treacherous, figure prominently in the account by the Catholic John Gerard, *The Autobiography of an Elizabethan*, trans. Philip Caraman (London: Longmans, Green and Co., 1951).

83 Tasso, *The Housholders Philosophie*, sig. D3v. Compare Basse, *Sword and Buckler*, sig. B2v (stanza 14), I. M., *A Health to the Gentlemanly Profession of Servingmen* (1598), in *Shakespeare Association Facsimiles* 3 (Oxford: Oxford University Press, 1931), sig. C2v, and William Vaughan, *The Golden-Grove, Moralized in Three Books*, 2nd ed. (London, 1608), sig. P8r. On John Hoskyn's emblem of the all-purpose "Trusty Servant" which he had painted on a wall at Winchester School, see Mark Thomton Burnett, "The 'Trusty Servant': A Sixteenth-Century English Emblem," *Emblematica* 6 (1992), 237–53.

84 Erich Segal, *Roman Laughter: The Comedy of Plautus* (Cambridge, Mass.: Harvard University Press, 1968), 133, refers to the "savior" cliché. Houlbrooke's *English Family Life*, ch. 4, records from diaries incidents of success and failure in saving children. For other examples of rescue and assistance see Hutchinson, *Memoirs of the Life of Colonel Hutchinson*, 37 and Dorothea Townshend, *Life and Letters of Mr. Endymion Porter: Sometime Gentleman of the Bedchamber to King Charles the First* (London: T. Fisher Unwin, 1897), 228.

85 See Cousin, *Of the Office of Servauntes*, sig. C3r, Thomas Howell, *Howell's Devises* (1581), intro. Walter Raleigh (Oxford: Clarendon Press, 1906), 51 (his hope that long service will "shrowde" him), and William Fleetwood, *The Relative Duties of Parents and Children, Husbands and Wives, Masters and Servants* (London, 1705), 384–5. The experience of Adam Martindale's eldest daughter, run down by a coach on her first service, then killed through overwork and exposure while employed by a woman "that had a deare love to her," is a reminder of how variable such security would have been. See Adam Martindale, *The Life of Adam Martindale, Written by Himself*, ed. Richard Parkinson, Chetham Society, old ser. 4 (1845), 207–8.

86 A. R. Braunmuller ed., *The Life and Death of King John* (Oxford: Oxford University Press, 1989).

87 See Ann Blake, "Children and Suffering in Shakespeare's Plays," *The Yearbook of English Studies* 23 (1993), 293–304 on his achievement in representing pathos and horror while avoiding sentimentality.

88 L. A. Beurline ed., "Introduction" to *King John* (Cambridge: Cambridge University Press, 1990), 52.

WIVES AND SERVANTS

1 The common law doctrine of *potestas* subordinates children, wives and servants to masters. See Edward Chamberlayne, *Angliae Notitia: Or the Present State of England* (London, 1669), 452: "a Wife in England is *de jure* but the best of servants." Common law coincides with Genesis in this regard according to T. E. in *The Law's Resolutions of Women's Rights*, excerpted by Joan Larsen Klein ed. in *Daughters Wives and Widows: Writings by Men about Women and Marriage in England, 1500–1640* (Urbana: University of Illinois Press, 1992), 32.

2 Robert Cleaver is cited by John C. Bean in "Comic Structure and the Humanizing of Kate in *The Taming of the Shrew*," in *The Woman's Part: Feminist Criticism of Shakespeare*, ed. Carolyn Ruth Swift Lenz *et al.* (Urbana: University of Illinois Press, 1980), 69–70. See also Dorothy Leigh, cited by Susan Dwyer Amussen, *An Ordered Society: Gender and Class in Early Modern England* (Oxford: Basil Blackwell, 1988), 41. Michael Roberts surveys attitudes toward women's work, including its interchangeability with that of servants, in "'Words they are women, and deeds they are men': Images of Work and Gender in Early Modern England," in *Women and Work in Pre-Industrial England*, ed. Lindsey Charles and Lorna Duffin (Dover, NH: Croom Helm, 1985), 132, 172 n. 118.

3 William Gouge, *Of Domesticall Duties: Eight Treatises* (London, 1622), 389.

4 Thomas Gataker, *Marriage Duties Briefly Couched Togither* (London, 1620), 15. Compare Gouge, *Of Domesticall Duties*, 302. Francis Dillingham, *Christian Oeconomy or Houshold Government* (London, 1609), sig. 11r, distinguishes the "politique" subjection of wives from the "servile" subjection of servants (meaning that wives work for their own good, servants for that of others).

5 See Margaret J. M. Ezell, *The Patriarch's Wife: Literary Evidence and the History of the Family* (Chapel Hill: The University of North Carolina Press, 1987), 16, 34, Linda A. Pollock, "Teach her to live under obedience: The Making of Women in the Upper Ranks of Early Modern England," *Continuity and Change* 4 (1989), 231–58, Amussen, *An Ordered Society*, 119–22, and Constance Jordan, "Renaissance Women and the Question of Class," in *Sexuality and Gender in Early Modern Europe: Institutions, Texts, Images*, ed. James Grantham Turner (Cambridge: Cambridge University Press, 1993), 90–106. Amy Louise Erickson, *Women and Property in Early Modern England* (London: Routledge, 1993), describes women's acumen in financial matters, Laura Gowing, *Domestic Dangers: Women, Words, and Sex in Early Modern London* (Oxford: Clarendon Press, 1996), their familiarity with legal procedures.

6 Prescribers often associate the afflictions of service with those of marriage or urge the wife to work hard as an example for servants. See Dillingham, *Christian Oeconomy*, sig. 14v, William Whately, *A Care-Cloth: Or a Treatise of the Cumbers and Troubles of Marriage* (London, 1624), sig. E4r, and Xenophon, *Xenophon's Treatise of Housholde*, trans. Gentian Hervet (London, 1534), sig. E3r–v.

7 Frances E. Dolan, *Dangerous Familiars: Representations of Domestic Crime in England 1550–1700* (Ithaca: Cornell University Press, 1994), 59–88, considers petty treason on the part of criminal servants, some of whom plot against masters with wives.

8 See Thomas Carter, *Carter's Christian Commonwealth: Domesticall Dutyes Deciphered* (London, 1627), 48, Thomas Fossett, *The Servants Dutie or the Calling and Condition of Servants* (London, 1613), 51, Giovanni M. Bruto, *The Necessarie, Fit and Convenient Education of a Yong Gentlewoman*, trans. W. P.

(London, 1598; rpt. Amsterdam: Da Capo Press, 1969), sig. H2v, and Gouge, *Of Domesticall Duties*, 592–3.

9 Other works which stress fusions of these roles are *Westward Ho* by John Webster and Thomas Dekker, *The Witch of Edmonton* by Dekker, John Ford and William Rowley, and *The Changeling* by Thomas Middleton and Rowley.

10 See Peter Erickson, *Patriarchal Structures in Shakespeare's Drama* (Berkeley: University of California Press, 1985), 16, 21.

11 Anthony Fletcher, *Gender, Sex and Subordination in England 1500–1800* (New Haven: Yale University Press, 1995), 107.

12 Edmund Spenser, *Spenser's Faerie Queene* (1596), ed. J. C. Smith (Oxford: The Clarendon Press, 1964), canto 1, xxv.7, vol.1, 350. For Geoffrey Chaucer's "The Franklin's Tale" see *The Complete Poetry and Prose of Geoffrey Chaucer*, ed. John H. Fisher (New York: Holt, Rinehart and Winston, 1977), 200.

13 Anon., *The Tragedy of Master Arden of Faversham* (1592), ed. M. L. Wine (London: Methuen, 1973). Subsequent references are to this text of the play.

14 Compare Wine ed., "Introduction" to *Arden of Faversham*, lxxiii. Frank Whigham stresses converging social changes in *Seizures of the Will in Early Modern English Drama* (Cambridge: Cambridge University Press, 1996), 63–120.

15 Geoffrey Bullough ed. reprints *A Shrew* in *Narrative and Dramatic Sources of Shakespeare* (London: Routledge and Kegan Paul, 1957), vol. 1, 69–108.

16 Margaret Lael Mikesell, "'Love Wrought These Miracles': Marriage and Genre in *The Taming of the Shrew*," *Renaissance Drama* 20 (1989), 146–9, argues that rebellion in the "new comedy" plot seems to perpetuate the *status quo*.

17 Thomas Moisan treats the theatrical "pedagogical mendacity" of the schooling sequence as "a practicum and frame for the training of a shrew" in "Interlinear Trysting and 'Household Stuff': The Latin Lesson and the Domestication of Learning in *The Taming of the Shrew*," *Shakespeare Studies* 23 (1995), 103.

18 Ann Thompson ed., *The Taming of the Shrew* (Cambridge: Cambridge University Press, 1984), note to 4.1.65–6.

19 Kate Mertes, maintains that these establishments were predominantly male in *The English Noble Household 1250–1600: Good Governance and Politic Rule* (Oxford: Basil Blackwell, 1988), 6, 43, 57. Compare Alice T. Friedman, *House and Household in Elizabethan England: Wollaton Hall and the Willoughby Family* (Chicago: University of Chicago Press, 1989), 46–7.

20 See John Hoskyns, *The Life, Letters, and Writings of John Hoskyns 1566–1638*, ed. Louise Brown Osborn (New Haven: Yale University Press, 1937), 75, 81, 87.

21 Henry Percy, "Instructions by Henry Percy, Ninth Earl of Northumberland, to his Son Algernon Percy, Touching the Management of His Estate, Officers, etc." (1609), *Archaeologia* 27 (1838), 337, 339.

22 On the changes in women's work see Susan Cahn, *Industry of Devotion: The Transformation of Women's Work in England 1500–1660* (New York: Columbia University Press, 1987).

23 Anne Clifford, *The Diaries of Lady Anne Clifford* (1603–76), ed. D. J. H. Clifford (Wolfeboro Falls, NH: Alan Sutton, 1991), 54; compare 52, 57, 60, 61, 66.

24 Joan and Maria Thynne, *Two Elizabethan Women: Correspondence of Joan and Maria Thynne 1575–1611*, ed. Alison D. Wall, Wiltshire Record Society Publication 38 (1982), 2 (by Joan), 31–3 (by Maria).

25 Friedman, *House and Household in Elizabethan England*, 53, 59–70.

26 Anon., *A Breviate Touching the Order and Governmente of a Nobleman's House* (1605), ed. Joseph Banks, *Archaeologia* 13 (1800), 323.

27 John Manningham, *The Diary of John Manningham of the Middle Temple 1602–3*, ed. Robert Parker Sorlien (Hanover, NH: The University Press of New England, 1976), 44.

28 In one possible source or analogue, *A Merry Jest of a Shrewde and Curste Wife*, as Mikesell points out in "'Love Wrought These Miracles,'" 151, conflict between husband and wife derives from the wife's very unwillingness to look after the hired help.

29 Erich Segal, *Roman Laughter: The Comedy of Plautus* (Cambridge, Mass.: Harvard University Press, 1968), 122; compare 105–6, 110.

30 For similar misogynous severity see Carter, *Carter's Christian Commonwealth*, 58–60: Vasta, the Queen of Ahashueroth, refused to come when summoned on a feast day and was consequently abandoned and replaced.

31 In George Gascoigne's *Supposes* (where a Count Hercules rules) the heroine chooses "a poore servaunt" of her father's as a lover before he identifies himself as an aristocrat in disguise. Bullough reprints *Supposes* in *Narrative and Dramatic Sources of Shakespeare*, vol.1, 111–58.

32 Bruce Robbins', *The Servants Hand: English Fiction from Below* (New York: Columbia University Press, 1986), 47, making a similar argument on how traditional elements in Dickens' fiction work as critiques of the cash nexus. See also 43, 45.

33 Compare Thompson ed., "Introduction" to *The Taming of the Shrew*, 17: "the psychological transformation of Katherina is a deeper, more internalised 'suppose' than any of the costume-changes in the sub-plot."

34 Grumio has been treated as thoroughly servile by Moisan, "'Knock me here soundly': Comic Misprision and Class Consciousness in Shakespeare," *Shakespeare Quarterly* 42 (1991), 279 and as the object of a brutality displaced from the wife of sources and analogues onto the servant by Mikesell, "'Love Wrought These Miracles,'" 153.

35 "For it is only as members somewhere," writes Michael Walzer in *Spheres of Justice: A Defence of Pluralism and Equality* (New York: Basic Books, 1983), 63, "that men and women can hope to share in all the other social goods – security, wealth, honor, office, and power – that communal life makes possible."

36 Subsequent references are to John Fletcher, *The Woman's Prize or the Tamer Tam'd* (1611), in *The Dramatic Works in the Beaumont and Fletcher Canon*, ed. Fredson Bowers (Cambridge; Cambridge University Press, 1979), vol. 4, 1–148.

37 Subsequent references are to Thomas Dekker, Henry Chettle, and William Haughton, *Patient Grissil* (1603), in *The Dramatic Works of Thomas Dekker*, ed. Fredson Bowers (Cambridge: Cambridge University Press, 1953), vol. I, 207–98.

38 Gouge, *Of Domesticall Duties*, 369.

39 Edward Pechter relates Gwalter's obsessive testing to his insecurity as a ruler; given the context of the Catholic menace to Protestant England, "a ruler's paranoia about his subjects' loyalty may seem like a normal, reasonable and fully justified mode of feeling." See *"Patient Grissil* and the Trials of Marriage," in *The Elizabethan Theatre XIV*, ed. A. L. Magnusson and C. E. Mcgee (Toronto: P. D. Meany, 1996), 92.

40 For a late medieval example of this symbolism, see Michael Goodich, *"Ancilla Dei*: The Servant as Saint in the Late Middle Ages," in *Women of the Medieval World: Essays in Honor of John H. Mundy*, ed. Julius Kirshner and Suzanne F. Wemple (Oxford: Basil Blackwell, 1985), 132–3.

41 Susan Snyder's line gloss in her edition of *All's Well That Ends Well* (Oxford: Oxford University Press) describes "Helen's balanced paradox of a vessel measurelessly capable of (or desirous of) taking in and measurelessly incapable of retaining."

42 See Carter, *Carter's Christian Commonwealth* 62 and Gouge, *Of Domesticall Duties* 274–5, 594–7. Torquato Tasso, *The Housholders Philosophie*, trans. T. K. (London, 1588), sig. C4r, warns that a young wife denied honest recreation may "hate or feare thee with y dread wherewith base slaves or servaunts are kept under by theyr Maisters."

43 Gataker, *Marriage Duties*, 12.

44 Guido Ruggiero, *Binding Passions: Tales of Magic, Marriage, and Power at the End of the Renaissance* (New York: Oxford University Press, 1993), 104.

45 William Fleetwood, *The Relative Duties of Parents and Children, Husbands and Wives, Masters and Servants*, 3 ed. (London, 1722), 290–1.

46 See Robert Cleaver, *A Godly Form of Householde Government* (London, 1598), 382 and Tasso, *The Housholders Philosophie*, sig. D3r. On reason by "participation" see Tasso sig. D3r.

47 Emphasizing the essential identity of sun and moon, Gouge writes that "the wife (as well as the husband) is . . . both a servant, and a mistresse, a servant to yeeld her body, a mistresse to have the power of his" (*Of Domesticall Duties*, 357).

48 Sheldon P. Zitner, *All's Well That Ends Well* (Boston: Twayne Publishers, 1989), 14.

49 Paula Neuss, "The Sixteenth-Century English 'Proverb' Play," *Comparative Drama* 18 (1984), 14–15.

50 Michael Taylor, "Persecuting Time with Hope: The Cynicism of Romance in *All's Well That Ends Well*," *English Studies in Canada* 11 (1985), 287, reads her mention of a "body" in 1.1.181 as referring only to Bertram's body, not as Neuss and I do, to her potential agency.

51 R. B. Parker, "War and Sex in 'All's Well That Ends Well'," *Shakespeare Survey* 37 (1984), 108.

52 Barbara Everett ed., "Introduction" to *All's Well That Ends Well* (Harmondsworth: Penguin Books, 1970), astutely compares Helena's situation as an attendant with Maria's in *Twelfth Night* (21), and as a virgin with Ophelia's in *Hamlet* (25).

53 Parker, "War and Sex in 'All's Well That Ends Well,'" 110.

54 According to A. L. Beier in *Masterless Men: The Vagrancy Problem in England, 1560–1640* (New York: Methuen, 1985), 110, the passport, one of four types of license issued to beggars, was intended for "convicted vagrants" to travel home on.

55 G. K. Hunter ed., *All's Well That Ends Well* (London: Methuen, 1959), line gloss.

56 See David Ellis, "Finding a Part for Parolles," *Essays in Criticism* 39 (1989), 294, 291. Ellis shows how directors and theater-commentators have often scape-goated Parolles to make Bertram more appealing and Parolles more coherent.

57 In his discussion of the original story, Giovanni Boccacio's tale of Giletta and Beltramo in *The Decameron*, Zitner, *All's Well That Ends Well*, 10, 17, brings out the greater proximity in status between hero and heroine.

58 Richard P. Wheeler, *Shakespeare's Development and the Problem Comedies: Turn and Counter-Turn* (Berkeley: University of California Press, 1981), 42.

59 For striking examples of this view see Lyndal Roper on witchcraft beliefs in *Oedipus and the Devil: Witchcraft, Sexuality and Religion in Early Modern Europe* (London: Routledge, 1994), 25 and Margreta De Grazia on the representation of the dark lady in "The Scandal of Shakespeare's Sonnets," *Shakespeare Survey* 46 (1994), 47–9.

60 I. M., *A Health to the Gentlemanly Profession of Servingmen* (1598), in *Shakespeare Association Facsimiles* 3 (Oxford: Oxford University Press, 1931), sig. C1r. A. R. Braunmuller, "'Second Means': Agent and Accessory in Elizabethan Drama," in *The Elizabethan Theatre XI*, ed. A. L. Magnusson and C. E. Mcgee (Port Credit: P. D. Meany, 1990), 177–203 explores connections between plays and legal formulas identifying master and servant in numerous transactions.

61 Parolles' dress and conduct might illustrate David Kuchta's association of effeminacy ("cat" suggesting prostitution) with idolatry and semiotic instability. See "The Semiotics of Masculinity in Renaissance England," in Turner ed., *Sexuality and Gender in Early Modern Europe*, 238.

62 David Scott Kastan, "*All's Well That Ends Well* and the Limits of Comedy," *English Literary History* 52 (1985), 580.

63 Camille Wells Slights, "Slaves and Subjects in *Othello*," *Shakespeare Quarterly* 48 (1997), 377–90 proposes that both Iago and Othello emerge from civic, humanistic contexts which fostered qualities conducive to the growth of the slave trade. See also Michael Neill, "Servant Obedience and Master Sins: Shakespeare and the Bonds of Service," in *Putting History to the Question:*

Power, Politics, and Society in English Renaissance Drama (New York: Columbia University Press, 2000), 46.

64 Nicole Loraux, *Tragic Ways of Killing a Woman*, trans. Anthony Forster (Cambridge, Mass.: Harvard University Press, 1987), 62.

65 Neill, "Servant Obedience and Master Sins," 27.

66 William Wentworth, "Sir William Wentworth's Advice to his Son," in *Wentworth Papers 1597–1628*, ed. J. P. Cooper, Camden Society, 4th series (London: Royal Historical Society, 1973), vol. 12, 15.

67 Among other interpretations suggested for this line are those of Norman Sanders ed., *Othello* (Cambridge: Cambridge University Press, 1984), line gloss: that, in effect, if I were in the Moor's position, I could see through my pretense of service; Emily C. Bartels, "Making More of the Moor: Aaron, Othello, and Renaissance Refashionings of Race," *Shakespeare Quarterly* 41 (1990), 450–1: "a conflicted desire to be and not to be the Moor" who is both noble and detestable; and E. A. J. Honigmann ed., *Othello* (Walton-on-Thames: Thomas Nelson and Sons, 1997), line gloss: "Were I the Moor, I would not wish to be Iago."

68 "Evill language of their master behinde his backe" comes eleventh in Gouge's list of servant vices (*Of Domesticall Duties*, 599–600).

69 Virginia Mason Vaughan, *Othello: A Contextual History* (Cambridge: Cambridge University Press, 1994), 49, observes that "A military ethics ... permeates Othello's thinking and his discourse even in the depths of his seemingly private, domestic crisis."

70 Characters are sentenced to the galleys in Jonson's *Volpone* and in Webster's *The White Devil* and *The Devil's Law Case*.

71 Cited by Anthony Gerard Barthelemy, *Black Face Maligned Race: The Representation of Blacks in English Drama from Shakespeare to Southerne* (Baton Rouge: Louisiana State University Press, 1987), 55. See also Patricia Parker, "Fantasies of 'Race' and Gender: Africa, *Othello*, and Bringing to Light," in *Women, "Race", and Writing in the Early Modern Period*, ed. Margo Hendricks and Patricia Parker (London: Routledge, 1994), 90, on how Iago's name links him to the Iberian slave-trade. Several critics have associated Iago with the eleventh-century Spaniard Saint James or Santiago who slew Moors.

72 On the presence of black slaves in London see James Walvin, *Slaves and Slavery: The British Colonial Experience* (Manchester: Manchester University Press, 1992), 35–7 and *Black and White: The Negro and English Society, 1555–1945* (London: Penguin Press, 1973), 7–10. Compare Peter Fryer, *Staying Power: The History of Black People in Britain* (London: Pluto Press, 1985), 8–13. Roslyn L. Knutson questions this presence in "A Caliban in St. Mildred Poultry," *Shakespeare and Cultural Traditions*, ed. Tetsuo Kishi *et al.* (Newark: University of Delaware Press, 1994), 116.

73 Knutson, "Elizabethan Documents, Captivity Narratives, and the Market for Foreign History Plays," *English Literary Renaissance* 26 (1996), 75–110, shows how London parishes record the gathering of alms with which to buy English captives out of slavery in North Africa and the Near East.

74 Defenses of general subordination often make this distinction. See the useful discussion of Stoic and Christian apologies for contemporary slavery in Carolyn Prager, "The Problem of Slavery in *The Custom of the Country*," *Studies in English Literature* 28 (1988), 308–10.

75 Gerrard Winstanley writes, "I am assured that, if it be rightly searched into, the inward bondages of the mind . . . are all occasioned by the outward bondage that one sort of people lay upon another." See "The Law of Freedom in a Platform: Or, True Magistracy Restored," (1652) in *The Law of Freedom and Other Writings*, ed. Christopher Hill (Harmondsworth: Penguin Books, 1973), 296.

76 Bernard Williams, *Shame and Necessity* (Berkeley: University of California Press, 1993), 15.

77 This motive for despair would be intensified by Iago's skill in using the forces of racism and sexism against Othello. See Barthelemy, *Black Face Maligned Race*, 154–8 and Ania Loomba, *Gender, Race, Renaissance Drama* (Manchester: Manchester University Press, 1989), 58–60.

78 F. L. Lucas, *Euripides and His Influence* (New York: Longmans, Green, 1928), 36.

79 Lois Potter, *Shakespeare in Performance: Othello* (Manchester: Manchester University Press, 2002), 178, describing Janet Suzman's 1987 production in Johannesburg, sees as significant for a "race-dominated society" "the fact that Emilia reaches out her hand toward Othello as she dies, and that he himself closes her eyes." For Edward Pechter, *Othello and Interpretive Traditions* (Iowa City; University of Iowa Press, 1999), 116–21, Emilia's transformation, showing remarkable thoughtfulness, is important in itself; she is no mere surrogate or foil.

80 Jean Bodin, *Six Books of the Commonwealth* (1576), abridged and trans. M. J. Tooley (Oxford: Basil Blackwell, 1955), 17–18.

81 See Richard Strier. "Faithful Servants: Shakespeare's Praise of Disobedience," in *The Historical Renaissance: New Essays on Tudor and Stuart Literature and Culture*, ed. Heather Dubrow and Richard Strier (Chicago: University of Chicago Press, 1988), 111, 124.

82 Compare Lady Julia's praise for wives wise enough to "dissemble" when they cannot obey their husbands in Edmund Tilney's dialogue, *The Flower of Friendship: A Renaissance Dialogue Contesting Marriage*, ed. and intro. Valerie Wayne (Ithaca: Cornell University Press, 1992), 135.

83 Paulina's strong influence has been emphasized by feminist critics including Carolyn Asp, "Shakespeare's Paulina and the *Consolatio* Tradition," *Shakespeare Studies* 11 (1978), 145–58, M. Lindsay Kaplan and Katherine Eggert, "'Good queen, my lord, good queen': Sexual Slander and the Trials of Female Authority in *The Winter's Tale*," *Renaissance Drama* 25 (1994), 89–118 and Carol Thoma Neely, *Broken Nuptials in Shakespeare's Plays* (New Haven: Yale University Press, 1985), 199–201.

84 Laurie Shannon, *Sovereign Amity: Figures of Friendship in Shakespearean Contexts*, ch. 6 (Chicago: University of Chicago Press, 2002), approaches

Camillo and Paulina through classical and humanistic discourses as political friends and councillors rather than as customary servants (or in Paulina's case, a wife).

FRIENDS AND SERVANTS

1 Some women in service married their masters; the daughters or widows of wealthy merchants might marry country gentlemen. Ann Jennalie Cook, *Making a Match: Courtship in Shakespeare and His Society* (Princeton: Princeton University Press, 1991), 47, cautions against exaggerating the "limited" number of marriages unequal in "rank, wealth, or personal gifts."
2 I have been influenced, however, by S. N. Eisenstadt and L. Roniger who maintain in *Patrons, Clients and Friends: Interpersonal Relations and the Structure of Trust in Society* (Cambridge: Cambridge University Press, 1984), that tensions in patron–client obligations are mitigated by "ritualized personal relationships" (9) and mediated by symbolism in the absence of firm structural relations (13, 206).
3 Lena Cowen Orlin, *Private Matters and Public Culture in Post-Reformation England* (Ithaca: Cornell University Press, 1994), 165, believes that traditional values of friendship were declining. Compare 140–1 and 172. But Laurie Shannon in *Sovereign Amity: Figures of Friendship in Shakespearean Contexts* (Chicago: University of Chicago Press, 2002), finds that an association between the "logics" of ideal male friendship and of advice to monarchs often shapes public polity and promotes freer speech.
4 Mario DiGangi, *The Homoerotics of Early Modern Drama* (Cambridge: Cambridge University Press, 1997), 102.
5 Giorgio Melchiori ed., "Introduction" to *The Second Part of King Henry IV* (Cambridge: Cambridge University Press, 1989), 5, n. 3. See also John Jowett, "The Thieves in *1 Henry IV*," *The Review of English Studies* 38 (1987), 326–7.
6 Melchiori ed., "Introduction" to *The Second Part of King Henry IV*, 11.
7 John Stow, citing Sir Thomas Elyot in *The Annales of England* (1592), excerpted in A. R. Humphreys ed., *The Second Part of King Henry IV* (London: Methuen, 1966), Appendix 1, 218; compare "one of his seruantes, whom he well fauored" in Humphreys' selection from Elyot's *The Boke named the Governour* (1531), 220.
8 See scene iv where the Prince repeats this identification several times. Geoffrey Bullough reprints *The Famous Victories* (1598) in *Narrative and Dramatic Sources of Shakespeare* (London: Routledge and Kegan Paul, 1962), vol. 4, 299–341.
9 See G. R. Batho ed., "Introduction" to *The Household Papers of Henry Percy Ninth Earl of Northumberland (1564–1632)* Camden Society, 3rd series, vol. 93 (London: Royal Historical Society, 1962), xxii–iii and J. P. Cooper, "Retainers in Tudor England," in J. P. Cooper, *Land, Men and Beliefs: Studies in Early-Modern History*, ed. G. E. Aylmer and J. S. Morrill (London: Hambledon Press, 1983), 85. On how household sizes fluctuated with

changing needs (hunting, hospitality), see Peter Clark. *English Provincial Society from the Reformation to the Revolution: Religion, Politics and Society in Kent 1500–1640* (Hassocks: Harvester Press, 1977), 123–4, Mary E. Finch, *The Wealth of Five Northamptonshire Families 1540–1640* (Oxford: Oxford University Press for the Northamptonshire Record Society, 1956), 81 and Felicity Heal, *Hospitality in Early Modern England* (Oxford: Clarendon Press, 1990), 92.

10 On the weakening of the code after the Rising of 1569 see Mervyn James, *Family, Lineage, and Civil Society: A Study of Society, Politics, and Mentality in the Durham Region, 1500–1640* (Oxford: Clarendon Press, 1974), 79; on the military profession see Lindsay Boynton, *The Elizabethan Militia 1558–1638* (London: Routledge and Kegan Paul, 1967), 104.

11 See I. M., *A Health to the Gentlemanly Profession of Servingmen*, in *Shakespeare Association Facsimiles* 3 (Oxford: Oxford University Press, 1931), sig. C3r. Immediately subsequent references are included in the text. *A Health* was printed in 1598, *Part 2* in 1600.

12 For a use of "accommodated" connoting military support see *Cymbeline* 5.3.32. Francis Walsingham indicates a capacity to support others when he commends Justice Manwood to Christopher Hatton as "well able for living to bear the countenance of a place of credit" in the Queen's service. See Christopher Hatton, *Memoirs of the Life and Times of Sir Christopher Hatton K.G.*, ed. Sir Harris Nicolas (London: Richard Bentley, 1847), 67–8.

13 This is Marc Bloch's definition of feudal reciprocity in *Feudal Society*, trans. L. A. Manyon (Chicago: University of Chicago Press, 1961), vol. 1, 228.

14 In *Shakespeare and Social Dialogue: Dramatic Language and Elizabethan Letters* (Cambridge: Cambridge University Press, 1999), Lynne Magnusson offers acute analyses of maintenance strategies in exchanges between speakers and writers who differ in social status.

15 Greeks believed that relatives who provide help unselfishly can be friends; fathers, according to Aristotle, cannot. See David Konstan, *Friendship in the Classical World* (Cambridge: Cambridge University Press, 1997), 58, 68. Compare Cicero, *De Amicitia*, trans. William Armistead Falconer (Cambridge, Mass.: Harvard University Press, 1971), 125–9, limiting sharply the numbers who can participate in a relation based on identity of outlook and good will. Michel de Montaigne's view is that, being "of one soul in two bodies, according to Aristotle's very apt definition, [friends] can neither lend nor give anything to each other." See "Of Friendship" (1572–6, 1578–80), in *The Complete Essays of Montaigne*, trans. Donald M. Frame (Stanford: Stanford University Press, 1958), 141.

16 Étienne de La Boétie, *The Politics of Obedience: The Discourse of Voluntary Servitude* (1548), intro. Murray N. Rothbard, trans. Harry Kurz (New York: Free Life Editions, 1975), 82–3. For a contrary view, see Francis Bacon's essay "Of Friendship" (1625), in *Francis Bacon: A Selection of his Works*, ed. Sidney Warhaft (Toronto: Macmillan of Canada, 1965), 115.

17 Konstan, *Friendship in the Classical World*, 18.

18 William Cecil, Lord Burghley, "Certain Precepts for the Well Ordering of a Man's Life" (1584), in *Advice to a Son: Precepts of Lord Burghley, Sir Walter Raleigh, and Francis Osborne*, ed. Louis B. Wright (Ithaca: Cornell University Press, 1962), 11.

19 Walter Raleigh, "Sir Walter Raleigh's Instruction to His Son and to Posterity," in *Advice to a Son*, 28.

20 Raleigh, "Sir Walter Raleigh's Instruction," 19–20. Compare Henry Percy, "Instructions by Henry Percy, Ninth Earl of Northumberland, to His Son Algernon Percy, Touching the Management of His Estate, Officers, etc" (1609), *Archaeologia* 27 (1838), 328.

21 Lawrence Stone, *The Family, Sex and Marriage in England 1500–1800* (Harmondsworth: Penguin Books, 1984), 79, de-emphasizes "emotional attachment" in use of the term "friends."

22 William Wentworth, "Sir William Wentworth's Advice to his Son," in *Wentworth Papers 1597–1628*, ed. J. P. Cooper, Camden Society, 4th series, vol. 12 (London: Royal Historical Society, 1973), 14–15.

23 Philip Sidney and Mary Sidney, *The Psalms of Sir Philip Sidney and the Countess of Pembroke*, ed. J. C. A. Rathmell (Garden City: Doubleday, 1963), 305.

24 See the concluding stanza of "Helpe best welcome, when most needefull," in Thomas Howell, *Howell's Devises*, intro. Walter Raleigh (Oxford: Clarendon Press, 1906), 53.

25 M. Steeven Guazzo, *The Civile Conversation of M. Steeven Guazzo*, trans. George Pettie (1581) and Barth. Young (1586), ed. Charles Whibley (New York: Knopf, 1925), vol. 2, 94.

26 Guazzo, *The Civile Conversation*, vol. 2, 95. In another context the dialogues elevate service to ideal friendship: "if thou have a trusty servaunt, let him be unto thee as thine owne soule" (vol. 2, 109).

27 Giovanni Della Casa, *The Arts of Grandeur and Submission: Or a Discourse Concerning the Behaviour of Great Men towards Their Inferiours; and of Inferiour Personages towards Men of Greater Quality*, trans. Henry Stubbe, second edition (London, 1670), 8, 14–15.

28 Thomas Whythorne, *The Autobiography of Thomas Whythorne*, ed. James M. Osborn (London: Oxford University Press, 1962), 28, 46.

29 Whythorne, *The Autobiography*, 81.

30 Robert Brain's terms in *Friends and Lovers* (New York: Basic Books, 1976), 109. Katharine Hodgkin, "Thomas Whythorne and the Problems of Mastery," *History Workshop Journal* 29 (1990), 26–7, emphasizes the "symbolic value" of the meagre concessions he has won.

31 Whythorne, *The Autobiography*, 138, 224.

32 Eve Kosofsky Sedgwick, *Between Men: English Literature and Male Homosocial Desire* (New York: Columbia University Press, 1985), 35.

33 Konstan, *Friendship in the Classical World* 14.

34 Alan Bray, "Homosexuality and the Signs of Male Friendship in Elizabethan England," *History Workshop Journal* 29 (1990), 11.

35 Richard Gough, *Human Nature Displayed in the History of Myddle* (1701), intro. W. G. Hoskins (Fontwell: Centaur Press, 1968), 76.

36 See Leonard Tennenhouse, "Sir Walter Ralegh and the Literature of Clientage," in *Patronage in the Renaissance*, ed. Guy Fitch Lytle and Stephen Orgel (Princeton: Princeton University Press, 1981), 243, n. 13. and David Starkey, "Intimacy and Innovation: The Rise of the Privy Chamber, 1495–1547," in *The English Court: From the Wars of the Roses to the Civil War*, ed. David Starkey *et al.* (London: Longman, 1987), 71–118.

37 On the continuity of this grievance from the Percy rebellion of 1403 to the Northern rising of 1569, and the Essex rebellion of 1601, see Herbert Weil and Judith Weil eds., "Introduction" to *The First Part of King Henry IV*, (Cambridge: Cambridge University Press, 1997), 29–30.

38 Laurens J. Mills, *One Soul in Bodies Twain: Friendship in Tudor Literature and Stuart Drama* (Bloomington: The Principia Press, 1937), 448, n. 117.

39 Ronald A. Sharp, *Friendship and Literature: Spirit and Form* (Durham, NC: Duke University Press, 1986), 38.

40 Niccolò Machiavelli, *The Discourses* (1519?), trans. Leslie J. Walker, ed. Bernard Crick (Harmondsworth: Penguin Books, 1970), 498–9.

41 Jean-Louis Flandrin, *Families in Former Times: Kinship, Household and Sexuality* (Cambridge: Cambridge University Press, 1979), 148–9.

42 I. M., *A Health*, sig. C1r.

43 Bacon, "Of Friendship" (1625), 118.

44 In Gail Kern Paster's readings, fluidity often functions as a sign of subjugation and effeminization (35) unless firmly controlled by males. See *The Body Embarrassed: Drama and the Disciplines of Shame in Early Modern England* (Ithaca: Cornell University Press, 1993), 23–63, 79–84, 98–9.

45 Linda Levy Peck, *Court Patronage and Corruption in Early Stuart England* (Boston: Unwin Hyman, 1990), 132.

46 Della Casa, *The Arts of Grandeur and Submission*, 11–13.

47 William Basse, *Sword and Buckler; Or, Servingmans Defence* (London, 1602), sig. D3r, stanza 66.

48 Emrys Jones ed., "Introduction" to *Antony and Cleopatra* (Harmondsworth: Penguin Books, 1977), 39. Paul A. Cantor's point that in a new imperial regime "fidelity to one's master is fast becoming the only virtue recognized" may suggest that assured friendship in the play could have resonated with Jacobean concerns over royal power and favoritism. See *Shakespeare's Rome: Republic and Empire* (Ithaca: Cornell University Press, 1976), 147–8.

49 According to Plutarch, "it was predestined that the government of all the world should fall into Octavius Caesar's hands." See "The Life of Marcus Antonius," in *Shakespeare's Plutarch*, ed. T. J. B. Spencer (Harmondsworth: Penguin Books, 1964), 245. Subsequent references to the "Life" are included in the text.

50 Plutarch, "How a Man May Discern a Flatterer from a Friend," in *Plutarch's Moralia: Twenty Essays*, trans. Philemon Holland (1603) (London: J. M.

Dent, 1911), 43. Subsequent references to this essay are included in the text. Shannon stresses the impact of the *Moralia* on Renaissance thought in *Sovereign Amity*, 22–3, 191. On flattery in *Timon of Athens* see James C. Bulman, *The Heroic Idiom of Shakespearean Tragedy* (Newark: The University of Delaware Press, 1985), 135–6.

51 The context for this critique in the "Life" is Cleopatra's under-handed strategy against Octavia's efforts to aid Antony and win him back by honorable means.

52 See Burghley, "Certain Precepts" 11, Laurence Humfrey, *The Nobles or of Nobilitye* (London, 1563), sig. U6r, Wentworth, "Advice to His Son" 15, Percy, "Instructions" 358. Percy's harangue against intermediaries and surrogates is particularly impassioned.

53 Guazzo, *The Civile Conversation*, vol. 1, 163.

54 Ibid., 210. Guazzo immediately replies, "Wee must consider on the other side, howe much the being in the Princes companie doeth countenance us."

55 For "Domitius Aenobarbus" see Plutarch, "The Life of Marcus Antonius" 228, 294; for "Domitius" 244 and also 252–3 (where, sick of an ague, he dies repenting his treasonous desertion of Antony). Enobarbus has usually been approached as a Roman soldier, a choral figure and a fool. See Elkin Calhoun Wilson, "Shakespeare's Enobarbus," in *Joseph Quincy Adams: Memorial Studies*, ed. James G. McManaway *et al.* (Washington, DC: The Folger Shakespeare Library, 1948), 391–408 and Ruth Nevo, *Tragic Form in Shakespeare* (Princeton: Princeton University Press, 1972), 331.

56 Domna C. Stanton "Difference on Trial: A Critique of the Maternal Metaphor in Cixous, Irigaray, and Kristeva," in *The Poetics of Gender*, ed. Nancy K. Miller (New York: Columbia University Press, 1986), 172. On women's mutability see Carol Thomas Neely, *Broken Nuptials in Shakespeare's Plays* (New Haven: Yale University Press, 1985), 138 and Ania Loomba, *Gender, Race, Renaissance Drama* (Manchester: Manchester University Press, 1989), 74.

57 Frank Whigham, *Ambition and Privilege: The Social Tropes of Elizabethan Courtesy Theory* (Berkeley: University of California Press, 1984), 116. It is hard to detect any sense of good will in this self-deprecating *topos* as dissected by Whigham.

58 Della Casa, *The Arts of Grandeur and Submission*, 34.

59 Janet Adelman, *The Common Liar: An Essay on Antony and Cleopatra* (New Haven: Yale University Press, 1973), 133.

60 Walter Darell, "A Pretie and Shorte Discourse of the Duetie of a Servingman" (1578), reprinted in "A Conduct Book for Malvolio," ed. Louis B. Wright, *Studies in Philology* 31 (1934), 129.

61 Baldesar Castiglione, *The Book of the Courtier* (1528), trans. Charles S. Singleton (Garden City: Anchor Books, 1959), 188.

62 Irena R. Makaryk, "'Dwindling into a Wife?' Cleopatra and the Desires of the (Other) Woman," in *The Elizabethan Theatre XIV*, ed. A. L. Magnusson and C. E. McGee (Toronto: P. D. Meany, 1996), 110. Compare Jyotsna

Singh, "Renaissance Antitheatricality, Antifeminism, and Shakespeare's *Antony and Cleopatra*," *Renaissance Drama* 20 (1989), 113.

63 Annibal in Guazzo's *The Civile Conversation*, vol.1, 88, also compares flatterers to people (presumably servants and women) who comfort us with pillows. Such verbal puffing and stuffing may belong with the "fat lady" tropes which, according to Patricia Parker, "dramatize . . . the limiting structures of [patriarchal] authority and control." See *Literary Fat Ladies: Rhetoric, Gender, Property* (London: Methuen, 1987), 31.

64 Guazzo, *The Civile Conversation*, vol. 1, 80–1.

65 In her fine account of this remarkably articulate ambassador, M. M. Mahood, *Bit Parts in Shakespeare's Plays* (Cambridge: Cambridge University Press, 1992), 193, writes that his lines "effect what is perhaps the most memorable of the play's many transitions from the trivial to the magnificent."

66 For a reading of the play which emphasizes homosocial rivalry rather than interdependency see Coppélia Kahn, *Roman Shakespeare: Warriors, Wounds, and Women* (London: Routledge, 1997), 110–43.

67 Guazzo, *The Civile Conversation*, vol. 2, 102 (with Annibal the speaker); the context is an ironic catalogue of the behavior a master has to tolerate from "persons of the house."

68 James, *Family, Lineage, and Civil Society*, 33.

TRAGIC DEPENDENCIES IN *KING LEAR*

1 Naomi Conn Liebler, *Shakespeare's Festive Tragedy: The Ritual Foundations of Genre* (London: Routledge, 1995), 197.

2 See Robert Pogue Harrison, *Forests: The Shadow of Civilization* (Chicago: University of Chicago Press, 1992), 77–81.

3 Daniel J. Kornstein, *Kill All The Lawyers?: Shakespeare's Legal Appeal* (Princeton: Princeton University Press, 1994), 212, points out references to law.

4 David Young's comment in *The Heart's Forest: A Study of Shakespeare's Pastoral Plays* (New Haven: Yale University Press, 1972), 76, on how characters are "forced to leave society" is representative.

5 Most useful have been Jonas A. Barish and Marshall Waingrow, "'Service' in *King Lear*," *Shakespeare Quarterly* 9 (1958), 347–55, for good service as reciprocity; M. M. Mahood, *Bit Parts in Shakespeare's Plays* (Cambridge: Cambridge University Press, 1992), 157–79, on service as a theatrical and formal resource in play design; Richard Strier, "Faithful Servants: Shakespeare's Praise of Disobedience," in *The Historical Renaissance: New Essays on Tudor and Stuart Literature and Culture*, ed. Heather Dubrow and Richard Strier (Chicago: University of Chicago Press, 1988), 104–33, for service as a means of radical socio-political action; and Rosalie L. Colie, "Reason and Need: King Lear and the 'Crisis' of the Aristocracy," in *Some Facets of King Lear: Essays in Prismatic Criticism*, ed. Rosalie L. Colie and F. T. Flahiff (Toronto: University of Toronto Press, 1975), 185–219, for the importance of Lear's entourage.

6 See the excerpt from *The Countesse of Pembrokes Arcadia* (1590) in Geoffrey Bullough ed., *Narrative and Dramatic Sources of Shakespeare* (London: Routledge and Kegan Paul, 1975), vol. 7, 409.

7 Michel de Montaigne, "Of Husbanding Your Will," *The Complete Essays of Montaigne*, trans. Donald M. Frame (Stanford: Stanford University Press, 1958), 772.

8 Montaigne, "Of Husbanding Your Will," 772.

9 Ibid., 767.

10 Montaigne, "Of Repentance," *The Complete Essays of Montaigne*, 615.

11 In *Shakespeare and Tragedy* (London: Routledge and Kegan Paul, 1981), 14, John Bayley argues, "Shakespearean tragedy never begins at home, as the modern spirit of sincerity feels it must do."

12 The "Knight" (F) is a "Servant" in Q. To conform with practice throughout this study, I have cited the text of *King Lear* in *The Riverside Shakespeare*. To avoid indiscriminate use of a conflated text, I have indicated when a passage derives only from Q in my line references, and have mentioned several passages where differences between the Quarto and Folio texts have significant implications for my argument. Throughout this chapter I have omitted as potentially confusing the brackets which the *Riverside Shakespeare* employs both for passages exclusive to the Quarto text and for terms that have commonly been emended.

13 Stanley Cavell, *Disowning Knowledge in Six Plays of Shakespeare* (Cambridge: Cambridge University Press, 1987), 60–2, 67–8.

14 Compare Leo Salingar's argument in *Dramatic Form in Shakespeare and the Jacobeans* (Cambridge: Cambridge University Press, 1986), 112 on the relevance of Montaigne's essay "Of the Affection of Fathers for Their Children" to Lear's relationships with his daughters.

15 A. C. Bradley, *Shakespearean Tragedy* (1904; reprinted New York: Meridian Books, 1957), 257.

16 Nicole Loraux, *Mothers in Mourning. With the Essay "Of Amnesty and Its Opposite"*, trans. Corinne Pache (Ithaca: Cornell University Press, 1998), 28.

17 See Dorothea Townshend, *Life and Letters of Mr. Endymion Porter: Sometime Gentleman of the Bedchamber to King Charles the First* (London: T. Fisher Unwin, 1897), 35.

18 Townshend, *Life and Letters*, 99–100.

19 Ibid., 228.

20 Ibid., 230.

21 Ibid, 245.

22 This point is considered in chapter 2, pp. 21–2 above. Royal wards certainly objected to their legal status. See for example the angry letter from Oxford to Burghley cited by Joel Hurstfield in *The Queen's Wards: Wardship and Marriage under Elizabeth I* (London: Longmans, Green and Co, 1958), 253.

23 Goneril later claims "You strike my people, / And your disordered rabble make servants of their betters," i.e. of the steward, Osric, and of Goneril herself (1.4.255–6).

24 Salingar, *Dramatic Form in Shakespeare and the Jacobeans*, 96.
25 These are the views respectively of Lynne Magnusson, *Shakespeare and Social Dialogue: Dramatic Language and Elizabethan Letters* (Cambridge: Cambridge University Press, 1999), 150–1, and of R. A. Foakes, *Hamlet versus Lear: Cultural Politics and Shakespeare's Art* (Cambridge: Cambridge University Press, 1993), 205.
26 Mahood, *Bit Parts in Shakespeare's Plays*, 167, defends the propriety of replacing Q "Doctor" with F "Gentleman," a figure who has been Lear's "faithful companion in persecution" and would be familiar to him as he recovers.
27 John Kerrigan, *On Shakespeare and Early Modern Literature: Essays* (Oxford: Oxford University Press, 2001), 21 believes that Cordelia herself replaces the Doctor in the Folio and revives Lear with her kiss: "Cerimon is, as it were, ousted by Marina."
28 *The True Chronicle Historie of King Leir* (1605), reprinted in Bullough, *Narrative and Dramatic Sources of Shakespeare*, vol. 7, 337–402. Subsequent references are in the text.
29 On the Fool's child-like long coat, see R. A. Foakes ed., "Introduction" to *King Lear* (Walton-on Thames: Thomas Nelson and Sons, 1997), 52.
30 For opposed views of the followers as riotous or orderly see Foakes ed., "Introduction" to *King Lear*, 67 and Mahood, *Bit Parts*, 162.
31 Bradley, *Shakespearean Tragedy*, 256.
32 Two additions or variations in the Folio text, 1.4.322–7 and 2.4.141–5, allow the sisters to emphasize the menace posed by Lear's train.
33 See Colie, "Reason and Need," 202.
34 William Basse, *Sword and Buckler: Or, Servingmans Defence* (London, 1602), sig. B2r, stanza 12.
35 See Ann Thompson, *King Lear* (Atlantic Highlands: Humanities Press International, 1988), 58. Compare Cavell, *Disowning Knowledge* 69 on how Lear finally gets, but feels he must hide, what he has wanted "from the beginning," a "partnership in a mystic marriage."
36 See Coppélia Kahn, "The Absent Mother in *King Lear*," in *Rewriting the Renaissance: The Discourses of Sexual Difference in Early Modern Europe*, ed. Margaret W. Ferguson *et al.* (Chicago: University of Chicago Press, 1986), 33–49. Janet Adelman, *Suffocating Mothers: Fantasies of Maternal Origin in Shakespeare's Plays, Hamlet to The Tempest* (London: Routledge, 1992), 298 n. 17, cites many critics who share this view of Lear. See also Marianne Novy, *Love's Argument: Gender Relations in Shakespeare* (Chapel Hill: University of North Carolina Press, 1984), 56.
37 Jay L. Halio ed., "Introduction" to *The Tragedy of King Lear* (Cambridge: Cambridge University Press, 1992), 31, terms Lear's entry "a kind of inverted *pietà*."
38 See F. W. Brownlow's analysis and edition of *A Declaration* in *Shakespeare, Harsnett, and the Devils of Denham* (Newark: University of Delaware Press, 1993), 223, 243. As often noted, Harsnett is a probable source for Tom's remarks on possessed maid-servants (Q 4.1.61–3).

39 Brownlow, *Shakespeare*, 86.

40 Harsnett, *A Declaration*, in Brownlow, *Shakespeare*, 218.

41 Brownlow, *Shakespeare*, 85 n.2, comments that because "mother" is commonly applied to men and "hysterica passio" to women, Lear's use of both is "an intentionally grotesque expression."

42 I have tried to extrapolate from a rich trove of feminist criticism on various birth metaphors to a more functional dramatic emphasis on agency and work.

43 Patricia Parker, *Shakespeare from the Margins: Language, Culture, Context* (Chicago: University of Chicago Press, 1996), 156.

44 See Elizabeth Sacks, *Shakespeare's Images of Pregnancy* (London: Macmillan, 1980), 76–7.

45 See John Kerrigan ed., *Motives of Woe: Shakespeare and 'Female Complaint'. A Critical Anthology* (Oxford: Clarendon Press, 1991), 56. Kerrigan mentions an "affluent" distrust of the begging, suffering, weeping woman and associates the "'diseased' maids" described by astrologer/physician Richard Napier with vagabondage and with the hysteria in *King Lear* (48).

46 Keith Wrightson, *English Society 1580–1680* (New Brunswick: Rutgers University Press, 1982), 86.

47 Martin Ingram, *Church Courts, Sex and Marriage in England 1570–1640* (Cambridge: Cambridge University Press, 1987), 285–6.

48 See Anthony Fletcher, *Gender, Sex and Subordination in England 1500–1800* (New Haven: Yale University Press, 1995), 222, Jack Goody, *Production and Reproduction: A Comparative Study of the Domestic Domain* (Cambridge: Cambridge University Press, 1976), 60, and Richard Adair, *Courtship, Illegitimacy and Marriage in Early Modern England* (Manchester: Manchester University Press, 1996), 9, 88. Mark Thornton Burnett, *Masters and Servants in English Renaissance Drama and Culture: Authority and Obedience* (London: Macmillan, 1997), 122–5, 133–8, focuses on abuses of women servants by masters and gentlemen.

49 See Marjorie K. McIntosh, "Servants and the Household Unit in an Elizabethan English Community," *Journal of Family History* 9 (1984), 20. Although Ilana Krausman Ben-Amos recognizes how fragile the situations of young workers could be in *Adolescence and Youth in Early Modern England* (New Haven: Yale University Press, 1994), 157, she emphasizes protective networks (181) and sexual self-discipline (204).

50 Paul Griffiths, *Youth and Authority: Formative Experiences in England 1560–1640* (Oxford: Clarendon Press, 1996), 271–89 gives the fullest, most detailed account. For other narratives see Fletcher, *Gender, Sex and Subordination in England 1500–1800*, 213–8, Michael MacDonald, *Mystical Bedlam: Madness, Anxiety, and Healing in Seventeenth-Century England* (Cambridge: Cambridge University Press, 1984), 86–7, and G. R. Quaife, *Wanton Wenches and Wayward Wives: Peasants and Illicit Sex in Early Seventeenth Century England* (New Brunswick: Rutgers University Press, 1979), 89–123.

51 See Peter C. Hoffer and N. E. H. Hull, *Murdering Mothers: Infanticide in England and New England, 1558–1803* (New York: New York University Press, 1981), 103, on how a judge freed a master responsible for the death of his child whose servant/mother he had put in a barn; juries often ignored the role of circumstances in causing mothers to injure babies or themselves (107). Compare Fletcher, *Gender, Sex and Subordination in England 1500–1800* 277–9.

52 Laslett, *The World We Have Lost* (London: Methuen, 1965), 157–8.

53 Adrian Poole, *Tragedy: Shakespeare and the Greek Example* (Oxford: Basil Blackwell, 1987), 233. Compare Philippa Berry, *Shakespeare's Feminine Endings: Disfiguring Death in the Tragedies* (Routledge, 1999), 155–9, on Lear's journey through a feminized otherworld. For a reading of Lear as a Proserpina to the Ceres of Cordelia, see Adelman, *Suffocating Mothers*, 306–7 n. 45.

54 Salingar, *Dramatic Form in Shakespeare and the Jacobeans*, 98, comments that Lear curses Cordelia as if he believed her to be a bastard. In *King Leir* he does call her "bastard Impe" (312).

55 Stanley Wells ed., *The History of King Lear* (Oxford: Oxford University Press, 2000), 280–5, reprints the ballad, "A Lamentable Song of the Death of King Lear and his Three Daughters."

56 See W. S. Holdsworth, *A History of English Law* (1903), 7th ed. (London: Methuen and Co. Ltd., 1956), vol. I, 559–63 on the slowly evolving law of the sea. Given the play's many references both to the sea and to outcasts (although "waif" still meant an abandoned piece of property), sea-law seems especially pertinent.

57 In an extant political ballad referred to by Wells ed., *The History of King Lear* (line gloss to scene 13.21), entitled "A songe betwene the Quenes majestie and Englande," the Queen ("bessy") is addressed as "the handmaid of the lord." See H. R. Woudhuysen ed., *The Penguin Book of Renaissance Verse 1500–1659*, selected and intro. by David Norbrook (London: Penguin Books, 1993), 94.

58 Quaife, *Wanton Wenches and Wayward Wives*, 218, 103.

59 Foakes ed., "Introduction" to *King Lear*, 86.

60 See Virginia Woolf, *A Room of One's Own* (London: Hogarth Press, 1929; rpt. London: Grafton Books, 1987), 48. Edgar associates the fiend "Flibbertigibbet" with "mopping and mowing" and the possession of chambermaids and waiting women (Q 4.1.61–3) when he begins to serve his blinded father. For the two references to this phrase in *Between the Acts* see Alice Fox, *Virginia Woolf and the Literature of the English Renaissance* (Oxford: Clarendon Press, 1990), 156.

61 Di Brandt, *Questions i asked my mother* (Winnipeg: Turnstone Press, 1987), 18, 4, 63.

62 Brandt, *Questions i asked my mother*, 13.

63 Jane Smiley, *A Thousand Acres* (New York: Ballantine Books, 1992), 51.

64 Edgar, in Berger's suspicious view, embraces a "victim's role that will enable him to shoot judgments at his father from his place of concealment." See

Making Trifles of Terrors: Redistributing Complicities in Shakespeare
(Stanford: Stanford University Press, 1997), 295.

65 William C. Carroll, *Fat King, Lean Beggar: Representations of Poverty in the Age of Shakespeare* (Ithaca: Cornell University Press, 1996), 197; compare 203.

66 See Stephen Greenblatt, "Shakespeare and the Exorcists," in *Shakespearean Negotiation: The Circulation of Social Energy in Renaissance England* (Oxford: Clarendon Press, 1988), 119. Greenblatt's treatment of Harsnett emphasizes his anti-theatricality but ignores his strident opposition to the coercive behavior of the Jesuit priests.

67 See Lawrence Stone, *The Family, Sex and Marriage in England 1500–1800* (Harmondsworth: Penguin Books, 1984), 80.

68 See the excerpt from the beginning of the 1574 *Mirror* by John Higgins in Bullough, *Narrative and Dramatic Sources of Shakespeare*, vol. 7, 327, line 136.

69 William Warner, *Albion's England*, bk. 3, ch. 4 (1589), excerpted in Bullough, *Narrative and Dramatic Sources of Shakespeare*, vol. 7, 336, line 36; compare line 30.

70 Many readers discover a stern existential outlook in Lear's speech. Raman Selden situates it "beyond the realm of social criticism" altogether, in "King Lear and True Need," *Shakespeare Studies* 19 (1987), 161. My view is closer to those of Colie and Dubrow. See Colie, "The Energies of Endurance: Biblical Echo in *King Lear*," in *Some Facets of King Lear*, 129, where "the thing itself" means "without conventional social and moral protections and disguises" and Dubrow, *Shakespeare and Domestic Loss: Forms of Deprivation, Mourning and Recuperation* (Cambridge: Cambridge University Press, 1999), 104 where "unaccommodated" means "cast out of their dwellings." Dubrow is aware that recovering homes may go with the agency of guarding others (107). Margreta De Grazia, however, restricts the sense of accommodation to superficial clothing in "The Ideology of Superfluous Things: *King Lear* as Period Piece," in *Subject and Object in Renaissance Culture*, ed. Margreta De Grazia *et al.* (Cambridge: Cambridge University Press, 1996), 23.

71 Liebler, *Shakespeare's Festive Tragedy*, 201.

72 See Judith Weil, "'Full Possession': Service and Slavery in *Doctor Faustus*," in *Marlowe, History, and Sexuality: New Critical Essays on Christopher Marlowe*, ed. Paul Whitfield White (New York: AMS Press, 1998), 145–8.

73 Carroll, *Fat King, Lean Beggar*, 7.

74 Caroline F. E. Spurgeon, *Shakespeare's Imagery and What It Tells Us* (1935; rpt. Cambridge: Cambridge University Press, 1966), 338 ff.

75 Keith Thomas, *Religion and the Decline of Magic: Studies in Popular Beliefs in Sixteenth- and Seventeenth-Century England* (Harmondsworth: Penguin Books, 1973), 585–6; compare 589.

76 Thomas, *Religion and the Decline of Magic*, 570.

77 Compare Greenblatt, "Shakespeare and the Exorcists," 119. He distinguishes witchcraft from possession by arguing that witchcraft was a crime controlled

by the courts whereas possession was a charismatic performance rivalling the authority of the church (98–9).

78 Adelman, *Suffocating Mothers*, 110. Diane Purkiss, *The Witch in History: Early Modern and Twentieth-Century Representations* (London: Routledge, 1996), 162, suggests that servants were well positioned to fashion themselves as witches.

79 See Steven Doloff, "'Cry you mercy, I took you for a joint-stool': A Note on King Lear's Trial of the Chairs," *Notes and Queries* 234 (1989), 331–2 and William Gulstad, "Mock-Trial or Witch-Trial In *King Lear*?," *Notes and Queries* 239 (1994), 494–7.

80 Brian P. Levack argues that practices of pricking and looking for numb marks could lead to torture and confession. See "State-Building and Witch-Hunting in Early Modern Europe," in *Witchcraft in Early Modern Europe: Studies in Culture and Belief*, ed. Jonathan Barry *et al.* (Cambridge: Cambridge University Press, 1996), 106–7. George W. Keeton, *Shakespeare and His Legal Problems* (London: A. and C. Black, 1930), 198, mentions two men imprisoned as late as 1895 for trying to exorcise the wife of one by holding her over a fire and "searing her with a red-hot poker."

81 In a performance commentary, J. S. Bratton ed., *Plays in Performance: King Lear* (Bristol: Bristol Classical Press, 1987), 151 points out that "Irving's Edgar delivered this as an aside, referring, therefore, to Lear rather than an invisible devil." On the power of evil eye beliefs in Shakespeare's society and in his plays, see Linda Woodbridge, *The Scythe of Saturn: Shakespeare and Magical Thinking* (Urbana: University of Illinois Press, 1994), 23–8; witches "were often credited with the evil eye" (222).

FREEDOM, SERVICE AND SLAVERY IN *MACBETH*

1 Barbara Everett, *Young Hamlet: Essays on Shakespeare's Tragedies* (Oxford: Clarendon Press, 1989), 88.

2 See William Arrowsmith, "Introduction to *Hecuba*," in *Euripides III*, ed. David Grene and Richmond Lattimore (Chicago: University of Chicago Press, 1960), 5.

3 Nicole Loraux, *Tragic Ways of Killing a Woman*, trans. Anthony Forster (Cambridge, Mass.: Harvard University Press, 1987), 62.

4 Nicholas Brooke ed., "Introduction" to *Macbeth* (Oxford: Oxford University Press, 1990), 53.

5 See Michael Hawkins, "History, Politics and Macbeth," in *Focus on Macbeth*, ed. John Russell Brown (London: Routledge and Kegan Paul, 1982), 160–1. The four types are pre-feudal kinship; a feudal hierarchy with ties to outsiders; a system which enhances the king's position; and a system wherein other institutions begin to limit royal power.

6 See Alan Sinfield, *Faultlines: Cultural Materialism and the Politics of Dissident Reading* (Oxford: Clarendon Press, 1992), 100–5.

7 David Norbrook, "*Macbeth* and the Politics of Historiography," in *Politics of Discourse*, ed. Kevin Sharpe and Steven N. Zwicker (Berkeley: University of California Press, 1987), 78–116.
8 This is one conclusion of Orlando Patterson's *Slavery and Social Death: A Comparative Study* (Cambridge, Mass.: Harvard University Press, 1982); it becomes his central argument in *Freedom* vol. 1, *Freedom in the Making of Western Culture* (London: Tauris and Co., 1991) where he explores the development of freedom as a "chord" of "personal, sovereignal, and civic" values (3). These shifting values derive from slavery and can be "either refined upward into a civilized ideal or backward to the primal domination of slavery" (365).
9 See Étienne de La Boétie, *The Politics of Obedience: The Discourse of Voluntary Servitude* (1548), intro. Murray N. Rothbard, trans. Harry Kurz (New York: Free Life Editions, 1975), 53.
10 Rothbard, "Introduction" to *The Politics of Obedience*, 12. For the Levellers see David Wootton, "Leveller Democracy and the Puritan Revolution," in *The Cambridge History of Political Thought 1450–1700*, ed. J. H. Burns (Cambridge: Cambridge University Press, 1991), 412–42. On pre-Civil war explorations of republican principles see Blair Worden, "English Republicanism," in *The Cambridge History of Political Thought 1450–1700*, 445–7.
11 La Boétie, *The Politics of Obedience: The Discourse of Voluntary Servitude*, 56, 59, 61.
12 La Boétie, *The Politics of Obedience: The Discourse of Voluntary Servitude*, 78–9, 85–6. "Dregs" corresponds closely to the French original ("tout le mauvais, toute la lie du royaume"). See La Boétie, *Discours de la Servitude Volontaire* (1548) (Paris: Editions Bossard, 1922), 91.
13 La Boétie, *The Politics of Obedience: The Discourse of Voluntary Servitude*, 80.
14 Ibid., 82.
15 According to Rebecca W. Bushnell, he loses the sexual passion more typical of tyrants. See *Tragedies of Tyrants: Political Thought and Theater in the English Renaissance* (Ithaca: Cornell University Press, 1990), 130. Worden, "English Republicanism", 448 observes that English writers "offered first and foremost a criticism of tyrants rather than of kings."
16 Quentin Skinner, *Liberty Before Liberalism* (Cambridge: Cambridge University Press, 1998), 41.
17 Skinner, *Liberty Before Liberalism*, 42–7, 61–2, 88–9.
18 Ibid., 84; his "Preface" ix–x, cites John Stuart Mill as an example of how the neo-Roman trend has survived.
19 In the inaugural Isaiah Berlin Lecture, "A Third Concept of Liberty," Skinner indicates that the view shared by Thomas Hobbes and Berlin (people are free to do what a state does not prevent) can be used to reduce rights. See *London Review of Books* 24: 7 (04/2002), 16–18. Concluding *Liberty Before Liberalism*, he warns against agents of the state "dressed in a little brief authority" (119).
20 See for example Martin Dzelzainis, "Milton's Politics," in *The Cambridge Companion to Milton*, 2nd edn., ed. Dennis Danielson (Cambridge:

Cambridge University Press, 1999), 77, pointing out that Milton "drew a clear line between due process and discretionary power."

21 For examples of how traditional liberties, such as the use of common ground, lost out to legal rights, see Christopher Hill, *Liberty Against the Law: Some Seventeenth-Century Controversies* (London: Penguin Books, 1996). The radical reformer Gerrard Winstanley, who wanted to guarantee universal freedom through shared possession of the soil and the abolition of wages, also believed in restricting the vote to right-thinking men over twenty and insisted that masters must have "served seven years." Those who abused their freedom would be temporarily enslaved. See "The Law of Freedom in a Platform" in *The Law of Freedom and Other Writings*, ed. and intro. Christopher Hill (Harmondsworth: Penguin Books, 1973), 295, 385, 389, 386–7.

22 See Robert J. Steinfeld, *The Invention of Free Labor: The Employment Relation in English and American Law and Culture, 1350–1870* (Chapel Hill: The University of North Carolina Press, 1991), 101.

23 Norbrook, "*Macbeth* and the Politics of Historiography," 115.

24 Ibid., 114.

25 Patterson, *Slavery and Social Death*, 340.

26 See Stephen Orgel ed., *The Tempest* (Oxford: Oxford University Press, 1987), note on "Weak masters," 5.1.41.

27 See Sarah C. Maza, *Servants and Masters in Eighteenth-Century France: The Uses of Loyalty* (Princeton: Princeton University Press, 1983), 134–5. Describing his first encounter with King James, Sir John Harrington recalls in *Nugae Antiquae*, "I made courtesie hereat, and withdrewe downe the passage, and out at the gate, amidst the manie varlets and lordlie servantes who stoode arounde." Harrington is cited by G. B. Harrison ed., "Introduction" to *King James the First: Daemonologie (1597), Newes From Scotland (1591)* (Edinburgh: Edinburgh University Press, 1966), viii.

28 Anon., *The English Courtier and the Countrey-gentleman* (1586), in *Inedited Tracts: Illustrating the Manners, Opinions, and Occupations of Englishmen During the Sixteenth and Seventeenth Centuries*, ed. W. Hazlitt (London: Roxburgh Library, 1868; rpt. New York: Burt Franklin, 1964), 40–1. Compare Felicity Heal, *Hospitality in Early Modern England* (Oxford: Clarendon Press, 1990), 95, showing that conventional attacks on crowds of idle drones echo Sir Thomas More's *Utopia*.

29 Edward Chamberlayne, *Angliae Notitia: Or the Present State of England* (London: 1669), 435; compare 462–3 referring to apprentices as "'Slaves' only for a time and by Covenant" but forced to "carry the Marks of pure Villans or Bondslaves." Ann Rosalind Jones and Peter Stallybrass, *Renaissance Clothing and the Materials of Memory* (Cambridge: Cambridge University Press, 2000), believe that livery clothing "inscribed obligations and indebtedness upon the body" (20).

30 Paul Van Brunt Jones, *The Household of a Tudor Nobleman*, in *University of Illinois Studies in the Social Sciences* (Urbana: University of Illinois Press,

1917), vol. 6, 62, suggests that masters furnished livery cloth both for pride and for self-defense. Richard Brathwaite suggests that if all wear livery in a household it will be easier to spy people running away with left-over meat, thereby depriving the poor. See *Some Rules and Orders for the Government of the House of an Earle* (1630), in *Miscellanea Antiqua Anglicana* (London: T. Bensley and Son, 1816), 24.

31 William Basse, *Sword and Buckler: Or, Servingmans Defence* (London, 1602), sig. Div–D2r, stanza 59.

32 The oft-cited biblical texts warning against "eyeservice" are Ephesians 6: 6 and Colossians 3: 22.

33 William Gouge, *Of Domesticall Duties: Eight Treatises* (London, 1622), 600–1; compare 628 on the need to keep secrets. "Covering" probably connotes protection in this context, as it does when the husband "veils" his wife's eyes (408).

34 Basse, *Sword and Buckler*, sig. Bir, stanzas 6–7.

35 Matthew Griffith, *Bethel, or a Forme for Families* (London, 1634), 387–8.

36 See Keith Thomas, *Religion and the Decline of Magic: Studies in Popular Beliefs in Sixteenth- and Seventeenth-Century England* (Harmondsworth: Penguin Books, 1973), 645 for recourse to witchcraft accusations as excuses for failures at work. Emmanuel Le Roy Ladurie, *Jasmine's Witch*, trans. Brian Pearce (Aldershot: Scolar Press, 1987), 64, 39 considers seemingly sincere complaints relating to what he terms "the onslaught on the arm," so essential in producing rural wealth.

37 On how ordinary people used witchcraft to explain a range of afflictions see Barbara Rosen, *Witchcraft in England, 1558–1618* (Amherst: University of Massachusetts Press, 1991), 43.

38 Compare Adrian Poole, *Tragedy: Shakespeare and the Greek Example* (Oxford: Basil Blackwell, 1987), 41 on how Macbeth "wants to execute thought."

39 It is worth noting that the Romans cited by Skinner in *Liberty Before Liberalism*, 42–5 (Sallust, Seneca, Tacitus, and Livy) are not challenging the institution of chattel slavery. See Peter Garnsey, *Ideas of Slavery from Aristotle to Augustine* (Cambridge: Cambridge University Press, 1996), 128–52; on Seneca as a possible exception, see 131, 144–5.

40 See John Turner, "Macbeth," in *Shakespeare: The Play of History*, ed. Graham Holderness *et al.* (Iowa City: University of Iowa Press, 1988), 141. Terry Eagleton's attempt in *William Shakespeare* (Oxford: Basil Blackwell, 1986) to champion the sisters as subversive "heroines" (2) and "radical separatists" (3) is unconvincing.

41 Gary Wills, *Witches and Jesuits: Shakespeare's Macbeth* (Oxford: Oxford University Press, 1995), 38–9, suggests that what they do need is body parts from battlefields in order to perform necromancy.

42 Paul A. Jorgensen, *Our Naked Frailties: Sensational Art and Meaning in 'Macbeth'* (Berkeley: University of California Press, 1971), 2, 23–4.

43 Jorgensen, *Our Naked Frailties*, 140, 148.

44 See especially the essays in Part I, "The Rhetoric of Politeness" by Lynne Magnusson, *Shakespeare and Social Dialogue: Dramatic Language and Elizabethan Letters* (Cambridge: Cambridge University Press, 1999).

45 Deborah Willis, *Malevolent Nurture: Witch-hunting and Maternal Power in Early Modern England* (Ithaca: Cornell University Press, 1995), 222–3.

46 See Richard Strier, "Faithful Servants: Shakespeare's Praise of Disobedience," in *The Historical Renaissance: New Essays on Tudor and Stuart Literature and Culture*, ed. Heather Dubrow and Richard Strier (Chicago: University of Chicago Press, 1988), 116, citing Martin Luther to explain the dynamics of loyalty to villains.

47 John Bayley, *Shakespeare and Tragedy* (London: Routledge and Kegan Paul, 1981), 70.

48 She treats him "at times as pure instrument" writes Cleanth Brooks, "The Naked Babe and the Cloak of Manliness," in *The Well Wrought Urn: Studies in the Structure of Poetry* (New York: Reynal and Hitchcock, 1947), 40.

49 See the excerpt from William Stewart in Kenneth Muir ed., *Macbeth* (Cambridge, Mass.: Harvard University Press, 1957), Appendix B, 191–2.

50 Stewart, excerpt in Muir ed., *Macbeth*, 194.

51 Wills, *Witches and Jesuits*, 87–8; compare 60, 189 n. 16, 192 n. 33.

52 Brooks, "The Naked Babe and the Cloak of Manliness," 37, 42.

53 Willis, *Malevolent Nurture*, 226.

54 John Boswell, *The Kindness of Strangers: The Abandonment of Children in Western Europe from Late Antiquity to the Renaissance* (New York: Pantheon Books, 1988), 27.

55 According to Kate Mertes, *The English Noble Household 1250–1600: Good Governance and Politic Rule* (Oxford: Basil Blackwell, 1988), 30, the position of "groom" or *garcio* referred to low status, not to work with horses.

56 Commentary note in Brooke's edition of *Macbeth*; "breech'd" could refer to a bloody flogging as well as to a boy's transition from skirts to breeches.

57 In this connection it is notable that E. A. J. Honigmann, *Shakespeare: Seven Tragedies: The Dramatist's Manipulation of Response* (London: Macmillan, 1976), 133 (stressing Macbeth's self-alienation as a criminal) terms him a "sorcerer's apprentice"!

58 A. R. Braunmuller ed., *Macbeth* (Cambridge: Cambridge University Press, 1997), notes a connection between Macbeth's argument to Banquo's assassins here and his later assault on Macduff.

59 See G. K. Hunter ed., "Introduction" to *Macbeth* (Harmondsworth: Penguin Books, 1967), 21. He supports his argument for this "archaic" sense by citing the memorial account of a lost interlude, "The Cradle of Security," in which a spritually lazy monarch puts off preparing to meet his maker until it is too late (21–3).

60 Bernice W. Kliman, *Shakespeare in Performance: Macbeth* (Manchester: Manchester University Press, 1992), 60–1, 83–4 refers to productions which treat Seyton as a more sinister figure.

61 La Boétie, *The Politics of Obedience: The Discourse of Voluntary Servitude*, 83.

Bibliography

Adair, Richard, *Courtship, Illegitimacy and Marriage in Early Modern England,* Manchester, 1996.

Adelman, Janet, *The Common Liar: An Essay on Antony and Cleopatra,* New Haven, 1973.

Suffocating Mothers: Fantasies of Maternal Origin in Shakespeare's Plays, Hamlet to The Tempest, London, 1992.

Aers, David, *Community, Gender, and Individual Identity: English Writing 1360–1430,* London, 1988.

Amussen, Susan Dwyer, *An Ordered Society: Gender and Class in Early Modern England,* Oxford, 1988.

Anderson, Michael, *Approaches to the History of the Western Family, 1500–1914,* London, 1980.

Anon., *A Breviate Touching the Order and Governmente of a Nobleman's House* (1605), ed. Joseph Banks, *Archaeologia* 13 (1800), 315–89.

The English Courtier and the Countrey-gentleman (1586), in *Inedited Tracts: Illustrating the Manners, Opinions, and Occupations of Englishmen During the Sixteenth and Seventeenth Centuries,* ed. W. Hazlitt, London, 1868; rpt. New York, 1964, 1–93.

The Famous Victories of Henry the Fifth (1598), in *Narrative and Dramatic Sources of Shakespeare,* ed. Geoffrey Bullough, London, 1962, vol. 4.

The Taming of A Shrew (1594), in *Narrative and Dramatic Sources of Shakespeare,* ed. Geoffrey Bullough, London, 1957, vol. 1.

The Tragedy of Master Arden of Faversham (1592), ed. M. L. Wine, London, 1973.

The True Chronicle Historie of King Leir (1605), in *Narrative and Dramatic Sources of Shakespeare,* ed. Geoffrey Bullough, London, 1975, vol. 7.

Archer, Ian W., *The Pursuit of Stability: Social Relations in Elizabethan London,* Cambridge, 1991.

Aristotle, *Aristotle's Poetics: Translation and Analysis,* trans. Kenneth A. Telford, Chicago, 1961.

Arrowsmith, William, "Introduction to *Hecuba,*" *Euripides III,* ed. David Grene and Richmond Lattimore, Chicago, 1960, 2–7.

Asp, Carolyn, "Shakespeare's Paulina and the *Consolatio* Tradition," *Shakespeare Studies* 11 (1978), 145–58

Bacon, Francis, "Of Friendship" (1625), in *Francis Bacon: A Selection of his Works*, ed. Sidney Warhaft, Toronto, 1965, 112–19.

Barber, C. L. and Richard P. Wheeler, *The Whole Journey: Shakespeare's Power of Development*, Berkeley, 1986.

Barish, Jonas A. and Marshall Waingrow, "'Service' in *King Lear*," *Shakespeare Quarterly* 9 (1958), 347–55.

Barnett, Richard C, *Place, Profit, and Power: A Study of the Servants of William Cecil, Elizabethan Statesman*, Chapel Hill, 1969.

Barry, Jonathan, "Introduction: Keith Thomas and the Problem of Witchcraft," in *Witchcraft in Early Modern Europe: Studies in Culture and Belief*, ed. Jonathan Barry *et al.*, Cambridge, 1996, 1–45.

Bartels, Emily C., "Making More of the Moor: Aaron, Othello, and Renaissance Refashionings of Race," *Shakespeare Quarterly* 41 (1990), 433–54.

Barthelemy, Anthony Gerard, *Black Face Maligned Race: The Representation of Blacks in English Drama from Shakespeare to Southerne*, Baton Rouge, 1987.

Barton, Anne, "Livy, Machiavelli and Shakespeare's *Coriolanus*" (1985), in *Essays, Mainly Shakespearean*, Cambridge, 1994, 136–60.

The Names of Comedy, Toronto, 1990.

Basse, William, *Sword and Buckler: Or, Servingmans Defence*, London, 1602.

Batho, G. R., ed., *The Household Papers of Henry Percy Ninth Earl of Northumberland (1564–1632)*, Camden Society, 3rd series, vol. 93, London, 1962.

Bayley, John, *Shakespeare and Tragedy*, London, 1981.

Bean, John C., "Comic Structure and the Humanizing of Kate in *The Taming of the Shrew*," in *The Woman's Part: Feminist Criticism of Shakespeare*, ed. Carolyn Ruth Swift Lenz *et al.*, Urbana, 1980, 65–78.

Beier, A. L., *Masterless Men: The Vagrancy Problem in England, 1560–1640*, New York, 1985.

Belsey, Catherine, *The Subject of Tragedy: Identity and Difference in Renaissance Drama*, London, 1985.

Ben-Amos, Ilana Krausman, *Adolescence and Youth in Early Modern England*, New Haven, 1994.

Berger, Jr., Harry, *Making Trifles of Terrors: Redistributing Complicities in Shakespeare*, Stanford, 1997.

Berry, Edward, *Shakespeare's Comic Rites*, Cambridge, 1984.

Berry, Philippa, *Shakespeare's Feminine Endings: Disfiguring Death in the Tragedies*, London, 1999.

Bevington, David, *Action is Eloquence: Shakespeare's Language of Gesture*, Cambridge, Mass., 1984.

Blake, Ann, "Children and Suffering in Shakespeare's Plays," *The Yearbook of English Studies* 23 (1993), 293–304.

Bloch, Marc, *Feudal Society*, trans. L. A. Manyon, Chicago, 1961, vol. I.

Bodin, Jean, *Six Books of the Commonwealth* (1576), abridged and trans. M. J. Tooley, Oxford, 1955.

Boswell, John, *The Kindness of Strangers: The Abandonment of Children in Western Europe from Late Antiquity to the Renaissance*, New York, 1988.

Boynton, Lindsay, *The Elizabethan Militia 1558–1638*, London, 1967.

Braden, Gordon, *Renaissance Tragedy: Anger's Privilege*, New Haven, 1985.

Bradley, A. C. *Shakespearean Tragedy* (1904), New York, rpt. 1957.

Brain, Robert, *Friends and Lovers*, New York, 1976.

Brandt, Di, *Questions i asked my mother*, Winnipeg, 1987.

Brathwaite, Richard, *Some Rules and Orders for the Government of the House of an Earle* (1630), in *Miscellanea Antiqua Anglicana*, London, 1821, 1–46.

Braunmuller, A. R., "'Second Means': Agent and Accessory in Elizabethan Drama," in *The Elizabethan Theatre XI*, ed. A. L. Magnusson and C. E. Magee, Port Credit, 1990, 177–203.

Bray, Alan, "Homosexuality and the Signs of Male Friendship in Elizabethan England," *History Workshop Journal* 29 (1990), 1–19.

Bristol, Michael D, *Carnival and Theater: Plebeian Culture and the Structure of Authority in Renaissance England*, London, 1985.

Brooks, Cleanth, "The Naked Babe and the Cloak of Manliness," in *The Well Wrought Urn: Studies in the Structure of Poetry*, New York, 1947, 21–47.

Brownlow, F. W., *Shakespeare, Harsnett, and the Devils of Denham*, Newark, 1993.

Bruto, Giovanni M., *The Necessarie, Fit and Convenient Education of a Yong Gentlewoman*, trans. W. P., London, 1958, rpt. Amsterdam, 1969.

Bullough, Geoffrey ed., *Narrative and Dramatic Sources of Shakespeare*, London, 1975, vol. 7.

Bulman, James C., *The Heroic Idiom of Shakespearean Tragedy*, Newark, 1985.

Burghley, William Cecil, Lord, "Certain Precepts for the Well Ordering of a Man's Life" (1584), in *Advice to a Son: Precepts of Lord Burghley, Sir Walter Raleigh, and Francis Osborne*, ed. Louis B. Wright, Ithaca, 1962, 9–13.

Burnett, Mark Thornton, *Masters and Servants in English Renaissance Drama and Culture: Authority and Obedience*, London, 1997.

    "'The Trusty Servant': A Sixteenth-Century English Emblem," *Emblematica* 6 (1992), 237–53.

Bushnell, Rebecca W., *Tragedies of Tyrants: Political Thought and Theater in the English Renaissance*, Ithaca: Cornell, 1990.

Cahn, Susan, *Industry of Devotion: The Transformation of Women's Work in England 1500–1660*, New York, 1987.

Calderwood, James L., *To Be And Not To Be: Negation and Metadrama in Hamlet*, New York, 1983.

Cantor, Paul A., *Shakespeare's Rome: Republic and Empire*, Ithaca, 1976.

Carroll, William C., *Fat King, Lean Beggar: Representations of Poverty in the Age of Shakespeare*, Ithaca, 1996.

Carter, Thomas, *Carters Christian Commonwealth: Domesticall Dutyes Deciphered*, London, 1627.

Castiglione, Baldesar, *The Book of the Courtier* (1528), trans. Charles S. Singleton, Garden City, 1959.

Cavell, Stanley, *Disowning Knowledge in Six Plays of Shakespeare*, Cambridge, 1987.

Chamberlayne, Edward, *Angliae Notitia: Or the Present State of England*, London, 1669.

Chaucer, Geoffrey, *The Complete Poetry and Prose of Geoffrey Chaucer*, ed. John H. Fisher, New York, 1977.

Cheyney, E. P., "The Disappearance of English Serfdom," *English Historical Review* 15 (1900), 20–37.

Cicero, Marcus Tullius, *De Amicitia*, trans. William Armistead Falconer, Cambridge, Mass., 1963.

Clark, Peter, *English Provincial Society from the Reformation to the Revolution: Religion, Politics and Society in Kent 1500–1640*, Hassocks, 1977.

Cleaver, Robert, *A Godly Form of Householde Government*, London, 1598.

Clifford, Anne, *The Diaries of Lady Anne Clifford* (1603–76), ed. D. J. H. Clifford, Wolfeboro Falls, NH, 1990.

Coleman, D. C., "Labour in the English Economy of the Seventeenth Century," *Economic History Review* ser. 2, 8 (1956), 280–95.

Coleridge, Samuel Taylor, *Coleridge's Writings on Shakespeare*, ed. Terence Hawkes, New York, 1959.

Colie, Rosalie L., "The Energies of Endurance: Biblical Echo in *King Lear*," in *Some Facets of King Lear: Essays in Prismatic Criticism*, ed. Rosalie L. Colie and F. T. Flahiff, Toronto, 1974, 117–44.

"Reason and Need: *King Lear* and the 'Crisis' of the Aristocracy," in *Some Facets of King Lear: Essays in Prismatic Criticism*, ed. Rosalie L. Colie and F. T. Flahiff, Toronto, 1975, 185–219.

Cook, Ann Jennalie, *Making a Match: Courtship in Shakespeare and His Society*, Princeton, 1991.

Cooper, J. P., "Retainers in Tudor England," in J. P. Cooper, *Land, Men and Beliefs: Studies in Early-Modern History*, ed. G. E. Aylmer and J. S. Morrill, London: Hambledon Press, 1983, 78–96.

Cousin, Gilbert, *Of the Office of Servauntes, A Boke Made in Latine by One Gylbertus Cognatus and Newely Englysed* (1534), trans. T. Chaloner, London, 1543.

Cressy, David, "Foucault, Stone, Shakespeare and Social History," *English Literary Renaissance* 21 (1991), 121–33.

"Kinship and Kin Interaction in Early Modern England," *Past and Present* 113 (1986), 38–69.

Crowley, Robert, *The Voyce of the Laste Trumpet, Blowen bi the Seventh Angel*, London, 1549.

Darell, Walter, "A Pretie and Shorte Discourse of the Duetie of a Servingman" (1578), rpt. in *"A Conduct Book for Malvolio,"* ed. Louis B. Wright, *Studies in Philology* 31 (1934), 115–32.

Davidoff, Leonore, "Mastered for Life: Servant and Wife in Victorian and Edwardian England," *Journal of Social History* 7 (1974), 406–28.

Davis, David Brion, *The Problem of Slavery in Western Culture*, Ithaca, 1966.

Dawson, Anthony B., "Making a Difference? Shakespeare, Feminism, Men," *English Studies in Canada* 15 (1989), 427–40.

De Grazia, Margreta, "The Ideology of Superfluous Things: *King Lear* as Period Piece," in *Subject and Object in Renaissance Culture*, ed. Margreta De Grazia *et al.*, Cambridge, 1996, 17–42.

"The Scandal of Shakespeare's Sonnets," *Shakespeare Survey* 46 (1994), 35–49.

Dekker, Thomas, with Henry Chettle and William Haughton, *Patient Grissil* (1603), in *The Dramatic Works of Thomas Dekker*, ed. Fredson Bowers, Cambridge, 1953, vol. 1.

Della Casa, Giovanni, *The Arts of Grandeur and Submission: Or a Discourse Concerning the Behaviour of Great Men towards Their Inferiours; and of Inferiour Personages towards Men of Greater Quality*, trans. Henry Stubbe, 2nd ed., London, 1670.

Deloney, Thomas, *Thomas of Reading. Or Six Worthy Yeomen of the West* (1612), Menston, 1969.

Derby, Edward and Henry, *The Household Regulations and Expenses of Edward and Henry, Third and Fourth Earls of Derby* (1561, 1568, 1586–90), ed. F. R. Raines, Manchester, 1853.

Desainliens, Claude, *The French Schoole-Maister* (1573), in *English Linguistics 1500–1800* (no. 315), ed. R. C. Alston, Menston, 1972.

D'Ewes, Simonds, *The Autobiography and Correspondance of Sir Simonds D'Ewes*, ed. James Orchard Halliwell, London, 1845.

DiGangi, Mario, *The Homoerotics of Early Modern Drama*, Cambridge, 1997.

Dillingham, Francis, *Christian Oeconomy or Houshold Government*, London, 1609.

Dolan, Frances E., *Dangerous Familiars: Representations of Domestic Crime in England 1550–1700*, Ithaca, 1994.

Doloff, Steven, "'Cry you mercy, I took you for a joint-stool': A Note on King Lear's Trial of the Chairs," *Notes and Queries* 234 (1989), 331–2.

Dubrow, Heather, *Shakespeare and Domestic Loss: Forms of Deprivation, Mourning and Recuperation*, Cambridge, 1999.

Dzelzainis, Martin, "Milton's Politics," in *The Cambridge Companion to Milton*, 2nd edn., ed. Dennis Danielson, Cambridge, 1999, 70–83.

Eagleton, Terry, *William Shakespeare*, Oxford, 1986.

Eisenstadt, S. N. and L. Roniger, *Patrons, Clients and Friends: Interpersonal Relations and the Structure of Trust in Society*, Cambridge, 1984.

Elliott, Vivian Brodsky, "Single Women in the London Marriage Market: Age, Status and Mobility, 1598–1619," in *Marriage and Society: Studies in the Social History of Marriage*, ed. R. B. Outhwaite, New York, 1981, 81–101.

Ellis, David, "Finding a Part for Parolles," *Essays in Criticism* 39 (1989), 289–304.

Erickson, Amy Louise, *Women and Property in Early Modern England*, London, 1993.

Erickson, Peter, *Patriarchal Structures in Shakespeare's Drama*, Berkeley, 1985.

Everett, Barbara, *Young Hamlet: Essays on Shakespeare's Tragedies*, Oxford, 1989.
Ezell, Margaret J. M., *The Patriarch's Wife: Literary Evidence and the History of the Family*, Chapel Hill, 1987.
Ferguson, Margaret W., "*Hamlet*: Letters and Spirits," in *Shakespeare and the Question of Theory*, ed. Patricia Parker and Geoffrey Hartman, London, 1985, 292–309.
Finch, Mary E., *The Wealth of Five Northamptonshire Families 1540–1640*, Oxford, 1956.
Finley, Moses I., *Ancient Slavery and Modern Ideology*, Harmondsworth, 1980.
Fit John, J., *A Diamonde Most Precious, Worthy to be Marked: Instructing All Maysters and Servauntes, how They Ought to Lead Their Lyves*, London, 1577.
Flandrin, Jean-Louis, *Families in Former Times: Kinship, Household and Sexuality*, Cambridge 1979.
Fleetwood, William, *The Relative Duties of Parents and Children, Husbands and Wives, Masters and Servants*, 3rd edn., London, 1722.
Fletcher, Anthony, *Gender, Sex and Subordination in England 1500–1800*, New Haven, 1995.
Fletcher, John, *The Woman's Prize or the Tamer Tam'd* (1611), in *The Dramatic Works in the Beaumont and Fletcher Canon*, ed. Fredson Bowers, Cambridge, 1979, vol. 4.
Flint, M. K. and E. J. Dobson, "Weak Masters," *Review of English Studies* 10 (1959), 58–60.
Foakes, R. A., *Hamlet versus Lear: Cultural Politics and Shakespeare's Art*, Cambridge, 1993.
Fossett, Thomas, *The Servants Dutie or the Calling and Condition of Servants*, London 1613.
Fox, Alice, *Virginia Woolf and the Literature of the English Renaissance*, Oxford, 1990.
Friedman, Alice T., *House and Household in Elizabethan England: Wollaton Hall and the Willoughby Family*, Chicago, 1989.
Fryer, Peter, *Staying Power: The History of Black People in Britain*, London, 1985.
Fuss, Diana, *Essentially Speaking: Feminism, Nature and Difference*, New York, 1989.
Garnsey, Peter, *Ideas of Slavery from Aristotle to Augustine*, Cambridge, 1996.
Gascoigne, George, *Supposes* (1566), in *Narrative and Dramatic Sources of Shakespeare*, ed. Geoffrey Bullough, London, 1957, vol. 1.
Gataker, Thomas, *Marriage Duties Briefly Couched Togither*, London, 1620.
Gerard, John, *The Autobiography of an Elizabethan*, trans. Philip Caraman, London, 1951.
Gieskes, Edward, "'He is but a bastard to the time': Status and Service in *The Troublesome Reign of John* and Shakespeare's *King John*," *English Literary History* 65 (1998), 779–98.
Girouard, Mark, *Life in the English Country House: A Social and Architectural History*, New Haven 1978.
Goldhill, Simon, *Reading Greek Tragedy*, Cambridge, 1986.

Goldman, Michael, "Characterizing Coriolanus," *Shakespeare Survey* 34 (1981), 73–84.

Goodich, Michael, "*Ancilla Dei*: The Servant as Saint in the Late Middle Ages," in *Women of the Medieval World: Essays in Honor of John H. Mundy*, ed. Julius Kirshner and Suzanne F. Wemple, Oxford, 1985, 119–36.

Goody, Jack, *Production and Reproduction: A Comparative Study of the Domestic Domain*, Cambridge, 1976.

Gouge, William, *Of Domesticall Duties: Eight Treatises*, London, 1622.

Gough, Richard, *Human Nature Displayed in the History of Myddle* (1701), intro. W. G. Hoskins, Fontwell, 1968.

Gowing, Laura, *Domestic Dangers: Women, Words, and Sex in Early Modern London*, Oxford, 1996.

Greenblatt, Stephen, "Shakespeare and the Exorcists," in *Shakespearean Negotiation: The Circulation of Social Energy in Renaissance England*, Oxford, 1988, 94–128.

Griffith, Matthew, *Bethel, or A Forme for Families*, London, 1634.

Griffiths, Paul, *Youth and Authority: Formative Experiences in England 1560–1640*, Oxford, 1996.

Guazzo, M. Steeven, *The Civile Conversation of M. Steeven Guazzo*, trans. George Pettie (1581) and Barth. Young (1586), ed. Charles Whibley, New York, 1925, vols. 1–2.

Gulstad, William, "Mock-Trial or Witch-Trial in *King Lear*?," *Notes and Queries* 239 (1994), 494–7.

Hajnal, John, "Two Kinds of Pre-Industrial Household Formation System," in *Family Forms in Historic Europe*, ed. Richard Wall *et al.*, Cambridge, 1983, 65–104.

Hall, Joseph, *Salomons Divine Arts of Ethickes, Politickes, Oeconomicks*, London, 1609.

Hanawalt, Barbara A., *The Ties that Bind: Peasant Families in Medieval England*, New York, 1986.

Harrison, Robert Pogue, *Forests: The Shadow of Civilization*, Chicago, 1992.

Harrison, William, *The Description of England* (1587), ed. George Edelen, Ithaca, 1968.

Hatton, Christopher, *Memoirs of the Life and Times of Sir Christopher Hatton K. G.*, ed. Sir Harris Nicolas, London, 1847.

Hawkins, Michael, "History, Politics and *Macbeth*," in *Focus on Macbeth*, ed. John Russell Brown, London, 1982, 155–88.

Heal, Felicity, *Hospitality in Early Modern England*, Oxford, 1990.

Hecht, J. Jean, *The Domestic Servant Class in Eighteenth-Century England*, London, 1956.

Hill, Christopher, *Liberty against the Law: Some Seventeenth-Century Controversies*, London, 1996.

"Pottage for Freeborn Englishmen: Attitudes to Wage Labour in the Sixteenth and Seventeenth Centuries," in *Change and Continuity in Seventeenth Century England*, London, 1974, 219–38.

"The Spiritualization of the Household," in *Society and Puritanism in Pre-Revolutionary England*, London, 1964, 443–81.

Hodgdon, Barbara, *The End Crowns All: Closure and Contradiction in Shakespeare's History*, Princeton, 1991.

Hodgkin, Katharine, "Thomas Whythorne and the Problems of Mastery," *History Workshop Journal* 29 (1990), 20–41.

Hoffer, Peter C. and N. E. H. Hull, *Murdering Mothers: Infanticide in England and New England, 1558–1803*, New York, 1981.

Holderness, Graham, *Shakespeare's History*, New York, 1985.

Holdsworth, W. S., *A History of English Law* (1903), London, 1956, vol. 1.

Holland, Peter, "Film Editing," in *Shakespeare Performed: Essays in Honor of R. A. Foakes*, ed. Grace Ioppolo, Newark, 2000, 273–98.

Honigmann, E. A. J., *Shakespeare: Seven Tragedies. The Dramatist's Manipulation of Response*, London, 1976.

Hoskyns, John, *The Life, Letters, and Writings of John Hoskyns 1566–1638*, ed. Louise Brown Osborn, New Haven, 1937.

Houlbrooke, Ralph A., *The English Family 1450–1700*, London, 1984.

   ed., *English Family Life 1576–1716: An Anthology from Diaries*, Oxford, 1988.

Howell, Thomas, *Howell's Devises* (1581), intro. Walter Raleigh, Oxford, 1906.

Humfrey, Laurence, *The Nobles or of Nobilitye*, London, 1563.

Hunt, Maurice, *Shakespeare's Labored Art: Stir, Work, and the Late Plays*, New York, 1995.

Hunter, G. K., "Flatcaps and Bluecoats: Visual Signals on the Elizabethan Stage," *Essays and Studies* ns. 33 (1980), 16–47.

Hurstfield, Joel, *The Queen's Wards: Wardship and Marriage under Elizabeth I*, London, 1958.

   and Alan G. R. Smith, eds., *Elizabethan People: State and Society*, London, 1972.

Hutchinson, Lucy, "The Life of Mrs. Lucy Hutchinson Written by Herself," in *Memoirs of The Life of Colonel Hutchinson*, London, 1908, 1–15.

Ingram, Martin, *Church Courts, Sex and Marriage in England 1570–1640*, Cambridge, 1987.

James I, King of England, *King James the First: Daemonologie (1597), Newes from Scotland (1591)*, ed. G. B. Harrison, Edinburgh, 1966.

James, Mervyn, *Family, Lineage, and Civil Society: A Study of Society, Politics, and Mentality in the Durham Region, 1500–1640*, Oxford, 1974.

   Society, Politics, and Culture: Studies in Early Modern England, Cambridge, 1986.

Johnson, Samuel, *Samuel Johnson on Shakespeare*, ed. W. K. Wimsatt, Jr., New York, 1960.

Jones, Emrys, *The Origins of Shakespeare*, Oxford, 1977.

Jones, Paul Van Brunt, *The Household of a Tudor Nobleman*, Urbana, 1917.

Jones, Ann Rosalind and Peter Stallybrass, *Renaissance Clothing and the Materials of Memory*, Cambridge, 2000.

Jordan, Constance, "Renaissance Women and the Question of Class," in *Sexuality and Gender in Early Modern Europe: Institutions, Texts, Images*, ed. James Grantham Turner, Cambridge, 1993, 90–106.

Jorgensen, Paul A., *Our Naked Frailties: Sensational Art and Meaning in 'Macbeth',* Berkeley, 1971.

Jowett, John, "The Thieves in *1 Henry IV,*" *The Review of English Studies* 38 (1987), 325–33.

Kahn, Coppélia, "The Absent Mother in *King Lear,*" in *Rewriting the Renaissance: The Discourses of Sexual Difference in Early Modern Europe,* ed. Margaret W. Ferguson *et al.,* Chicago, 1986, 33–49.

Roman Shakespeare: Warriors, Wounds, and Women, London, 1997.

Kaplan, M. Lindsay and Katherin Eggert, "'Good queen, my lord, good queen': Sexual Slander and the Trials of Female Authority in *The Winter's Tale,*" *Renaissance Drama* 25 (1994), 89–118.

Kastan, David Scott, "*All's Well That Ends Well* and the Limits of Comedy," *English Literary History* 52 (1985), 575–89.

Keeton, George W., *Shakespeare and His Legal Problems,* London, 1930.

Kelso, Ruth, *Doctrine for the Lady of the Renaissance,* Urbana, 1956.

Kerrigan, John, ed., *Motives of Woe: Shakespeare and 'Female Complaint'. A Critical Anthology,* Oxford, 1991.

On Shakespeare and Early Modern Literature: Essays, Oxford: Oxford University Press, 2001.

Klein, Joan Larsen, ed., *Daughters, Wives and Widows: Writings by Men about Women and Marriage in England, 1500–1640,* Urbana, 1992.

Kliman, Bernice W., *Shakespeare in Performance: Macbeth,* Manchester, 1992.

Knutson, Roslyn L., "A Caliban in St. Mildred Poultry," in *Shakespeare and Cultural Traditions,* ed. Tetsuo Kishi *et al.,* Newark, 1994, 110–26.

"Elizabethan Documents, Captivity Narratives, and the Market for Foreign History Plays," *English Literary Renaissance* 26 (1996), 75–110.

Konstan, David, *Friendship in the Classical World,* Cambridge, 1997.

Kornstein, Daniel, J., *Kill All The Lawyers?: Shakespeare's Legal Appeal,* Princeton, 1994.

Kuchta, David, "The Semiotics of Masculinity in Renaissance England," in *Sexuality and Gender in Early Modern Europe: Institutions, Texts, Images,* ed James Grantham Turner, Cambridge, 1993, 233–46.

Kussmaul, Ann, *Servants in Husbandry in Early Modern England,* Cambridge, 1981.

La Boétie, Étienne de, *Discours de la Servitude Volontaire* (1548), Paris, 1922.

The Politics of Obedience: The Discourse of Voluntary Servitude (1548), intro. Murray N. Rothbard, trans. Harry Kurz, New York, 1975.

Ladurie, Emmanuel Le Roy, *Jasmin's Witch,* trans. Brian Pearce, Aldershot, 1987.

Laslett, Peter, *Family Life and Illicit Love in Earlier Generations: Essays in Historical Sociology,* Cambridge, 1977.

"Mean Household Size in England since the Sixteenth Century," in *Household and Family in Past Time,* ed. Peter Laslett, Cambridge, 1972, 125–58.

The World We Have Lost, London, 1965.

The World We Have Lost: Further Explored, revised 3rd ed. of *The World We Have Lost,* London, 1983.

"The Wrong Way through the Telescope: A Note on Literary Evidence in Sociology and in Historical Sociology," *British Journal of Sociology* 27 (1976), 319–42.

Levack, Brian P., "State-Building and Witch-Hunting in Early Modern Europe," in *Witchcraft in Early Modern Europe: Studies in Culture and Belief*, ed. Jonathan Barry *et al.*, Cambridge, 1996, 96–115.

Levenson, Jill L., "'Hamlet' Andante/'Hamlet' Allegro: Tom Stoppard's Two Versions," *Shakespeare Survey* 36 (1983), 21–8.

Liebler, Naomi Conn, *Shakespeare's Festive Tragedy: The Ritual Foundations of Genre*, London, 1995.

The Lisle Letters, ed. Muriel St. Clare Byrne, Chicago, 1981, vol. 3.

Livy, *From the Founding of the City [Ab Urbe Condita]*, trans. B. O. Foster, London, 1925, vol. 1.

Loomba, Ania, *Gender, Race, Renaissance Drama*, Manchester, 1989.

Loraux, Nicole, *Mothers in Mourning. With the Essay "Of Amnesty and Its Opposite,"* trans. Corinne Pache, Ithaca, 1998.

Tragic Ways of Killing a Woman, trans. Anthony Forster, Cambridge, Mass., 1987.

Lucas, F. L., *Euripides and His Influence*, New York, 1928.

M., I., *A Health to the Gentlemanly Profession of Servingmen* (1598), in *Shakespeare Association Facsimiles* 3, Oxford, 1931.

McBride, Theresa, *The Domestic Revolution: The Modernization of Household Service in England and France, 1820–1920*, New York, 1976.

McCracken, Grant, "The Exchange of Children in Tudor England: An Anthropological Phenomenon in Historical Context," *Journal of Family History* 8 (1983), 303–13.

MacCulloch, Diarmaid, "Bondmen Under the Tudors," in *Law and Government Under the Tudors*, ed. Claire Cross *et al.*, Cambridge, 1988, 91–109.

MacDonald, Michael, *Mystical Bedlam: Madness, Anxiety, and Healing in Seventeenth Century England*, Cambridge, 1984.

MacFarlane, Alan, *The Family Life of Ralph Josselin a Seventeenth-Century Clergyman: An Essay in Historical Anthropology*, Cambridge, 1970.

Marriage and Love in England: Modes of Reproduction 1300–1840, Oxford, 1986.

Machiavelli, Niccolò, *The Discourses* (1519?), trans. Leslie J. Walker, ed. Bernard Crick, Harmondsworth, 1970.

McIntosh, Marjorie K., "Servants and the Household Unit in an Elizabethan English Community," *Journal of Family History* 9 (1984), 3–23.

Macpherson, C. B., "Servants and Labourers in Seventeenth-Century England," In *Democratic Theory: Essays in Retrieval*, Oxford, 1973, 207–23.

Magnusson, Lynne, *Shakespeare and Social Dialogue: Dramatic Language and Elizabethan Letters*, Cambridge, 1999.

Mahood, M. M., *Bit Parts in Shakespeare's Plays*, Cambridge, 1992.

Makaryk, Irena R., "'Dwindling into a Wife?' Cleopatra and the Desires of the (Other) Woman," in *The Elizabethan Theatre XIV*, ed. A. L. Magnusson and C. E. McGee, Toronto, 1996, 109–25.

Manningham, John, *The Diary of John Manningham of the Middle Temple 1602–3*, ed. Robert Parker Sorlien, Hanover, NH, 1976.

Marcus, Leah Sinanoglou, *Childhood and Cultural Despair: A Theme and Variations in Seventeenth-Century Literature*, Pittsburgh, 1978.

Marshall, Cynthia, "Wound-Man: *Coriolanus*, Gender, and the Theatrical Construction of Interiority," in *Feminist Readings of Early Modern Culture: Emerging Subjects*, ed. Valerie Traub *et al.*, Cambridge, 1996, 93–118.

Marshall, Dorothy, *The English Domestic Servant in History*, London, 1949.

Martindale, Adam, *The Life of Adam Martindale, Written by Himself*, ed. Richard Parkinson, Chetham Society, old ser. 4 (1845).

Maza, Sarah C., *Servants and Masters in Eighteenth-Century France: The Uses of Loyalty*, Princeton, 1983.

Mertes, Kate, *The English Noble Household 1250–1600: Good Governance and Politic Rule*, Oxford 1988.

Mikalachki, Jodi, *The Legacy of Boadicea: Gender and Nation in Early Modern England*, London, 1998.

Mikesell, Margaret Lael, "'Love Wrought These Miracles': Marriage and Genre in *The Taming of the Shrew*," *Renaissance Drama* 20 (1989), 141–67.

Mills, Laurens J., *One Soul in Bodies Twain: Friendship in Tudor Literature and Stuart Drama*, Bloomington, 1937.

Mitterauer, Michael, "Servants and Youth," *Continuity and Change* 5 (1990), 11–38.

Moisan, Thomas, "Interlinear Trysting and 'Household Stuff': The Latin Lesson and the Domestication of Learning in *The Taming of the Shrew*," *Shakespeare Studies* 23 (1995), 100–19.

"'Knock me here soundly': Comic Misprision and Class Consciousness in Shakespeare," *Shakespeare Quarterly* 42 (1991), 276–90.

Montaigne, Michel de, "Of the Education of Children" (1579–80), in *The Complete Essays of Montaigne*, trans. Donald M. Frame, Stanford, 1958, 106–31.

"Of Friendship" (1572–6), in *The Complete Essays of Montaigne*, trans. Donald M. Frame, Stanford, 1958, 135–44.

"Of Repentance" (1585–8), in *The Complete Essays of Montaigne*, trans. Donald M. Frame, Stanford, 1958, 610–21.

"Of Husbanding Your Will" (1585–8), in *The Complete Essays of Montaigne*, trans. Donald M. Frame, Stanford, 1958, 766–84.

Morgan, Edmund S., *The Puritan Family: Religion and Domestic Relations in Seventeenth-Century New England*, New York, 1966.

Neely, Carol Thomas *Broken Nuptials in Shakespeare's Plays*, New Haven, 1985.

Neill, Michael. "'He that thou knowest thine': Friendship and Service in *Hamlet*," in *A Companion to Shakespeare's Works*, vol. 1 *The Tragedies*, ed. Richard Dutton and Jean E. Howard, Oxford, 2003, 319–38.

"Servant Obedience and Master Sins: Shakespeare and the Bonds of Service," in *Putting History to the Question: Power, Politics, and Society in English Renaissance Drama*, New York, 2000, 13–48.

"'Servile Ministers'" *Othello, King Lear* and the Sacralization of Service," the 2003 Garnett Sedgwick Memorial Lecture at the University of British Columbia, Vancouver, 2003.

Neuss, Paula, "The Sixteenth-Century English 'Proverb' Play," *Comparative Drama* 18 (1984), 1–18.

Nevo, Ruth, *Tragic Form in Shakespeare*, Princeton, 1972.

Newton, Judith, and Deborah Rosenfelt eds., "Introduction," *Feminist Criticism and Social Change: Sex, Class and Race in Literature and Culture*, New York, 1985, xv–xxxix.

Norbrook, David, "*Macbeth* and the Politics of Historiography," in *Politics of Discourse*, ed. Kevin Sharpe and Steven N. Zwicker, Berkeley, 1987, 78–116.

Novy, Marianne L., *Love's Argument: Gender Relations in Shakespeare*, Chapel Hill, 1984.

O'Day, Rosemary, *The Family and Family Relationships, 1500–1900. England, France and the United States of America*, New York, 1994.

Orlin, Lena Cowen, *Private Matters and Public Culture in Post-Reformation England*, Ithaca, 1994.

Orme, Nicholas, *Education and Society in Medieval and Renaissance England*, London, 1989.

From Childhood to Chivalry: The Education of the English Kings and Aristocracy 1066–1530, London, 1984.

Osborne, Francis, "Advice to a Son" (1656), in *Advice to a Son: Precepts of Lord Burghley, Sir Walter Raleigh, and Francis Osborne*, ed. Louis B. Wright, Ithaca, 1962, 33–114.

Oxford English Dictionary

Parker, Patricia, "Fantasies of 'Race' and 'Gender': Africa, *Othello*, and Bringing to Light," in *Women, "Race", and Writing in the Early Modern Period*, ed. Margo Hendricks and Patricia Parker, London, 1994, 84–100.

Literary Fat Ladies: Rhetoric, Gender, Property, London, 1987.

Shakespeare from the Margins: Language, Culture, Context, Chicago, 1996.

Parker, R. B., "War and Sex in 'All's Well That Ends Well'," *Shakespeare Survey* 37 (1984), 99–113.

Paster, Gail Kern, *The Body Embarrassed: Drama and the Disciplines of Shame in Early Modern England*, Ithaca, 1993.

Patterson, Orlando, *Freedom*, vol. 1, *Freedom in the Making of Western Culture*, London, 1991.

Slavery and Social Death: A Comparative Study, Cambridge, Mass., 1982.

Pechter, Edward, *Othello and Interpretive Traditions*, Iowa City, 1999.

"*Patient Grissil* and the Trials of Marriage," in *The Elizabethan Theatre XIV*, ed. A. L., Magnusson, and C. E., McGee, Toronto, 1996, 83–108.

Peck, Linda Levy, *Court Patronage and Corruption in Early Stuart England*, Boston, 1990.

Percy, Henry, "Instructions by Henry Percy, Ninth Earl of Northumberland, to His Son Algernon Percy, Touching the Management of His Estate, Officers, etc." (1609), *Archaeologia* 27 (1838), 306–58.

Perkins, William, *[Christian] Oeconomie: Or Houshold-Government. A Short Survey of the Right Manner of Erecting and Ordering a Family, According to the Scriptures*, in *Collected Works*, London, 1631, vol. 3, 667–700.

Pinchbeck, Ivy and Margaret Hewitt, *Children in English Society*, London, 1969, vol. 1.

Platter, Thomas, *Thomas Platter's Travels in England* (1599), trans. Clare Williams, London, 1937.

Plumpton Correspondence: A Series of Letters, Chiefly Domestick, Written in the Reigns of Edward IV, Richard III, Henry VII, and Henry VIII, ed. Thomas Stapleton, Camden Society 4, London, 1839.

Plutarch, "How a Man May Discern a Flatterer from a Friend," in *Plutarch's Moralia: Twenty Essays*, trans. Philemon Holland (1603), London, 1911, 36–101.

"The Life of Marcus Antonius," in *Shakespeare's Plutarch*, ed. T. J. B., Spencer, Harmondsworth, 1964, 174–295.

"The Life of Martius Coriolanus," in *Shakespeare's Plutarch*, ed. T. J. B. Spencer, Harmondsworth, 1964, 296–362.

Pollock, Linda, A., *Forgotten Children: Parent-Child Relations from 1500–1900*, Cambridge, 1983.

ed., *A Lasting Relationship: Parents and Children over Three Centuries*, London, 1987.

"Teach her to live under obedience: The Making of Women in the Upper Ranks of Early Modern England," *Continuity and Change* 4 (1989), 231–58.

With Faith and Physic: The Life of a Tudor Gentlewoman Lady Grace Mildmay 1552–1620, London, 1993.

Poole, Adrian, *Tragedy: Shakespeare and the Greek Example*, Oxford, 1987.

Potter, Lois, *Shakespeare in Performance: Othello*, Manchester, 2002.

Powell, Thomas, *Tom of All Trades. Or the Plaine Path-Way to Preferment* (1631), ed. F. J. Furnivall, The New Shakspere Society Publications, series 6, nos. 2–3: *Shakespeare's England*, rpt. Vadus, 1965.

Prager, Carolyn, "The Problem of Slavery in *The Custom of the Country*," *Studies in English Literature* 28 (1988), 301–17.

Purkiss, Diane, *The Witch in History: Early Modern and Twentieth Century Representations*, London, 1996.

Quaife, G. R., *Wanton Wenches and Wayward Wives: Peasants and Illicit Sex in Early Seventeenth Century England*, New Brunswick, 1979.

Raleigh, Walter, "Sir Walter Raleigh's Instruction to His Son and to Posterity" (1632), in *Advice to a Son: Precepts of Lord Burghley, Sir Walter Raleigh, and Francis Osborne*, ed. Louis B. Wright, Ithaca, 1962, 15–32.

Robbins, Bruce, *The Servant's Hand: English Fiction from Below*, New York, 1986.

Roberts, Michael, "'Words they are women, and deeds they are men': Images of Work and Gender in Early Modern England," in *Women and Work in Pre-Industrial England*, ed. Lindsey Charles and Lorna Duffin, Dover, NH, 1985, 122–80.

Rollins, Judith, *Between Women: Domestics and Their Employers*, Philadelphia, 1985.

Romano, Dennis, *Housecraft and Statecraft: Domestic Service in Renaissance Venice, 1400–1600*, Baltimore, 1996.

Roper, Lyndal, *Oedipus and the Devil: Witchcraft, Sexuality and Religion in Early Modern Europe*, London, 1994.

Rosen, Barbara, ed., *Witchcraft in England, 1558–1618*, Amherst, 1991.

Rosenberg, Marvin, *The Masks of Hamlet*, Newark, 1992.

Rowe, Katherine, *Dead Hands: Fictions of Agency, Renaissance to Modern*, Stanford, 1999.

Ruggiero, Guido, *Binding Passions: Tales of Magic, Marriage, and Power at the End of the Renaissance*, New York, 1993.

Sacks, David Harris, "Searching for 'Culture' in the English Renaissance," *Shakespeare Quarterly* 39 (1988), 465–88.

Sacks, Elizabeth, *Shakespeare's Images of Pregnancy*, London, 1980.

Salingar, Leo, *Dramatic Form in Shakespeare and the Jacobeans*, Cambridge, 1986.

Schochet, Gordon J., *Patriarchalism in Political Thought: The Authoritarian Family and Political Speculation and Attitudes Especially in Seventeenth Century England*, Oxford, 1975.

Seaver, Paul, *Wallington's World: A Puritan Artisan in Seventeenth-Century London*, Stanford, 1985.

Sedgwick, Eve Kosofsky, *Between Men: English Literature and Male Homosocial Desire*, New York, 1985.

Segal, Erich, *Roman Laughter: The Comedy of Plautus*, Cambridge, Mass., 1968.

Selden, Raman, "King Lear and True Need," *Shakespeare Studies* 19 (1987), 143–69.

Seneca, Lucius Annaeus, "Epistle no. 47," in *The Epistles of Seneca* [*Epistulae Morales*], vol. 1, trans. Richard M. Gummere, London, 1967.

Shakespeare, William, *The Riverside Shakespeare*, 2nd edn., ed. G. Blakemore Evans, Boston, 1997.

All's Well That Ends Well, ed. G. K. Hunter, London, 1959.

All's Well That Ends Well, ed. Barbara Everett, Harmondsworth, 1970.

All's Well That Ends Well, ed. Susan Snyder, Oxford, 1993.

Antony and Cleopatra, ed. Emrys Jones, Harmondsworth, 1977.

Coriolanus, ed. Philip Brockbank, London, 1976.

Coriolanus, ed. R. B. Parker, Oxford, 1994.

Coriolanus, ed. Lee Bliss, Cambridge, 2000.

Hamlet, ed. Harold Jenkins, London, 1982.

The Three-Text Hamlet: Parallel Texts of the First and Second Quartos and First Folio, ed. Bernice W. Kliman and Paul Bertram, intro. Eric Rasmussen, New York, 1991.

The First Part of King Henry IV, ed. Herbert Weil and Judith Weil, Cambridge, 1997.

The Second Part of King Henry IV, ed. A. R. Humphreys, London, 1966.

The Second Part of King Henry IV, ed. Giorgio Melchiori, Cambridge, 1989.

King John, ed. E. A. J. Honigmann, London, 1954.

The Life and Death of King John, ed. A. R. Braunmuller, Oxford, 1989.

King John, ed. L. A. Beaurline, Cambridge, 1990.

Plays in Performance: King Lear, ed. J. S. Bratton, Bristol, 1987.
King Lear, ed. R. A. Foakes, Walton-on-Thames, 1992.
The Tragedy of King Lear, ed. Jay L. Halio, Cambridge, 1992.
The History of King Lear, ed. Stanley Wells, Oxford, 2000.
Macbeth, ed. Kenneth Muir, Cambridge, Mass., 1957.
Macbeth, ed. G. K. Hunter, Harmondsworth, 1967.
Macbeth, ed. Nicholas Brooke, Oxford, 1990.
Macbeth, ed. A. R. Braunmuller, Cambridge, 1997.
Othello, ed. Norman Sanders, Cambridge, 1984.
Othello, ed. E. A. J. Honigmann, Walton-on-Thames, 1997.
The Taming of the Shrew, ed. Ann Thompson, Cambridge, 1984.
The Tempest, ed. Stephen Orgel, Oxford, 1987.
Shannon, Laurie, *Sovereign Amity: Figures of Friendship in Shakespearean Contexts*, Chicago, 2002.
Sharp, Ronald A., *Friendship and Literature: Spirit and Form*, Durham, NC, 1986.
Shell, Marc, *Children of the Earth: Literature, Politics, and Nationhood*, Oxford, 1993.
Sidney, Philip and Mary Sidney, *The Psalms of Sir Philip Sidney and the Countess of Pembroke*, ed. J. C. A. Rathmell, Garden City, 1963.
Sinfield, Alan, *Faultlines: Cultural Materialism and the Politics of Dissident Reading*, Oxford, 1992.
Singh, Jyotsna, "Renaissance Antitheatricality, Antifeminism, and Shakespeare's *Antony and Cleopatra*," *Renaissance Drama* 20 (1989), 99–121.
Skinner, Quentin, *Liberty Before Liberalism*, Cambridge, 1998.
"A Third Concept of Liberty," *London Review of Books* 24:7 (04/2002), 16–18.
Slater, Miriam, *Family Life in the Seventeenth Century: The Verneys of Claydon House*, London, 1984.
Slights, Camille Wells, "Slaves and Subjects in *Othello*," *Shakespeare Quarterly* 48 (1997), 377–90.
Smiley, Jane, *A Thousand Acres*, New York, 1992.
Smith, Steven R., "The Ideal and Reality: Apprentice-Master Relationships in Seventeenth Century London," *History of Education Quarterly* 21 (1981), 449–69.
Spenser, Edmund, *Spenser's Faerie Queene* (1596), vol. I, ed. J. C. Smith, Oxford, 1964.
Spevack, Marvin, ed., *The Harvard Concordance to Shakespeare*, Cambridge, Mass., 1973.
Spurgeon, Caroline F. E., *Shakespeare's Imagery and What It Tells Us*, Cambridge, rpt. 1966.
Stanton, Domna C., "Difference on Trial: A Critique of the Maternal Metaphor in Cixous, Irigaray, and Kristeva," in *The Poetics of Gender*, ed. Nancy K. Miller, New York, 1986, 157–82.
Starkey, David, "Intimacy and Innovation: The Rise of the Privy Chamber, 1485–1547," in *The English Court: From the Wars of the Roses to the Civil War*, ed. David Starkey *et al.*, London, 1987, 71–118.

States, Bert O., *Hamlet and the Concept of Character*, Baltimore, 1992.

Steinfeld, Robert J., *The Invention of Free Labor: The Employment Relation in English and American Law and Culture, 1350–1870*, Chapel Hill, 1991.

Stevenson, Laura Caroline, *Praise and Paradox: Merchants and Craftsmen in Elizabethan Popular Literature*, Cambridge, 1984.

Stone, Lawrence, *The Family, Sex and Marriage in England 1500–1800*, Harmondsworth, 1984.

Strier, Richard, "Faithful Servants: Shakespeare's Praise of Disobedience," in *The Historical Renaissance: New Essays on Tudor and Stuart Literature and Culture*, ed. Heather Dubrow and Richard Strier, Chicago, 1988, 104–33.

Tasso, Torquato, *The Housholders Philosophie*, trans. T. K., London, 1588.

Taylor, Michael, "Persecuting Time with Hope: The Cynicism of Romance in *All's Well That Ends Well*," *English Studies in Canada* 11 (1985), 282–94.

Tennenhouse, Leonard, "Sir Walter Ralegh and the Literature of Patronage," in *Patronage in the Renaissance*, ed. Guy Fitch Lytle and Stephen Orgel, Princeton, 1981, 235–57.

Thomas, Keith, *Religion and the Decline of Magic: Studies in Popular Beliefs in Sixteenth- and Seventeenth-Century England*, Harmondsworth, 1973.

Thompson, Ann, *King Lear*, Atlantic Highlands, 1988.

Thompson, E. P., "Eighteenth-Century English Society: Class Struggle without Class?" *Social History* 3 (1978), 133–65.

"The Grid of Inheritance: A Comment," in *Family and Inheritance: Rural Society in Western Europe, 1200–1800*, ed. Jack Goody *et al.*, Cambridge, 1976, 328–60.

Thynne, Joan and Maria Thynne, *Two Elizabethan Women: Correspondence of Joan and Maria Thynne 1575–1611*, ed. Alison D. Wall, Wiltshire Record Society Publication 38, 1982.

Tilley, Morris Palmer, *A Dictionary of the Proverbs in England in the Sixteenth and Seventeenth Centuries*, Ann Arbor, 1950.

Tilney, Edmund, *The Flower of Friendship: A Renaissance Dialogue Contesting Marriage* (1573), ed. Valerie Wayne, Ithaca, 1992.

Townshend, Dorothea, *Life and Letters of Mr. Endymion Porter: Sometime Gentleman of the Bedchamber to King Charles the First*, London, 1897.

Turner, John, "King Lear," in *Shakespeare: The Play of History*, ed. Graham Holderness *et al.*, Iowa City, 1988, 89–118.

"Macbeth," in *Shakespeare: The Play of History*, ed. Graham Holderness *et al.*, Iowa City, 1988, 119–49.

Vaughan, Virginia Mason, *Othello: A Contextual History*, Cambridge, 1994.

Vaughan, William, *The Golden-Grove, Moralized in Three Books*, 2nd ed., London, 1608.

Walvin, James, *Black and White: The Negro and English Society, 1555–1945*, London, 1973.

Slaves and Slavery: The British Colonial Experience, Manchester, 1992.

Walzer, Michael, *Just and Unjust Wars: A Moral Argument with Historical Illustrations*, New York, 1977.

Spheres of Justice: A Defense of Pluralism and Equality, New York, 1983.

Weil, Judith, "'Full Possession': Service and Slavery in *Doctor Faustus*," in *Marlowe, History, and Sexuality: New Critical Essays on Christopher Marlowe*, ed. Paul Whitfield White, New York, 1998, 143–54.

"Visible Hecubas," in *The Female Tragic Hero in English Renaissance Drama*, ed. Naomi Conn Liebler, New York, 2002, 51–69.

Weisman, Ronald F. E., "Reconstructing Renaissance Sociology: The 'Chicago School' and the Study of Renaissance Society," in *Persons in Groups: Social Behavior as Identity Formation in Medieval and Renaissance Europe*, ed. Richard C. Trexler, Binghampton, 1985, 39–46.

Wentworth, William, "Sir William Wentworth's Advice to his Son," in *Wentworth Papers 1597–1628*, ed. J. P. Cooper, Camden Society, 4th series, vol. 12, London, 1973, 9–25.

Whately, William, *A Care-Cloth: Or a Treatise of the Cumbers and Troubles of Marriage*, London, 1624.

Wheeler, Richard P., *Shakespeare's Development and the Problem Comedies: Turn and Counter-Turn*, Berkeley, 1981.

Whigham, Frank, *Ambition and Privilege: The Social Tropes of Elizabethan Courtesy Theory*, Berkeley, 1984.

Seizures of the Will in Early Modern English Drama, Cambridge, 1996.

Whythorne, Thomas, *The Autobiography of Thomas Whythorne*, ed. James M. Osborn, London, 1962.

Williams, Bernard, *Shame and Necessity*, Berkeley, 1993.

Williams, Raymond, *The Country and the City*, London, 1985.

Marxism and Literature, Oxford, 1977.

Willis, Deborah, *Malevolent Nurture: Witch-Hunting and Maternal Power in Early Modern England*, Ithaca, 1995.

Wills, Gary, *Witches and Jesuits: Shakespeare's Macbeth*, Oxford, 1995.

Wilson, Adrian, "The Ceremony of Childbirth and its Interpretation," in *Women as Mothers in Pre-Industrial England: Essays in Memory of Dorothy McLaren*, ed. Valerie Fildes, London, 1990, 68–107.

"A Critical Portrait of Social History," in *Rethinking Social History: English Society 1570–1920 and Its Interpretation*, ed. Adrian Wilson, Manchester, 1993, 9–58.

Wilson, Elkin Calhoun, "Shakespeare's Enobarbus," in *Joseph Quincy Adams: Memorial Studies*, ed. James G. McManaway *et al.*, Washington, DC, 1948, 391–408.

Winstanley, Gerrard, "The Law of Freedom in a Platform: Or, True Magistracy Restored," (1652), in *The Law of Freedom and Other Writings*, ed. Christopher Hill, Harmondsworth, 1973, 273–389.

Woodbridge, Linda, *The Scythe of Saturn: Shakespeare and Magical Thinking*, Urbana, 1994.

Woolf, Virginia, *A Room of One's Own*, London, 1929, rpt. 1987.

Wootton, David, "Leveller Democracy and the Puritan Revolution," in *The Cambridge History of Political Thought 1450–1700*, ed. J. H. Burns, Cambridge, 1991, 412–42.

Worden, Blair, "English Republicanism," in *The Cambridge History of Political Thought 1450–1700*, ed. J. H. Burns, Cambridge, 1991, 443–75.

Woudhuysen, H. R., ed., *The Penguin Book of Renaissance Verse*, selected and intro. by David Norbrook, London, 1993.

Wright, Louis B., ed., *Advice to a Son: Precepts of Lord Burghley, Sir Walter Raleigh, and Francis Osborne*, Ithaca, 1962.

Wrightson, Keith, *English Society 1580–1680*, New Brunswick, 1992.

"Estates, Degrees and Sorts in Tudor and Stuart England," *History Today* 37 (1987), 17–22.

and David Levine, *Poverty and Piety in an English Village: Terling, 1525–1700*, New York, 1979.

Xenophon, *Xenophon's Treatise of Housholde*, trans. Gentian Hervet, London, 1534.

Young, David, *The Heart's Forest: A Study of Shakespeare's Pastoral Plays*, New Haven, 1972.

Zeitlin, Froma I., *Playing the Other: Gender and Society in Classical Greek Literature*, Chicago, 1996.

Zitner, Sheldon P., *All's Well That Ends Well*, Boston, 1989.

Index